Praise for *The Game from Where I Stand*

"Doug Glanville was always different from other baseball players—in a good way. . . . He was more like one of us (regular folks) than one of them (exalted athletes). He saw himself the way you would if you made the majors: full of self-awareness and humanity, traits that are otherwise in short supply in the VIP-treated, image-conscious world of pro sports. It stood to reason, then, that Glanville's baseball memoir, *The Game from Where I Stand,* would be different as well. . . . [Glanville] is a witty, insightful writer. . . . Many times during the steroids scandal, it has seemed as if the players were on one side of the battle and the baseball writers were on the other. In Glanville, finally, we have someone who is of both camps, and everyone on either side would benefit from hearing what he has to say."
— *The Washington Post*

"My favorite baseball book of the year."
—Jayson Stark, ESPN.com

"Generous, perceptive, wise (he's a Penn graduate, after all), and thoughtful, Glanville further distinguishes his career with this rich and rewarding look back at it."
—*Boston Herald*

"Thoughtful and intelligent."
—*New York Post*

"Glanville hits for the cycle with an elegantly written, up-close-and-personal, deliciously detailed, sidesplitting, and sad account of the day-to-day life of a journeyman ballplayer. . . . He reveals, as no one before has, what it's like to be a 'boy of summer.'"
—*Tulsa World*

"Like a player peering from dugout steps, surveying the field and the game, Glanville has a wonderful vantage."
—*The Plain-Dealer*

"An engaging and thoughtful detailing of the way a smart, feeling player processed and parried with the realities of megabyte-era Major League Baseball."
—*Chicago Sun-Times*

"*The Game from Where I Stand* is a book of uncommon grace and elegance. ... [It is] a book about baseball unlike any I have ever read, filled with insight and a certain kind of poetry in its spare and haunting prose."
—Buzz Bissinger, author of *Friday Night Lights* and *Three Nights in August*

"Most fans know us only by what they see in the highlights on television. But as Doug Glanville knows so well, being a professional athlete doesn't make us exempt from the world that exists outside the lines—we are very much a part of it, but we can't let it show. (That's not professional!) In this book, Doug goes beyond the playing field to bring into view the full reality of being in the major leagues."
—Jimmy Rollins

"When I was a teenager, Jim Brosnan's *The Long Season* changed the way I looked at baseball, but over the years I tended to read books by players and managers as studies in self-interest. Doug Glanville's book is different. *The Game from Where I Stand* is an honest, thoughtful, and insightful perspective on baseball, and Glanville's unadulterated respect for the sport and its people never wavers. This isn't good, it is brilliant."
—Peter Gammons

"Doug Glanville wants to tell fans about the texture of life—its stresses and pleasures—in the big leagues. Glanville, just your basic Ivy League-educated outfielder, has done fans a nifty favor."
—George F. Will

"I have known Doug Glanville for many years and always enjoyed competing against him. Doug was a great student of the game and someone who seemed to enjoy his playing career and took a lot from it. That is demonstrated in *The Game from Where I Stand*. Doug paints a very entertaining and accurate picture of the game that we love. This book will make you laugh and provides wonderful insights about our national pastime."
—Cal Ripken Jr.

THE GAME

——— *from* ———

WHERE I STAND

FROM BATTING PRACTICE
TO THE CLUBHOUSE
TO THE BEST BREAKFAST ON THE ROAD,
AN INSIDE VIEW OF A BALLPLAYER'S LIFE

DOUG GLANVILLE

ST. MARTIN'S GRIFFIN

NEW YORK

www.stmartins.com

Designed by Kelly Too

The Library of Congress has cataloged the Henry Holt edition as follows:

Glanville, Doug.
    The game from where I stand : a ballplayer's inside view / Doug Glanville.—1st ed.
        p. cm.
    Includes index.
    ISBN 978-0-8050-9159-5
    1. Baseball players—United States—Social conditions.   2. Baseball players—Professional
relationships—United States.   3. Baseball players—United States—Attitudes.   4. Glanville,
Doug.   5. Baseball players—United States—Biography.   I. Title.
    GV867.64.G58 2010
    796.357'640973—dc22

                                                                                2009043578

ISBN 978-0-312-57309-6 (trade paperback)

Originally published in hardcover in 2010 by Times Books,
an imprint of Henry Holt and Company

First St. Martin's Griffin Edition: April 2011

10   9   8   7   6   5   4   3   2   1

LOST AND FOUND

Trust me, we have looked
To no avail
In pendants, in photos
Symbols that are not you
We lost you before
For your time had come
And our time frozen
In wait
But we found warmth
In the words you left behind
Words you used to counsel the heavens
Words that thaw the ice
Of our trying state
And now the family
You never knew
Knows you
And I know you again
Now that I have
Found your voice
In mine

. . .

To my father, the angels' therapist,
still counseling from the heavens

CONTENTS
• • •

INTRODUCTION

• • •

"Now batting, the center fielder, number six, Doug Glanville."

For fifteen professional seasons, nine of them in the major leagues, those words (or some variation of them) began my workday. I heard them in tiny small-town ballparks and in triple-decker urban stadiums that seated fifty thousand people or more. I heard them in spring training; I heard them in the playoffs; I may have even heard them in my sleep. The sound never got old.

I was a center fielder, and once I got a taste of what that meant, I never wanted to play any other position. There is no other place on the field with such uninhibited sight lines to take in all that baseball has to offer. My job as the center fielder was to run down everything hit in my direction, but it was also to lead, to make sure my fellow outfielders knew where to play before the ball was hit.

There is an immense beauty in standing in the center of the outfield and being able to see everything. From center field you can see where the catcher is setting up and, based on your knowledge of your team's pitching staff, know to a high degree of accuracy what is about to happen. You can watch a pickoff play about to develop and anticipate that the base runner is about to erase a potential run by being too jumpy. You can even see what is happening in the stands and note that your dad just got back to his seat after buying a big bag of popcorn.

A center fielder has to fully understand where the other players are relative to one another before every pitch. If I had a speedy right fielder playing alongside me, I could feel confident giving him more room. I had to know the abilities and range of everyone on the field to maximize our chance to record an out on any given play. If I was too close, I cut down our range as a team; if I was too far away, balls fell in safely. I had to be able to look at my teammates and keep our spacing constant, accounting for the count, the wind, the speed of my fellow outfielders, even my sore hamstring.

These calculations became second nature to me, because unlike most ballplayers, I am an engineer by training. When I was drafted by the Chicago Cubs in the first round of the 1991 amateur draft, I was a junior at the University of Pennsylvania, studying systems engineering. Not that many Ivy League student athletes are scouted by the pros, but the Cubs must have seen something they liked, because they picked me twelfth overall, one slot ahead of a high school phenom from New York City named Manny Ramirez. (Hmmm, wonder what ever happened to him.)

Once I signed on the dotted line accepting the Cubs' signing bonus offer, dream met reality and I began my journey to the big leagues.

As a first-round draft pick, all eyes are on you and there is no other place to be but center stage. In July 1991, I reported to the Geneva Cubs, who played in a college town in upstate New York. I lived on Main Street and remember hearing the light change from green to yellow to red. My rite of passage began.

In 1992, I made a stop in the Carolina League in Winston-Salem, complete with three roommates. We seemed to have a revolving door out front since every other day one of us was affected by a front-office move. Released, demoted, promoted.

After the season, the front-office executives who had drafted me were fired, and the new regime sent me back to the same level in 1993 with a promise of advancement midseason. True to their word, I was promoted to the Double-A Orlando Cubs. Welcome to the world of Disney.

I would play in Orlando for two seasons, and my once-promising career seemed to be stuck in neutral. But in the fall of 1994, I received an invitation to play in the Arizona Fall League. It was here where it all started to come together. A player-of-the-week award gave me optimism that I was seeing progress. I was performing well against the best the minor leagues had to offer.

When the final tallies were counted, my performance in the fall league solidified a spot for me on the Cubs' Triple-A team in Des Moines, Iowa. I did not know it at the time, but it was here that I would face an unexpected test. The manager of the Iowa Cubs, Ron Clark, and I did not get along. Our differences had begun the year before, when I was in Orlando. Clark was the minor league director of instruction at the time, and after one game he called me into the office to discuss a base-running decision I had made. Clark told me that I had made the wrong choice. I disagreed, but we didn't agree to disagree; we just fought for the last word. He would file this act of insubordination away.

In Iowa, every day was a battle. It was a year of constant badgering and a lot of tentative mistakes on the field, but one of the things that kept me going was the encouragement of our hitting coach, Glenn Adams. *Keep working, keep your head up*, he told me.

At season's end, my numbers were unimpressive. By now, I was twenty-five years old, which is ancient for a minor leaguer, and the Cubs asked me to play in the Instructional League that fall, an opportunity typically reserved for much younger players and a sign that my future had to be now. Fortunately, I met Tom Gamboa, a manager who would take me to Puerto Rico to play for his Mayaguez Indios in winter ball. It was there that I found my stride, winning an MVP trophy and, the next year, a championship.

To play so well after being buried in Triple-A was striking, even to the Cubs' front office. What was in the water in Puerto Rico? Part of the problem was that my Triple-A manager never took the time to know my story.

That story was one of determination. I chose to complete my

college education after I was drafted, to fulfill a promise to my family. I had taken a leave of absence during the spring semester of my senior year to play for Winston-Salem, but when the fall came, it was my time to finish what I started and graduate.

My parents had set the tone for education. Growing up as the son of a math teacher and a practicing psychiatrist gave me a strong academic base.

My mom, who hailed from Rocky Mount, North Carolina, was the oldest of four children and a born teacher. She followed this knack for leadership right through the public school system in my hometown of Teaneck, New Jersey, where she taught for over twenty years. She thrust herself directly into Teaneck's commitment to introduce diverse groups of people to one another by organizing cottage parties and by participating in cross-cultural social events like "Friendship Day." She had the strength common to the most uncommon teachers: a sense for making her audience know that she was talking to each person individually.

My father left his homeland of Trinidad and Tobago at the age of thirty-one in the midst of a political shakeup in the school system, where he had served as an assistant headmaster. His journey would take him to Howard University in Washington, D.C., where he would attend medical school. His skill in critical thinking helped shape the way I evaluated situations and people. His vast array of responses to scenarios and his unwavering ability to disarm anyone with one cool phrase were transformational for me. Through genuine humility, he brought everyone into a common space.

He was also a true Renaissance man. His primary passion was writing poetry, and after his passing he left a collection of poems for everyone to continue to learn from and find joy in.

But it was my brother who was all about baseball. He laid out a plan for my baseball destiny by listing the steps to major league glory. He is still playing baseball today, at the age of forty-seven; he is the one member of our family who has always passionately followed his heart, whatever the expense.

My parents had many choices of where to build their life, but they chose Teaneck, a blossoming beacon of diversity in the homogeneous, wealthy suburbs of Bergen County.

No place shaped my perspective as much as Teaneck. In the 1960s Teaneck had been at the forefront of integration, bringing black and white students together to learn in the same space, setting the expectation that diversity would be embraced. Diplomacy became a huge part of my worldview as I witnessed people of all walks learning how to communicate with one another.

It was also this experience that made the major leagues feel like home once I got my first call-up to the Cubs on June 9, 1996. I was sent down once, but by September I would be back up for what would be the remainder of my career.

But I would not stay with the Cubs for long. They traded me on December 23, 1997, to the Philadelphia Phillies, which opened up my career. I would be going back to the East Coast, playing for my childhood favorite team, going back to my college town, and—best of all—starting. (Yes, the Phillies were my favorite team growing up. You would think that a northern New Jersey kid would love either the Mets or the Yankees, but my brother got me into sports so young that I chose my favorite team simply by the color of their uniform. Nothing could beat those powder blue road uniforms of the Phillies in the 1970s.)

My five seasons in Philadelphia embodied the complete major league experience. I came as the rising prospect, wise in years but still with much to prove. I left as the disgruntled and exhausted role player, whose role was mostly to teach my replacement how to play the game.

In between, I experienced all it is to be a major leaguer. I have been the disappointment, I have been the "can't miss," I have been the cornerstone, I have been the underpaid, I have been the overpaid, I have been the marginalized veteran, I have been the "lost a step," I have been the "traded for," I have been the day-to-day, I have been the comeback kid, I have been the free agent, but most of all, I have been a fan, friend, son, little brother, and hometown hero. There were good years and bad years, I was a hero and a goat, but through it all I was only human.

My life was turned upside down in 2000, when I received news on the last day of spring training that my father had suffered the first of a series of strokes. With a season about to start, I had no idea what to do. I played on, but with a heavy heart.

In August 2002, after many anxious times, things took a turn for the worse. With an already deadly cocktail of strokes, a lung cancer diagnosis, a previous heart attack, and diabetes, my father experienced yet another major stroke. When my mother spoke to me on the phone that morning, she was trying to stabilize him in the Hackensack Medical Center emergency room. She later told me that after my father had been declared "nonresponsive," he had recovered consciousness when, during her conversation with me, she said the word *baseball*. So, to me, his condition had gone from grave to horrible—and that was progress. I was optimistic. I sensed he would still be with us when I got there.

I drove up from Philadelphia, essentially on autopilot the whole way. My dad was semicomatose when I entered his hospital room, but he straightened up and smiled—and then went back into his coma. The doctor, a close family friend, spat out unrecognizable (to us) figures to explain my father's state that, when translated into layman's terms, basically told us that he was on borrowed time. Yet my father defiantly showed us that numbers were only for the emotionally conservative.

I hugged my mother, and I told her that I had to get back to the team. On the drive back to Philadelphia, I felt a renewed strength. I turned up the radio and cruised down the highway. Something told me that my father would be in my life for a little while longer. The numbers hadn't suggested that, but his spirit did. The music reached a crescendo, and I unwittingly blew past the speed limit. Sirens blared, and as I slowly pulled over, I thought, *I have a pretty good excuse.* But I didn't have time to give it. The officer, a Phillies fan at heart, recognized me and—as he wrote me up—started telling me, "You're having a tough year, but numbers are not important; your value to our community is priceless."

I never had been so thankful to receive a speeding ticket. It was a small price to pay for having someone remind me of what amazing blessings and gifts I'd had in my life. I had so much to smile about. After all, my father was still smiling.

From that point on, I proceeded to play the best baseball I had played in years. My paltry .200 batting average rose nearly fifty points, and by season's end I was two hits away from my 1,000th career hit. I sensed that I was going to be fine. When I arrived at Pro Player Stadium in Miami for the last game of the season, my name was penciled in atop the batting order. I wasted no time. I got a hit in my first at-bat for number 999, and in my next turn, I smoked a single into left for my 1,000th. I felt unstoppable that day, as if something bigger than me was swinging the bat on my behalf.

At 7:15 p.m., it was over; the Phillies had fallen short, but I had collected not only my 1,000th hit but my 1,001st as well. At that precise moment, my father passed away.

Maybe his work was done here; maybe he felt that peace within that all men long for but are afraid to court. Somehow, deep down, I knew it was a good thing. I also knew that he gave me the confidence and faith that when my turn came, I would embrace it, too.

I would leave Philadelphia that winter, signing as a free agent with the Texas Rangers. I thought it would be a new start, but I tore a hamstring in April, spent six weeks on the disabled list, and in late July, I found myself traded back to my first team, the Chicago Cubs. Though I was no longer a starter, the Cubs did give me an opportunity to play in the postseason that fall, and even though it ended badly (as it so often seems to for the Cubs), it was still an unforgettable experience.

I returned to the Phillies for the 2004 season, but I was now firmly entrenched as a bench player, which was not where I wanted to be. I figured that if I was going to be a reserve, I might as well play for a team with a chance to win a championship. So in February 2005 I reported to spring training with the New York Yankees, hoping to win a reserve outfield spot.

The Yankees ran me out there every day during the exhibition games. To combat any wearing down, I was in the gym at least twice a day working on my body.

I was playing fairly well, not lighting the world on fire, but steady. My competition for the last slot, Bubba Crosby, was battling leg problems, and I thought I might get a few points for staying healthy. But Crosby soon regained his health and came back on fire—as I cooled off.

A week before Opening Day, we played the Phillies at their camp, and just as my career had begun with a base hit to left off the Phillies' Terry Mulholland at Veterans Stadium, on this day I smacked a base hit to left off the Phillies' Tim Worrell. After the game, the Yankees' general manager, Brian Cashman, and manager, Joe Torre, brought me into the office to tell me that I had been released. They were giving me a week's head start to catch on with another team. I didn't say much other than to thank them for the opportunity. I thought I was a good fit for the Yankees: a player who had been a starter, able to play all fields, and young enough to run out there a lot. But I was trumped.

I would no longer take my place in center field, at least not as a major leaguer, although I still believed I belonged there. Not because I was bitter about my rejection, but because the spirit of what makes center field so special is within me.

It was where I could make the best use of my skills, which is what my parents expected most from me. A center fielder is at once a player, a strategist, an observer, and a thinker—good preparation for writing a book.

This book is my attempt to open up the hidden world of baseball players, to reveal the human side of the game and the human side of the men who play it. There is a richness to the experience of playing baseball that is not visible to fans or commentators, and by sharing it with you, I hope to bring you a greater appreciation of what happens on the field and off, and to give you a taste of what it's like to sit in the dugout, to relax in the clubhouse, to stand in the on-deck circle, to run the bases, to position yourself in the outfield.

The book is distilled from my observations, sentiments, assumptions, and reflections from standing at the heart of the diamond, to paint a complete picture of what a life in baseball is like. You'll meet the teammates, opponents, managers, coaches, girlfriends, buddies, and other people who populate a ballplayer's world, and you'll see the game from behind the scenes, a perspective that gets left out of most coverage of this sport. You'll get a better idea of what goes on inside a player's head as he digs in at the plate, stands ready in the field, or rides the bench. The stories I tell are every player's story and are testimonials to the human condition in all its glory and frailties, something not exclusive to baseball.

In fact, if I have done this great game justice, you will find that whether or not you have ever picked up a bat or thrown a ball, this book could be your story as well.

THE GAME FROM WHERE I STAND

1

...

BEFORE THE FIRST GAME

Had the front office lied to me? I seriously doubted it, but why was Lenny Dykstra, the wounded veteran whom I was to replace, in the batting cage looking like he was in midseason form?

I had just arrived at my first spring training with the Philadelphia Phillies in 1998 with a mixture of excitement, caution, and awe. I was lugging my old Chicago Cubs bag, the only one I owned that was major league caliber. In the sea of red that adorned the Phillies clubhouse, the Cubbie blue stood out like a deep-dish pizza in a buffet of cheese steaks.

My journey to Philadelphia had begun two days before Christmas when the Cubs traded me like a set of steak knives for second baseman Mickey Morandini. It was the first time I became exchanged goods, and, like every other player who has gone through the experience, I grappled with the idea of being wanted and not being wanted in the same transaction. It was difficult to process or put in perspective, particularly because my grandfather had passed away a few hours before I got the call from Cubs general manager Ed Lynch telling me of the trade.

Soon, however, I could appreciate the upside. I couldn't think of a better place to put on a new uniform. I would now be playing for my favorite team from childhood and in my college town.

The key word was *playing*. It looked like I'd be trading in the label of *platoon player* for *starter*, replacing the often-injured, thirty-four-year-old Dykstra. Thirty-four is not that old by most standards—even in baseball you should have a few more solid years in front of you—but Lenny was dealing with a degenerative back problem. With that knowledge, maybe the Cubs were doing me a favor by shipping me to a place where I could see my name in the lineup every day.

As a relatively young player, I couldn't fully understand what it was like to be in Lenny's spikes. He must have heard that this new kid from the Cubs was coming to be the next Phillies center fielder and thought, *What about me?*

A few years earlier, I had watched another veteran face the abyss. Willie Wilson was a legend who was nearing the end of his career but still had something to contribute. He had years of experience and had won a World Series with the Kansas City Royals, back when his speed and base-stealing abilities were second to none. His young rival at the Cubs spring training, Karl "Tuffy" Rhodes, personified the inevitable. Rhodes had just come off of an amazing year in the minor leagues, and all signs suggested that the center field job was his to lose.

Wilson was frustrated by even the possibility of being displaced. He did what he could to outplay Rhodes, but one time his uncertainty would spill into a shoving match between the two players. The veteran seemed to be looking for a fight at all times.

Our teammate, the veteran shortstop Shawon Dunston, discussed the Wilson-Rhodes battle with me, and his wisdom shone through. He spoke of what happens to players when that door is closing on them—how you feel when the game rips that uniform off your back before you quit, how the anxiety and panic begin when the game starts peeling off a small piece to get the process under way. The pressure can make any player lose it.

Time cannot be stopped, not for Willie Wilson, not for Lenny Dykstra. It eventually becomes someone else's turn, like it or not.

Dykstra continued to take solid swings in the cage, and I began to understand that I would be better off if I just played my game instead of worrying about how his back was doing.

When players are pitted against each other, they still have a relationship. It may be touch and go like Rhodes and Wilson, but Glanville and Dykstra got along fine. I had learned that Lenny liked Strat-O-Matic, a baseball board game that I played as a kid, so I had a set delivered to camp and shared with him the cards from the Phillies team of the previous year.

Lenny was the kind of player whose full worth to a team did not show up on a Strat-O-Matic card. He was "Nails" to the fans of Philadelphia, embodying grit and determination and a "do whatever it takes" approach to the game. Yes, he was a character—his lore preceded him, like the story of how he would discard his entire uniform for a new one if he didn't get on base in his first at-bat—but he was one smart cookie on the field and in the clubhouse. Many of those who loved his attitude and eccentricity often underestimated how well he understood the game and what a great tactician he was. He had amazing discipline at the plate and always seemed to be thinking a few steps ahead of his opponent.

When your physical abilities desert you, your savvy can keep you in the picture, at least for a while. Replacing a legend—even one with a bad back—is not easy. I knew I had to bring my best game to earn this job. The Phillies may have had a clear plan, but I needed to help myself by playing well, to make it an easier choice for them. Entrenched experience trumps anything a young buck can do in spring training. As our third base coach, John Vukovich, would say, "Let's see what the kid does when there is a third deck in the stadium."

I proceeded to play some of my best baseball that spring while staying as far below the radar as possible. The press and talk radio were at work trying to stir the pot about how this was the old versus the new, the gritty versus the graceful, the muddy versus the cleancut. In many ways, Lenny and I were very different people, but in the end, each of us would take your head off on the baseball field if you were trying to take our job.

Just as on the first day of school, every player has an opportunity in spring training, and not merely the kind of opportunity that can propel you from the minors to the majors, but a chance to be someone new, a chance to reinvent yourself.

Spring training provides fertile ground for a metamorphosis, for rookies and veterans alike. A player often tries to transform himself into a new "me"—at least until he or someone else wants the old "me" back.

Thanks to having way too much time to think during the vacuum we call the off-season, players figure out the answer to just about every question under the sun. Thus they inevitably come into camp hopeful that they can turn over a new leaf and change perceptions and results just by showing up different in some way.

New leaves come in many forms. A player might report twenty-five pounds heavier—possibly from natural means, possibly not. He might sport a new batting stance or lose the mustache. As for me, during the spring of 1996, I decided to break out a new way to wear my baseball pants.

The expression goes: We all put our pants on the same, one leg at a time. For many years in baseball, team dress codes dictated that players also *wore* their pants (as well as the rest of their uniform) the same. There was a time, for example, when all the Minnesota Twins had to wear those stirrups that showed the Twin Cities emblem, a combination of the letters *T* and *C*.

I played with teams that talked about the "three-finger" rule: you had to get three fingers worth of stirrup showing below the bottom of your pants. But over time, these rules were relaxed—as were the no-facial-hair rules of the Cincinnati Reds and other teams—and dressing up or down became a free-for-all.

As history of any kind will tell us, when human beings get an opportunity to express their individual selves, a few selves will go completely over the top. As the baseball dress code waned, players waxed creative. They studied historical photos, they talked to club-house managers with sewing skills, and they even made up their own style. *Project Runway* had nothing on us.

Royce Clayton and Juan Pierre would wear their pants just below the knee to celebrate the history of Negro League players and to proclaim their style. Other players often unknowingly imitated George Hendrick, who played in the 1970s and '80s and wore his pants all the way down to the tops of his spikes. Hendrick had a style that was equally suited to the ballpark or to a wedding, wear-ing what appeared to be baseball "slacks." Still, the Hendrick experience became popular for a period of time. Mickey Morandini of the Phillies took the style to the next level, adding stirrups to the bottom of his pants.

Of course, there were some who pushed the envelope a little too far. The Pirates' Derek Bell introduced a style that would best be described as "late twentieth-century jester." He wore pants that had to be at least eight sizes larger than what he required. It would be safe to say that I could have fit inside one of his pant legs. The league eventually said, "Pittsburgh, we have a problem." The offi-cials were probably afraid that if he ran into a ball girl chasing a ball down the line, she would end up engulfed in loose fabric.

My style of choice, "high waters"—so named because you could wear them in a flood and stay dry—was inspired by my time playing winter ball on the island of Puerto Rico. In the winter of 1995–96, the Mayaguez Indios provided only one pair of pants that ade-quately fit my waist. These pants were not too long, not too short, but unlike the bears' porridge, they weren't just right either. I looked as if I had left my pants in the dryer too long. But at the end of that winter league season, I was named the league's most valuable player, so high waters it was for spring training. I would wear my pants this way for the rest of my career.

Though some metamorphoses are permanent, any change a

player decides to make in spring training is understood to be retractable. The superstitious nature of the game allows for full refunds and reversible epiphanies. One spring I decided to use black bats instead of my typical reddish-brown, Walker finish. After a horrible first week at the plate, my black bat phase officially ended.

Sometimes a player chooses to reinvent himself by changing his wheels. Literally. But the ability of a new car to transform you depends on your team. When I joined the New York Yankees for spring training in 2005, I knew the bar would be high. This was a roster full of All Stars and legends like Derek Jeter, Alex Rodriguez, Gary Sheffield, Jorge Posada, Randy Johnson, and Mariano Rivera. I had recently splurged on a Range Rover that had enough gadgets and gizmos to look like it had been designed by NASA. This will stand tall in the Bronx Bombers' parking lot, I told myself.

Not so fast. My new teammates were buying vehicles that were works of art. They boasted limited-edition numbers and custom colors that only a Picasso could paint. My teammate Rey Sanchez chastened me: "You have been in the league long enough, splurge! Why only one car?" I guess that would be one way to revamp one's image. As Ernie Banks might have said, "Let's drive two."

I came to understand that making a strong entrance is a powerful way to show you mean business for the upcoming season. Vanity plates, suits, jewelry, houses, or even rare animals can also do the trick.

During a caucus in the Cincinnati Reds' batting cages, I listened as Ken Griffey Jr. talked about his hobbies. He clearly loved living on the edge, and like most players, he liked to have something that no one else could have had first. He shared some stories about how he loved to ride his souped-up motorcycle and push the speed envelope. He also said that his son was following suit with some off-road action. But what caught my ear was when he mentioned the rare exotic shark he had in a tank in his house. While most people, upon hearing that, would certainly be impressed about the uniqueness of having a pet shark, ballplayers are different. Our competitive nature instead prompts us to ponder: "I wonder where I can pick up a unicorn?"

I once thought I saw a unicorn on the baseball field. It happened when I was standing on first base in a game against the St. Louis Cardinals. I looked down to shortstop, and there was Ozzie Smith, one of the few players in history whose glove would carry him to Cooperstown (although he could hit, too). Still a green rookie, I dreamed of a double-play ball that would give me the chance to take him out and become one of the elite few who had knocked the "Wizard" back to Oz while breaking up "two."

Sure enough, Mark Grace hit the next pitch on the ground to second baseman Mike Gallego, who flipped it to Ozzie. I was sure he was headed across the bag toward right field, so in anticipation I slid in, knees flying. My accelerated breathing—or was it the glow from the shortstop's mitt?—temporarily stunned me. Ozzie gloved the ball at the exact moment he touched the base, changed direction from where I was headed, immaculately removed the ball from his mitt, and threw to first. I could only look up from the dirt, a mile away from my target. The Wizard had worked his magic. Had he teleported? Was his glove made out of unicorn leather?

While I've never really seen a mitt made out of unicorn, I have seen metal trees bearing baseball gloves standing under a cloudless sky in the middle of the Arizona desert. Every spring training, representatives from the major glove manufacturers descend upon each team's camp to showcase their wares. On the designated day, players young and old buzz around the makeshift flea market, set up in the complex's parking lot or on the stadium concourse.

Those who don't have a contract with a company might be able to score a free glove or appropriate one for a son or nephew who has just started Little League. For those with an existing deal, this is the day you can choose the type of glove you want for the upcoming season or decide to stay with the status quo.

Growing up, I paid little attention to all the options. I just grabbed whichever glove had the autograph of one of my favorite players. I sought Steve Carlton, Mike Schmidt, or anyone on the great Phillies teams of the 1970s and early 1980s. Once I had made my pick, my brother would run it over with my mom's car to break it in.

When you turn pro, those days are gone. Selecting a glove is a complicated business.

What length do you want? There were small, medium, large, and extra-large options for varying tastes. This dictated the length of the fingers and/or the depth of the pocket, where the ball should come to a comfortable rest.

Do you want a glove that has been "pre–broken in"?

Do you want a finger hole so your index finger can stick out? In theory the finger-out option provides more room for the ball to land in a bigger pocket.

Since I was with Rawlings for the bulk of my career, I had more specific questions. H-web or Trap-Eze? Your webbing could look like just about any window you have ever seen. You could get the four glass panes (H-web), or the opaque tinted kind, solid all around, or perhaps add the blinds with treatments (Trap-Eze web).

Don't forget the foam padding. Wilson used to have a dial on the outside of the finger holes that allowed you to adjust it to the mold of your hand.

If you are an exceptional case, you can add some color beyond the typical tan, brown, or black, maybe even spice it up with a number or nickname—the glove's equivalent of vanity plates.

I kept waiting for the GPS option, but it never arrived.

Fortunately, most players only play one general position: outfielder, infielder, catcher, first baseman, or pitcher. The poor soul who plays multiple positions will need a wheelbarrow on Glove Day. Outfielders' gloves tend to be a little longer, allowing extra room to catch the escaping fly ball. Infielders' gloves tend to be small, so that it's easy to get your throwing hand into the pocket to facilitate a quick release.

Smaller gloves also necessitate staying low to the ground—the preferred stance for infielders. Catchers are in their own world; they need padding and more padding to catch those ninety-five-mile-per-hour fastballs. First basemen have the biggest pocket in the bunch, to catch throws from infielders that might rise above the head or skip in the dirt. The pitchers? Well, let's save that for later.

In the minor leagues, the glove hierarchy is divided between the prospects and the suspects. High draft picks often sign glove contracts the day they turn pro. Lower picks have to scrounge around a little.

As a prospect, my experience with Jimmy Piersall, the Cubs' minor league outfield coach, kept my selection fairly simple. If he thought a glove was too big, too colorful, or, worst of all, had a Trap-Eze web, he kicked it around the outfield with a running commentary that was every bit as colorful as the offensive mitt. Why no Trap-Eze? He thought it to be "style before substance." The Trap-Eze web, he instructed us, was too long to be effective in fielding ground balls in the outfield because the ball tended to get caught in its decorative webbing. As a result, you often had to reach for the ball more than once, and that split second could be the difference between out and safe on a throw to the plate.

Heeding Jimmy, I'd place an order that went something like this: "Give me an outfield glove that is on the small side, soft leather so that it is practically broken in, black, and please no Trap-Eze web." The almighty H-web became my final choice. Thank goodness I didn't have to choose from the 2010 Rawlings collection. There are thirteen types of gloves on its Web site. Can someone tell me the difference between a Single Post Double Bar and a Horizontal Bar X-Laced? Ordering a Rawlings glove has gotten dangerously close to ordering at Starbucks.

Modern-day pitchers have had to deal with another wrinkle: television cameras. With the advent of the zoom lens, studying old videos suddenly took on a new meaning. You could watch a pitcher and find out what pitch he was throwing because you could see his fingers grip the ball or see him do something through the webbing of his glove. Most pitchers stay away from gloves with the finger-out option because the positioning or movement of the index finger can tip pitches. Then there was my Cubs teammate Steve Trachsel, who apparently found out that anyone near a TV who had a gift for lip reading could interpret what he was saying during a meeting on the mound. This could have been a big issue when he was pitching against opponents with some ingenuity. So he began to use the closed webbing as a shield over his mouth. He looked like Zorro with a baseball cap.

The better players adjusted. Greg Maddux was meticulous about making his glove practically bulletproof. He made sure his glove had no holes anywhere, to thwart any spy attempts. Forget about seeing the way he was gripping the ball through the webbing; X-rays couldn't penetrate it. Now virtually all pitchers choose gloves with webbing that is impervious to anyone's sight lines, and they should.

Once you make it to the major leagues, it is a given that you have some sort of glove supplier. Unless you are a superstar, this contract is rarely much more than an agreement that the company will supply all the gloves that you need, within reason. The money attached to the deal is not much more than a formality (certainly relative to major league contracts). You might receive some cash for your services or perhaps a gift certificate to order from a giant electronics store. I ordered a lot of digital cameras for gifts.

Eventually, the glove is chosen, and, in time, a couple of brand-new mitts will appear in your locker. Since this process is repeated year in and year out, you can accumulate quite a collection. Some gloves last for many years, creating a nice stockpile to donate to charity or to give to a clueless rookie who needs a head start.

Very few players get to have their signature emblazoned in the pocket of gloves that will be sold in stores for a world of kids to buy. But those who find themselves under contract with a glove company will at least have the chance to see their name in bold letters. I would get two gloves each year with DOUG GLANVILLE stitched in script across the thumb.

In some ways, this is a sign that you have arrived, an announcement to the baseball world that your name is official and that unless someone has a needle and a lot of time, no one can erase you from this moment. And that's as magical as a unicorn.

A couple of years ago an Internet site called comedy.com presented its "All-Ugly" Major League Baseball team. Official photos of current players were accompanied by commentary. I'm not going to throw anyone under the bus here and cause any more damage to their mugs or egos, but I will quote some of the comments and maybe you'll be able to put a face to a name: "There are Halloween masks that aren't as scary." "Face apparently caught on fire and they put it out with a bear trap." "Great hitter. Head shaped like a trash can."

If your head really is shaped like a trash can, there's probably not much you can do to avoid getting trashed, but for the rest of the players there's a lesson here: it's a good idea to take Photo Day seriously.

The baseball brass and the media certainly do. Perhaps years ago it was just an occasion for taking a team picture of forty players who can't sit still for seven minutes. No more. Photo Day is a grand affair involving props, costume changes, poses at multiple stations, and photographers willing to prostrate themselves or mount unstable police sawhorses to get the right shot. Fashion Week rolled into three hours.

For the players with the least seniority, Photo Day begins at about 7 a.m. Seasoned veterans are given later time slots so that they can grab a few more winks. Eventually, whether your face looks like a bear trap or a chick magnet, you get to the ballpark. No one wants to miss a mandatory session this early in the spring.

A full buffet of baseball wear is laid out for Photo Day. Complete uniform including jerseys of various styles and colors. Accessories, too: glove, bat, batting gloves, turf shoes, maybe even spikes. Caveat rookies: temper your excitement. It's only a slight exaggeration to say that if you don't bring your equipment bag, you risk throwing out your back hauling this mini–sports store from station to station.

Another warning to greenhorns: the morning dew is still present when the festivities begin. So for all those wonderful shots taken with you one knee, look out. Maybe you should kneel on your glove or bring an extra T-shirt to act as a knee coaster.

Photo Day seems to have more stations than Amtrak. Each stop is manned by a photographer from some entity that needs a picture of you for the season. Maybe it is ESPN, which will use the same picture if you blow away the opposition with a one-hundred-mile-per-hour fastball or get caught driving at the same speed at 3 a.m. in your Porsche (unless there is a police photo). Maybe it is your own team, which will take a headshot that will follow you all year on every scoreboard in every stadium.

It's no time to lose your focus when the team photographer takes this one. Entering the batter's box and seeing a twenty-five-foot-high photo of yourself on the big screen in the outfield is startling enough. If you've got a goofy grin or one eye closed, your stats on the board better be good enough to make everyone forget that you might make the "All-Ugly" team.

(My scoreboard headshot was decent enough, but I did have a beef with my bio up there. I was born in Hacksensack, New Jersey, but grew up in Teaneck, which I considered my hometown. Yet for my entire career, next to my Photo Day headshot, I had to read "Hackensack, N.J." It turned my stomach because Hackensack High School was Teaneck's archrival.)

As you go from one station to the next, you find a mass of teammates waiting for the next guy to finish his shoot. For some players, this time in front of the camera carries with it more pressure than, say, laying down a squeeze bunt. With your teammates watching, it's tough to lay down that smile that Mom would like. Instead, you are expected to intimidate the camera and thereby intimidate opponents who will eventually see you glaring down at them. Give a cheese-eating grin, and you'll be mocked to no end by the guys in your own clubhouse.

As technology has grown more complex, so has Photo Day. New stations seem to bloom every spring. One of my favorites was the video game station. Baseball on today's gaming systems is extremely realistic because the game makers get digital images of the actual players. A 3-D camera takes a full picture of your head. This image is then used on the digital character generated in the game. Young baseball fans can then play your avatar to their heart's content, never realizing that you lost thirty minutes of your life in a Photo Day vortex.

It may be as hard to make the All-Ugly team as it is to make the All-Star team, but Photo Day teaches ballplayers that a picture can be worth a thousand jibes. One bad showing at a photo station, and it will immortalize you not only in some baseball card set or in stadiums across the country, but in the minds and on the tongues of your brethren. I can't remember any of the pitching stats of my former Phillies teammate Jim Poole, but I still can picture one of his headshots for his baseball card that was taken when he was in the Los Angeles Dodgers' minor league system. Was that a dead muskrat on top of his head or, heaven forbid, Jim's own hair? As he explained, "I had just finished running my sprints; what do you expect?" *I expect you'll never get caught in that position again*, I thought.

When a camera appears, veteran baseball players—like veteran politicians—seem able to snap on a permafreeze grin without blinking or twitching. But this skill is not obtained overnight. The vast majority of players get sent down to the minors a few times before mastering a smile worthy of the Dental Hall of Fame. Sometimes the demotion is sudden or unexpected, as was the case with my Cubs teammate Kevin Roberson. He had made the team with bags packed and secured below the bus, confident that the car he had shipped to Wrigley Field gave him that stamped ticket to the promised land. Then the team removed him from his seat in a last-minute change of heart. Back to Triple-A.

For three consecutive springs, 1994, 1995, and 1996, I was one of those players. I never got the kind of break that would ultimately result in my departing from spring training to a major league city—but at least I wasn't removed publicly from a bus. Three times the end of March came, and I heard the all-too-familiar company line: "Good effort, but we don't feel you are quite ready. Keep working." Accompanying the line was a ticket to Orlando or Des Moines.

The line and the destination finally changed in 1997. The Cubs' manager, Jim Riggleman, took me aside and said, "Congratulations, you did a great job. You made the team." It was a surreal moment because even though I knew I had lit the Cactus League on fire, I had done that before. All that had yielded was a pat on the back and a minor league uniform.

Having been called up to Chicago twice during the 1996 season, I played it cool when Riggleman told me I'd made the team. I used that little taste of major league experience to put a look on my face that said, *I am happy, but I was expecting this.*

After getting the good news, I spoke to my family. In typical fashion, my mom looked at the schedule to see where we would celebrate my birthday (August 25) that year. I wasn't worried about a party or presents; I just wanted to survive with the club long enough to make it to late summer.

My taste of the big time from the year before helped me understand that after a minor league demotion, players are *actually* sent packing. You are responsible for your own equipment. And you better learn the system quickly. Spikes go on the bottom; otherwise you may rip your only T-shirt or find mud in your toothpaste. If you forget something, it's your own fault.

Not so in "the Show." Once the curtains lifted that spring, my equipment bag mysteriously was packed. I kept looking around for some practical jokester, but it was the real thing.

The behind-the-scenes crew of a major league team is similar to the staff at a five-star hotel. The clubhouse manager is the concierge. He oversees the locker room, supervising a staff of at least three or four people who provide numerous services. Packing a player's bag is just the tip of the iceberg. The locker room guys have an endless task list in their heads at all times. Most days they clean your spikes after games (polish them, too) and do errands requested by the players. These guys work hard.

Your blue undershirt got a little faded? Go to Frank, the equipment manager. Need a room for your cousin in Baltimore or some extra tickets for a friend? Talk to Jimmy, the traveling secretary. Running out of bats? Talk to Phil, the assistant clubhouse manager. Need a dental appointment for your wife? Tap Jeff, the head trainer, on the shoulder. Need an assistant to help you with your fan mail? Done, after a quick call to the PR department.

The Texas Rangers may never have won the World Series, but if there were a competition for best home team clubhouse, there'd be several banners flying over the Ballpark in Arlington. When I was with the team in 2003, Tom Hicks's big Texan hospitality extended from his owner's box all the way to the locker room. The Rangers' crew didn't just pick up every article of your uniform from the floor; they practically took the shirt off your back before you could do it yourself. Take a basketball shot for the hamper and miss? Don't even think about getting the rebound; it was already tipped in by the assistant clubhouse manager.

The saying "You are what you eat" applies to professional baseball. In the low minors, the specialty du jour is sometimes peanut butter and jelly made by the chef—you. Such fare all but guarantees a postgame trip to the local Waffle House or Denny's, where "grand slam" has a very different meaning.

In the majors, pregame goodies await your arrival. Depending on the team, this spread could range from a George Foreman Grill menu, to those cool fruit bars with real fruit in them.

My last season with the Phillies, 2004, was the first time that I had heard about a cook being signed as a free agent. When we faced the Tampa Bay Devil Rays in interleague play, we raved about Joe Swanhart, the short-order cook in the visiting locker room. Joe took his work so seriously that he had a neon sign for his mini-restaurant ("Swanny's"). Everything was cooked on site and to order.

The Phillies were so impressed that they made Joe an offer he couldn't refuse. I never found out the terms, but it must have been generous enough for him to leave sunny Florida for chilly Philly. Multiyear deal with a no-trade clause, no doubt. He was worth it.

After seven months of the royal treatment, it is no wonder that it's hard for players to go from king to commoner and adjust to everyday life when the season is over. Services that were at your fingertips for the last seven months go into hibernation.

But none of that crossed my mind when I made the Cubs in 1997. After years of demotions, I was wide awake, eager to begin a journey, a luxurious, prestigious, and high-end ride shaping the beginning of the dream.

But I still needed a place to live.

In the minors, you're on your own when looking for lodging. The transaction wire rather than the local real estate listings provides the best leads. Just as you might assume the position of a player who has been demoted or promoted, you might also assume the lease of his studio or one bedroom. Or you might strike up a quick friendship in spring training, which could lead to a roommate.

In the big leagues, it's almost disingenuous to say you are "apartment hunting." The "hunting" we did for apartments at the tail end of spring training was more like what a lion does when a steak is thrown into his cage and lands three feet away from his front paws.

As spring training winds down and it appears you will make the team, a prearranged hidden network of brokers and building managers springs into action. Faxes, e-mails, and brochures pour in, touting apartment-finding services or particular apartment complexes in the city where you will live for the next six months. It can be overwhelming until you realize that most major league teams have a bread-and-butter list of places where players have stayed.

There are certain dealbreakers. Just as most teams have little interest in players who can't connect with a fastball, most major leaguers have little interest in apartments where they have to arrange to connect phone or gas service themselves. They're not necessarily above it; they're simply too busy before the season starts to wait for AT&T or Peco Energy to call or come by. If you like a place well enough, you might ask a family member or trusted surrogate to pinch hit. More likely, you'll find a place that is all-inclusive. Pay a flat amount that covers your energy, phone, water bill, and all incidentals in one simple statement. Caribbean resorts have nothing on a baseball player's all-inclusive rental agreements.

When I signed with Texas, I knew nothing about the Dallas–Fort Worth area. As spring training wound down, I had no clue where I should live. My next-door neighbor in the clubhouse in Surprise, Arizona, Alex Rodriguez, gave me tips on the rental market and a few ideas of good places to stay, but it is hard to take any advice when you haven't even been to the city.

I ended up renting from my friend Royce Clayton, who still owned the condo he had purchased when he played for the Rangers from 1998 to 2000. Royce had hooked up his Dallas pad with top-notch amenities. It had marble everything, shades that retracted with the push of a button, and it was walking distance from a phenomenal outdoor shopping mall. The front-desk team offered terrific service—and just as important, everything was rolled into one easy payment. Bills were consolidated, and other than the "inconvenience" of getting the phone put in my name, it was easy street. My one regret is that, because I was traded away in the middle of the night, I still owe the building staff a tip. What a deadbeat!

On occasion, the full-service route can be bumpy. My first two years in Philadelphia, I stayed in two different apartments. I had to put one of them together piece by piece, right down to renting the furniture. The other was a high-end setup, complete with doorman and cleaning service.

But the more people are doing for you, the more they know

about you. My teammate Mike Lieberthal also lived in the same high-end building. We agreed that our cleaning crew left a lot to be desired—not because they did a bad job in our apartments, but because they liked to spread dirt about us outside our apartments.

They gossiped that I wasn't spending enough on my suits and that Mike should be going out with the woman at the front desk instead of keeping his options open. Forget about bringing a date home. They discussed your love life the way fans discussed your batting average. Thank goodness this was before Facebook; there is no telling what kind of pictures of us may have come up on the Internet.

Dealing with the constant challenge of being on the road takes up enough brain space as it is. Early in their careers players learn that help with their domestic lives is readily available. Sure, there's a certain glamour in living in a place that takes care of all your needs, but practicality also comes into play. You don't want to miss a bunch of bills because your mailbox overflowed while you were on a twelve-day swing to the West Coast. Then people will really start talking about you!

The life of a baseball player brings with it the chronic sensation of being temporary. You can be traded at the drop of a hat; you can be sent down to the minors; you can have a great year and leave for free agency. Players are nomads, really, members of the same wandering tribe.

As such, it is difficult to commit to a space and put down any kind of roots. Once you move a bill into your name or put up that favorite picture of you with your brother, you have committed to a relationship with your surroundings, and the white walls and hotel art (which most players barely notice) now have color and an opinion. It is safer not to connect. It is easier to manage when you can just drop off one check at the front desk and not worry. Otherwise you are setting yourself up for a bad breakup.

There are exceptions—players who remain in the same city for a decade—but most players live with their suitcase open on the floor, waiting for the next road trip, waiting to go back to their real home when the season ends.

What matters most is what happens on the field. And that starts with Opening Day.

My first Opening Day in the majors was memorable but not action-packed. The 1997 Cubs opened the season in Miami, taking on the Florida Marlins, whose pitching rotation was virtually unhittable: Kevin Brown, Al Leiter, Alex Fernandez, Livan Hernandez. We didn't know it at the time, but this staff would help carry the Fish to their first World Series title that fall.

I didn't play that day. I was in a platoon; I was starting against left-handed pitchers, so I sat against Brown, a sinker-ball-throwing right-hander. Since sinker-ball-throwing right-handers usually meant I would foul at least one ball off my shin per game, I wasn't that upset about sitting this one out and just taking it all in.

Our home opener at Wrigley Field a week later was interesting, but in a different way. The Cubs were brave enough to play in sub-freezing temperatures (twenty-nine degrees, wind at twenty-two miles per hour) on the same day that the White Sox later canceled their night game. On these days my teammate Rey Sanchez would wear a ski mask that made him look like he was about to join a secret society of blue ninjas. Then there was Jeff Conine of the Marlins, who evidently despised the cold. He wore so many layers he looked like he would explode if his shoelace came undone. I kept thinking about bunting toward him just to see if he would even bother moving.

Even stranger was a surreal Opening Day experience a few years later at Olympic Stadium in Montreal. It was during one of the many seasons when hardly anyone was going to Expos games. Playing in Montreal was like entering a strange time-space wormhole. I would get out of bed at the team hotel, walk to the train station, travel underground to the bowels of the stadium, and take the elevator to the locker-room level. Once I got on the train, I did not see daylight. The game could have been at noon, it could have been at midnight, and I would not have known the difference.

With the domed stadium only partly filled with fans, everything echoed, and the sound system made the announcer sound as if he were speaking from a submarine twenty thousand leagues under the sea. To top it off, he spoke in two languages, English and French, and no one could tell which one he was speaking in. As far as I was concerned, we were on the surface of Mars.

To kick off their Opening Day, the Expos took a page from the hit show *Survivor*. They had dramatic drumming, a dance team, flaming tiki torches, and girls in grass skirts. The Expos players went out to their positions and snuffed out their torches as if they were eliminating someone. Since most Opening Days revolved around fireworks, Blue Angels, parachutes, and flying mascots, the burning tiki lamps really took us to a new place. It's really too bad that only a handful of people were at the game, because it was the most creative Opening Day I had ever seen.

Opening Day games themselves are also notable for the monumental effect they have on your stats. Once the game starts and you get that first at-bat, anticipation is high; you're squeezing the bat so hard, you might build a mound of sawdust at the plate. As one of my minor league teammates, Andrew Hartung, joked after grounding out in his inaugural at-bat, "Oh no! I'm batting zero; I'm oh-for-one!" One year I did manage to hit a home run on Opening Day (Ryan Dempster of the Marlins was my victim), and it was nice to peek at the newspaper the next day and see myself among the league leaders, knowing that it would last for about two days, at best.

But the start of a season isn't all roses. When players from all over the world descend into one locker room, sometimes a flu-like bug will hit everyone at once.

One season when I was with the Phillies, it hit us all during the last couple of days of spring training, and while I guess that was better than the year we had to get emergency hepatitis vaccines (one player, Pedro Valdes, had to start the season on the disabled list because the shot hurt his arm), the entire team was still knocked out with a horrible flu to kick off the year. Usually the season starts after an off-day that serves as a practice day (or, if you're opening at home, a "get settled into your apartment" day). Well, I spent that practice day lying on a hotel floor in midtown Manhattan. I finally crawled to the phone to call the team trainer, and hours later I was in the hospital hooked up to an IV. I played the next day against the Mets at Shea Stadium, but I might as well have been swinging a sledgehammer. All I could do was think about my bed and some chicken soup from Mom across the George Washington Bridge in Teaneck.

There was also the horror in 2000, when I got a phone call from my mom that my father had a stroke, just days before our opening game against Randy Johnson and the Arizona Diamondbacks. That was certainly a bad Opening Day—nothing like facing a one-hundred-mile-per-hour fastball when your father is hanging between life and death.

My last Opening Day was also the grand opening of the Phillies' new stadium, Citizens Bank Park. It was cold and rainy, but it was nice to see the changing of the guard from Veterans Stadium (where I got the first hit of my career) to this wonderful new ballpark.

This day that begins the new baseball season is more than just the start of something special. It is the renewal of the soul of the game. Looking back at his Opening Days, a player can mark all the stages of his life. The day also continues the journey of a life in baseball, with players reaffirming their vow to play the game with everything they have, while living a dream and enjoying a passion.

And judging from the faces of the fans I saw for so many years on Opening Day, I got the feeling it meant the same thing to them.

2
...

PREPARING FOR THE GAME

Once you come down from the excitement of making the team and moving into your new locker, class begins. Spending time in spring training working out, hitting off the tee, and playing exhibition games was important, but now the games count. Since every team is physically talented, finding every mental advantage is essential. Major League Baseball 101 is now in session.

Depending on the organizational philosophy and the manager, teams prepare for games in different ways. There are, however, several similarities. At the beginning of a series, every club has a meeting to determine how to position its defensive players according to each of the opposing hitters' patterns.

At the top of our reading list? Reports from those unsung heroes, the scouts who follow an upcoming opponent in the days before you play them. The scouts' skinny is presented in charts that map out each hitter's tendencies. A "spray chart" for each batter shows the path of every ball put in play. Lines representing the trajectory of the ball are coded based on the pitch thrown.

Is the guy at the plate a dead pull hitter? Does he hit ground balls to shortstop a lot? What does he do against left-handed pitchers? By looking at the most densely populated areas on the charts, you get an idea of where to station yourself.

After a player has been in the league for a while, there is substantially more data on him, and a clearer strategic defense initiative emerges. Over time, there are what seem to be a million lines on that spray chart showing where every ball he hit ended up. If you think of the spray chart as a fan over a mini–baseball diamond, then the players whose fans are wide-open are the most unpredictable hitters because they "spray" the ball all over the place. Ivan Rodriguez would drive you crazy because he hit the ball anywhere and everywhere. All you could do was play right in the middle of every field and hope you could run a ball down when it was hit away from your spot.

There weren't a lot of surprises on Gary Sheffield's chart, especially when the count was in his favor. He would "turn and burn," pulling the ball practically down the third baseman's throat. I took a lot of steps toward the left-center field gap to cut down the safe areas on the pull side of the field.

As a center fielder, I was captain of the outfield and responsible for positioning my left fielder and right fielder as well as myself. Mindful of this added duty, I tackled the charts as if I were studying for a final exam in my Transportation Systems Engineering course in college. Good thing. Some of my teammates blew off their homework from time to time.

My right fielder in Philadelphia was Bobby Abreu (a Gold Glover, by the way). He was a bona fide superstar and all-around good guy, but he had minimal interest in the charts, partly because he relied on his instincts so often. He would rather leave it up to me (or at times a white-towel-waving coach from the dugout) to tell him where to stand. This worked on most occasions—except when the wind was blowing twenty miles per hour, and yelling for his attention became fruitless. If he didn't take a peek at me to see if I had moved, we were vulnerable.

In general, outfield positioning is like that old Atari baseball game: we all move in unison. Spacing depends on the personnel, but it was a constant. With a faster outfielder like Bobby in right, the center fielder can leave a little bigger space. But speed means nothing without a plan and without focus.

Rewarded with huge contracts because of their offensive prowess, many players have developed a kind of attention deficit disorder when it comes to defense. There is nothing more inappropriate than an outfielder practicing his swing or batting stance in the outfield (shhhhh, we all have done it at one time or another), but then again, offense pays the bills.

If you put up tremendous offensive numbers year after year, the game will cut you a little slack when it comes to the glove. So, too, will those awarding the Gold Glove. Every year, it seems a few recipients are honored more for their hitting than for their fielding. In 1999, Rafael Palmeiro was named the American League's Gold Glove first baseman while playing only twenty-eight games in the field. (He was a designated hitter for most of that season and batted .324 with forty-seven home runs.)

When I joined the Texas Rangers in 2003, the starting lineup included a couple of Gold Glovers: Palmeiro and Alex Rodriguez. Our manager, Buck Showalter, expected both of them to join the rest of us at the defensive positioning meetings. Buck was serious about these rituals. The door to the meeting room was shut at exactly the time we were supposed to start. Latecomers were denied entry and fined.

The room in which we met could have doubled as the CIA's command center. There was a map of the world with pins marking our opponents in the league. When I first saw it, I thought we might be preparing to re-create Napoleon's sweep across Russia, not trying to sweep the Red Sox. There were also flags on the wall from every country our players represented. Buck was generous enough to include my late father's homeland of Trinidad, even though I wasn't born there.

Players sat in staggered rows of luxury leather chairs; Buck stood at his podium with his dossier. He demanded and commanded our full attention. This was all business. We broke down every player, practically to the type of toothpaste he used. Buck had information that only spies could have gathered—tidbits based on overheard conversations and analyses based on something that happened in a player's personal life which might affect his play. He waxed about how a snippet from John Olerud's conversation could be used to our advantage against the Seattle Mariners' pick-off plays, or he insisted that a player on the Devil Rays would be mentally unavailable because of an alleged off-the-field incident at home.

Showalter also invited us to put in our two cents: many of us on the team—including me—had recently arrived as free agents, and Buck was eager for our input about the hitting patterns, tendencies, likes, and dislikes of our former teammates. Armed with this inside knowledge, we were as prepared as any team in the league.

As hard as it is to *get* to the big leagues, it often takes just as much effort to *stay* there. Once your opponents know your number, you better change that number every so often or you'll soon be back in the minors. You have to keep opponents guessing by going against your pattern once in a while.

When leading off the game, I never swung at the first pitch. Pitchers saw the pattern and began laying in fat fastballs to start the game. I noticed, and one day I predetermined that I was going to swing as hard as I could to lead off the game. Result: a base hit up the middle.

The Rangers, like most teams, held a separate meeting for pitchers and catchers, where the pitching staff, pitching coach, bullpen coach, and bench coach compared notes on how to get each hitter out. Does he struggle against a curveball? Will he chase a bad pitch when he has two strikes against him? Does he have a "hole" in his swing that you can exploit?

On rare occasions, position players would be allowed to join the pitchers' meeting and share the knowledge they had about hitters from playing with them in the past. But for the most part, we shared what we knew less formally.

In Chicago, manager Jim Riggleman had a different system. He gathered the entire team to talk about how to pitch our opponent—in large part because there is nowhere to banish half the squad in the tiny Wrigley Field locker room. On one occasion, we were playing the Montreal Expos, who had just called up a young outfielder by the name of Vladimir Guerrero. No one knew anything about him, save Amaury Telemaco, who had seen Guerrero play in their native Dominican Republic. So we quizzed him.

"Can you throw him a curve?"

"No, he can hit that."

"How about working him away?"

"No, he has these long arms and can hit balls way out of the strike zone."

"What about hard fastballs inside?"

"No, he can catch up with anyone's fastball."

After Telemaco shot down a few more possible ways to get Guerrero out, Riggleman yelled, "Oh, come on! How good can this guy be? He just got here!"

The rookie showed us that day why we couldn't find a strategy. He smacked a home run against the wind and hit every other pitch we threw—hard.

These days there's a book on Vladimir Guerrero, but it's hardly the length of a Dostoyevsky novel. He still swings at everything and still hits the ball hard. Once he got a base hit after swinging at a ball that bounced before it reached the plate.

No amount of study can prepare you for a cricket shot. When that happens, all you can do is smile—and put it on his chart.

If there were a pie chart illustrating how players prepare for their opponents, scouting reports would only be one sliver. Pictures in motion is another. The video room allows pitchers and hitters to fine-tune their skills in a way that old-timers could never foresee.

I'm not referring to the latest PlayStation or Xbox. I'm talking about videotape—and, later, digital video—that allows players to study every tic and tactic of every opponent and, equally important, of themselves. Accompanying the video is a log and a record of every pitch, every at-bat, and every sequence of events during a game.

Forget HGH. When I broke into the big leagues with the Chicago Cubs, VHS was our hidden weapon. "Fast Eddie" was our video room guru. He would sit in the dungeon of Wrigley Field and stare at what seemed to be a hundred mini–video screens at one time. Then he would create tapes for each player so we could study our performance and scrutinize our opponents. We could even learn a thing or two about an umpire's tendencies. When I joined the Texas Rangers, I saw that Buck Showalter was just as serious. During batting practice Buck required us to dedicate one whole station to video. We watched our archives for fifteen minutes every day during our pregame routine.

Catchers in particular found VHS a very useful tool. My longtime Phillies teammate Mike Lieberthal would arrive early at the stadium every day to watch tape and read data on each hitter on the other team. This would give him a sense of how to call a game. He would then discuss options with each pitcher individually. Before they ever set foot on the field, they had an approach.

Because VHS tapes were easy to transport, we could carry clips to study on road trips. Soon, however, VHS was passé. The digital age was upon us, and our video station suddenly became a hard drive of data that allowed you to click and drag to obtain the desired information.

I could sit in front of the computer, click on GLANVILLE, then click on CURT SCHILLING, and voilà! Every at-bat where I faced Curt would come up. Did I want to know what he threw me on 2–2 counts? Do I want to see how I looked against his slider? I could sort the data by count, pitch type, player, pitcher, whatever I needed.

At one point I saw enough of Randy Johnson on the screen to realize that whenever there were runners in scoring position, he liked to throw a "get me over" slider for a strike as the first pitch in the sequence. For a while, he would freeze me on it, and the count would be 0 and 1 every time. After recognizing the pattern, I was able to guess slider, but you still have to be able to hit a pitch even if you know what's coming. Easier said than done against Randy, but once I did slap a first-pitch slider for a base hit into left field, scoring two runs.

Of course, pitchers could throw hitters for a loop, too. Greg Maddux was one of the smartest players at any position. Whenever I led off the game, I would do a ritual and enter the batter's box with my head down. (Shawon Dunston did something like this, too.) Eventually Maddux saw this pattern. One game while my head was down, the ball was halfway to home plate before I looked up. Easy strike. Advantage Maddux. From that day forth, I had to enter the batter's box with one eye on him.

But the quest for information about opposing players and managers does not end with the pregame meeting or the trip to the video room. I can still remember conversations in which we sought to expand our baseball IQs by asking such questions as: How in the world can Halle Berry be seeing David Justice? Do you think Derek Jeter will ever date someone who isn't on *Maxim*'s Top 100 Sexiest Women list? Did you see Bobby Abreu's latest toy? It's a customized Porsche complete with his number 53 embroidered all over the place. Did you catch Lou Piniella on SportsCenter? Does he really hate dirt that much? Despite our reputation for "spit first, ask questions later," this pepper game of personality spiced up our pregame stretching.

Ah, stretching. Once on the field, every player had to fall in line for a routine led by the strength and conditioning coach. Fortunately, we did have room to "interpret" the suggested stretch or, better yet, to focus on the areas that gave us the most trouble— because no doubt, we were all hurting somewhere.

The home team takes batting practice first, while the visitors stretch. This seems to violate the rules of etiquette; after all, when you have guests for dinner, you serve them first. But being served second can have its advantages. In the late 1990s, nothing drew more attention than Mark McGwire's thunderous batting practice. When we were in St. Louis and he was in the cage, the only thing we stretched was our necks. He turned the same batter's box we all hit in into a launching pad. (Of course, we now know he was using a different fuel than some of us.)

After stretching and agility drills (high knees, lunges, backpedaling), we played catch. Most of the time, you have a set catch partner over the course of a season. This arrangement makes it easier than drawing straws every day or just worrying that you might be the sad sap that has to "double up" and join an already established pair. Sounds like junior high, doesn't it?

My Phillies catch partner Desi Relaford and I bonded over the course of summers tossing the ball. We regularly subverted the drill by taking a few moments to try out some pitches—a fun attempt to return to our glory days in high school, when each of us had toed the rubber.

I featured the "Nasty," a smoldering cauldron of funk and twist. This pitch was a derivative of something the former big leaguer Jim Bouton showed me one day at my high school practice. The author of *Ball Four* had office space in my hometown, so he came out one day to my high school practice to show us all some pitching tips. (I actually played against him in a summer league and watched his cap fall off even then.) To throw the Nasty, you wrap your ring finger and thumb around the ball and pull down hard as you let the ball come up and out of your hand. It is as hard to master as it sounds, but once you get it, the bottom drops out of it and probably your elbow, too.

How good a high school pitcher was I? Not too shabby. Good velocity, no sense of the strike zone. I was blessed with a mean curve and a hard fastball and cursed with control so errant that I had no idea where the ball was going. In one game I achieved a rare feat. I hit two guys in the head, back to back. Then the next hitter fouled a ball off his face in self-defense. My pitching line: a lot of walks, a lot of strikeouts, a lot of hit batters, and a lot of ice.

In the majors, I never did try to lobby my way to pitching during a 17–2 blowout. I thought it could be fun, but I also remembered how my arm used to feel after games I pitched in high school. After an eleven-inning, 168-pitch performance against Don Bosco Prep, I couldn't lift my arm for days. No more pitching—hand me a bat, please.

Desi, an infielder, did want to take the mound, and he got his wish as a member of the New York Mets in 2001. He pitched a perfect inning, striking out one. After that, I would not have been surprised to hear that he lobbied to go into a 3–2 game when the closer had the flu.

I wasn't so brave. Who could forget José Canseco's miserable experience when he tried to ride to the rescue of the Texas Rangers' bullpen against the Boston Red Sox in 1993? He looked like The Rock holding a white pea in his hands. He ultimately blew out his elbow, requiring Tommy John surgery, and causing a huge void in the Rangers' lineup.

José should have stuck to hitting, an art perfected in batting practice, which follows the pregame catch. Most teams divide their players into four groups for this drill. Managers mix up how the groups are determined. Some prefer to keep the composition of these groups the same all season, while others send you up there in the order you'll be hitting in the game. All arrangements are subject to change on a whim.

The order in which you hit is less important than who is pitching to you. Teams have more than one batting practice pitcher, and on every team I played with, it was always an issue as to which group would get the best BP thrower. Juan "Porky" Lopez was everybody's favorite when I was with the Cubs. His pitches were straight as an arrow. It was like hitting a beach ball. If you had Porky, you were confident you'd have a good day at the plate.

Porky's bizarro world double was the late Phillies coach and field general John Vukovich. Vuk's likely multiple bone spurs in his elbow forced five hitches in his delivery before he finally released a cross between a slider and a fork ball. When he was on the mound, leaving the cage with a broken bat or two was inevitable, thanks to mistimed swings. His control was a factor, too. More than likely, someone was going to get plunked in the back or knee once a week when Vuk was pitching BP. We had so much love and respect for the man that we dared not say anything, but deep down we were worried that a poor showing in batting practice might ruin our confidence.

Depending on the team philosophy, the goal of batting practice varied. On hitting coach Tony Muser's watch in Chicago, we had an opening round of situational hitting. Tony wanted you to approach each pitch as a game scenario. Get the runner over, get the squeeze down, make the sacrifice bunt to third, hit-and-run. When Larry Bowa threw BP in Philly, he kept the ball away from you most of the time, making sure you used the whole field.

After the first round, it is up to the batter to decide what he wants to do with each pitch. A group leader will dictate the number of swings per round. I had that role often, since I was a leadoff hitter and needed to set the table at all times.

Once you get established, you can try to launch every ball into the stands. But don't try that as a rookie; you will be berated for not having much of a plan. Then again, sometimes it feels good to hit the ball a mile for confidence purposes. During my last season in Philly, when we played the Red Sox at Fenway Park, I tried to hit every ball over the Green Monster and onto the Mass Pike.

Occasionally contests pop up at the cage. My Cubs teammate Brian McRae watched pitcher Frank Castillo's anemic swing and determined that there was no way he would ever hit a ball over the fence, even in BP. In 1995 Brian had said that he would lease a Mercedes for Frank if he hit a ball over the fence in BP. And if Frank hit one in a game, Brian would lease his-and-her Benzes—one for Frank, one for his wife. Seemed like a safe bet until the pitcher got one up in the jet stream during batting practice at Wrigley in 1997, and it landed in the basket just above the outfield wall. Frank got his car.

After about ninety minutes of on-the-field preparation, it's time for a change—literally. Players return to the clubhouse, climb out of their pregame jerseys, and put on their game uniforms. Typically, the home team has more than an hour before it has to go back out. The visiting team has less than thirty minutes, since guests hit second (but they also can get to the park later).

What to do? Depending on the manager or how you played defense recently, you may not have a choice during this time. The coaching staff may call for "infield," which is a quick defensive session on the field that puts each player at his position. The coaches will hit grounders into the outfield, telling the outfielders to throw to each base as if a runner is trying to take the extra base. Infielders get different kinds of ground balls, and in this drill, the catchers will get a chance to fire the ball to each base, simulating a reaction to a would-be base stealer. So if "infield" is called, better get your arm loose. It would not be a stretch to declare that "infield" was the most complained-about pregame ritual. Especially when your arm was sore, or as we called it, "hanging."

But many days, players can use any free time however they see fit. It was a time for music—even if Sammy Sosa put his one song for the year on a perpetual loop. (I loved the remake of "Killing Me Softly" by the Fugees, but after Sammy got it on his boom box, he played it until it killed me softly.) It was time for ESPN—no other TV station seemed to exist. (But how many times can you see Barry Bonds hit a ball into McCovey Cove?) It was time for food—I could eat an entire pizza from Donatos in Cincinnati.

Of course, as you get a tad older, you probably have to spend a good portion of this time getting your body ready. The weight rooms in Philly were busy with guys on the treadmill, often accompanied by Randy Wolf's Linkin Park CD. Whatever it took to get into the zone and be ready for that grand entrance onto the field. The time flew by, since you may have done an interview or become engrossed replying to fan mail. Players are mostly creatures of habit, especially when they are on a good personal streak. Make that turkey sandwich again since you hit a home run yesterday; play another hand of pluck so that you can win bragging rights over Brian L. Hunter; head down to the media room to do a mini–photo shoot for the team paraphernalia catalog. Anything can happen during this time, until that bell rings telling you it's time to "get it on." For me that was twenty minutes before the game began.

At that time I liked to sit in the dugout for a few minutes, soaking in all the sights and sounds, scoping out the selection of sunflower seeds or Powerade flavors, hobnobbing with reporters, or chatting with a "famous" person who was about to throw out the first pitch. Jerry Rice, Russell Crowe, and Allen Iverson made for interesting conversations. (Or watching Marion Jones race the Phillie Phanatic—it looked like her feet never touched the ground.) Then at the fifteen-minute mark most of the starters were out on the closest foul line, getting into their individual rituals.

Keep in mind, on the way to either the right field or the left field line, we would have to pass fans looking to get an autograph, a photo, or share a "hello." The configuration of the stadium affected this dynamic. In San Diego's old Jack Murphy Stadium, we were so far away from the left field line that we had a lengthy jog to reach our supporters (not always supporters, but it is nice to think so). In Oakland, the fans behind the dugout could reach over the top and grab the cap off of your head.

I usually spent some time signing. But if it was a little late or if I needed more time to get loose thanks to a tight hamstring, I'd use the "Sandberg wave." Ryne Sandberg had perfected a gesture with his hand that conveyed, *I see you, but I have to get to work.* I would describe it as part Disney, part traffic officer stop.

Some players had to be dragged away from signing among the mass of humanity during the pregame. My short run with the Yankees showed a surprisingly patient Derek Jeter, who signed for extensive periods of times. Scott Rolen would be more tactical, catch a few fans earlier so that he could just focus on getting ready for the game during these fifteen minutes.

Maybe your willingness to sign had something to do with your signature. If you hadn't made the adjustment as a rookie to cut down on the letters in your name, you weren't learning. My name is fairly long, but after signing thousands of cards upon being drafted, I cut out more than half of the letters. It became more of a symbol than an actual signature.

I did save a base from the 2004 inaugural season at Citizens Bank Park in Philadelphia. On it were all my teammates' signatures. Todd Jones had immaculate handwriting. Years later, I can still read every letter. Then there is young gun Jason Michaels, whose autograph looked like a cross between my two-year-old son's signature with his less dominant hand, and a gerbil that got lost during water coloring. Not that mine was art, but over time, I was efficient. I remember when Jimmy Rollins was perfecting his signature, at first it took him the entire pregame to do one. Make no mistake about it, we practice for a while in the locker room before breaking out a new signature. It may take weeks.

Eventually I would saunter to the foul line, which I used as a starting block for short sprints. Later in my career, I would ask the strength and conditioning coach to help stretch my legs out before the running.

Because opposing players were also running sprints from their foul line, we were destined to meet in center field. Cubs skipper Jim Riggleman abhorred fraternization. He was one of the most positive, laid-back managers I ever played for, but he did not like us talking to the guys we were trying to beat.

He insisted we "banana" on our sprints. By that he meant that we should curve off toward the center field fence or just run at a diagonal to be sure we didn't cross paths with the players we would soon be facing. We also rubbed shoulders with opponents during stretching before batting practice. In those close quarters, the Cubs had you on the clock. We could say and do whatever we wanted with an opponent for a minute or so, maximum. Brian McRae would often announce when you were getting dangerously close to the finish and the fine that was assessed if you went overtime. And forget about crossing hitting coach Tony Muser. He was watching.

Seeing the umpires and the coaches congregate at home plate to exchange lineups and go over the ground rules, we knew we were on borrowed time. If the national anthem started when I was still down the left field line and penciled in to lead off the game, I knew I had to rush. I had to be ready for the first pitch, especially on the road. On the days I wasn't quite loose, I dreaded playing the Toronto Blue Jays or Montreal Expos, where a second anthem would make for some tightening muscles.

By now we'd all been at the park for over four hours. Loose or not, we knew the adrenaline would carry us through. It was time to play ball.

3

. . .

DURING THE GAME

Being a leadoff hitter is a relentless job. Your responsibility is to get on base and be a spark for your team's offense, and by the time you sit down after yet another game with five plate appearances, another one is coming at you. Your legs are probably killing you most of the year from dancing around the bases. You can't ease into the game or watch for a couple of pitches to see what the pitcher is throwing, because you are the trailblazer, with nothing but past experience, instincts, and a scouting report to create a plan for that first at-bat.

You could be at Dodger Stadium at twilight, when you can't see much of anything for the first few innings; you could be in an extra muddy Pro Player Stadium (now Sun Life Stadium) in Florida; you could be at home in Philadelphia, playing the Chicago Cubs, batting after Sammy Sosa has dug yet another hole in the batter's box the size of the Grand Canyon. You will find out how this plays out before anyone else on your team.

You are also the scout, responsible for relaying information back to your teammates and calming any pregame jitters.

"Hey, man, what's he throwing out there?"

Well, on one occasion, Kevin Brown was throwing darts, and from the first at-bat I said to myself, *We are in trouble.* I saw most of his pitches (part of what I was supposed to do, make him use his entire repertoire in that first plate appearance), and I realized that he was extra nasty on this day. But I kept my opinion to myself, even though in the end his five-hit complete-game victory was not shocking to me.

Since my silence didn't seem to help us, on another occasion I decided to be totally honest. We were in Dodger Stadium facing Chan Ho Park, on a day when he was at the top of his game. It was a dusky daytime start, and I could hardly see anything. Park struck me out on a 3–2 slider that was out of the strike zone. But I chased it.

When I got back to the dugout I told my teammates, "I'm not going to sugarcoat it. You can't see anything up there."

That approach didn't work either. Despite being major leaguers, everyone has a little bit of doubt that maybe today they won't have it anymore, that maybe staying out late last night will catch up to them today, that maybe this game will be their last before getting traded or sent back to Triple-A. They are looking to the leadoff hitter to remind them that it's going to be all right. My gloomy scouting report put the whole team in a funk, and we were no match for Park that night.

Every game is like the dial being reset to zero, and it is the leadoff hitter's job to help remind everyone that we can beat this guy. If I can lead off the game with a hit, the whole team will exhale. Give me the bat and let me turn up the dial for you.

The prototypical leadoff hitter, as I was reminded throughout my career, was supposed to get on base. You get a hit, you walk, or you get hit by a pitch. If you are doing that around 40 percent of the time, you are a star. If you reach on an error, a fielder's choice, or a dropped third strike, that doesn't count in the statistics column, even if you put so much pressure on the defense that you may have forced the mistake. Although the run you score counts just the same.

So what constitutes sparking an offense? Can you accomplish this feat even if you don't have a .400 on-base percentage? If your job is to score runs, it is hard to do that from the bench after another groundout to short, but I also know that infielders have to be a lot more on their toes when speedy guys come to the plate. Pitchers know that those guys drive you bananas once they get on base. Is that worth something that isn't quantifiable?

I was a middle-of-the-lineup hitter in high school and college, but in the pros my tools were seen as much more appropriate for a leadoff hitter. You need speed; you need to make contact; you need to get on base. I did the first two pretty well; it was the third part that hovered over me my entire career.

All along the way, there are people suggesting or telling you how to get better, from the head scout to the general manager to the hot dog guy, and a huge part of what makes you a professional is sifting through the millions of opinions and figuring out what is useful and what is not. I was told in the minor leagues that I chased too many high pitches and that "you can get away with it in the minors, but face Roger Clemens and you will never get on top of that pitch." Well, that guy was completely wrong, and I actually lived on high pitches my entire career. When I was with the Phillies, I got more than two hundred hits one season, but because my on-base percentage was lower than the threshold of effectiveness for leadoff hitters, I focused the next year on being more patient. The result was disappointing on both counts: I had fewer walks *and* fewer hits. Was the team better off for this new approach? I certainly wasn't.

In the end, you are responsible for your performance, and if you don't produce, you don't play. I listened to my evaluators and made a genuine effort to get better at my role, but there were diminishing returns, too. I had a couple of seasons scoring over a hundred runs. But I would never be that quintessential leadoff hitter, and my career on base percentage ended up a nonimpressive .315. Although I did average more than a hit a game when I was in the starting lineup.

There was one place where I couldn't buy a hit: Turner Field in Atlanta. My average there made Mario Mendoza look like Albert Pujols. You could have put the ball on a tee for me, and I would have gone oh-for-four with a couple of strikeouts.

Part of the blame goes to the Braves' staff of Cy Young winners and the team's phenomenal pitching coach, Leo Mazzone, who gave them a great plan to get me out. It wasn't tough to figure out. Never get beat inside, so they carved up the outside corner with ginsu-like precision.

I could hit the Braves' pitchers a lot better at Veterans Stadium or Wrigley Field. So I chalked up my failures at Turner Field to the lights and all the dark patches that were scattered about the field. There were no lights in the upper deck behind home plate, putting fielders at a disadvantage, too. It wasn't unusual for a center fielder to lose a ball in the pitch-black night sky. Does Nike make night vision goggles?

One night in Atlanta the worm finally turned. I managed to get a base hit to right field off a Jason Marquis fastball. Time out! I stopped the game to get the ball. The Braves' first baseman, B. J. Surhoff, asked me what this was for. I'm sure he expected that it must have been my five hundredth hit or something. "No reason," I told him. "I finally got a hit here."

I did have legitimate causes to get a game ball now and then. I got the first-ever hit at Enron Field (now Minute Maid Park) in Houston, and I got my one thousandth hit on the last day of the 2002 season. Good reasons. But I stared at and admired that Turner Field ball more often so I could survive the next series there without losing my mind.

Baseball players are creatures of habit. Even beyond all the superstitions that would put your neighborhood psychic to shame, players display patterns on the field that can be used against them. The video room did wonders in revealing these patterns, but there was nothing more useful then seeing a hand tipped in real time with your own eyes during a game.

I've heard that Hank Aaron often sat in the dugout peering

through the little hole at the top of his helmet. He created a tele-scope of sorts—not to look at the man in the moon, but the man on the mound. With such a narrow field of vision, he could focus exclu-sively on the pitcher, looking for any tendencies that could be exploited from the batter's box.

When I played, no one was better at finding a pitcher's tells than Bobby Abreu. It didn't matter who was on the mound; Bobby was a mile ahead of his opponent. He knew what was coming. No wonder he played so cool.

By the third or fourth inning, Bobby was onto something. Jeff D'Amico would curl his glove on his curveball; Carlos Perez would hook his leg when he was going home with a pitch. If Hideo Nomo was going to throw a splitter, the catcher would crouch higher in anticipation of the ball ending up in the dirt and bouncing high.

Information like this was pure gold. If you're at the plate and know that something off-speed is coming, you can wait on the pitch. If you're on first base itching to steal and know a slower pitch like a change-up or a splitter in the dirt is on its way, that's the time to take off. The additional fraction of a second a breaking ball takes to reach the plate is just the break you need.

One of my favorite players of all time, Roberto Alomar, was another master—and a generous one at that, in part, I'm sure, because his father, Sandy Alomar Sr., was my coach for years when I was in the Cubs system. Although we played on opposing teams in Puerto Rico during winter ball, Roberto gave me a clinic whenever we crossed paths (sometimes talking shop when I reached first base, his position that winter). He taught me how to time a pitcher after he comes set and before he throws to first on a pickoff attempt (not sell-ing out his own team, mind you). Soon, off the appropriate pitcher, I could steal second base blindfolded on a silent count. He explained in great detail how pitchers tipped their pitches or pickoff throws and even discussed how catchers give away pitches by the way they set up.

Knowledge is only one element of the equation. Discipline is the other. Once you've broken a code, you don't want to tip your own hand. If I start dancing around in my lead from first base, the entire stadium will know I'm stealing, and the opposing manager will call a pitchout. Disciplined hitting is even more difficult. You may get that pitch you knew was coming, but it is another thing to zone in and not swing at it when it is five inches out of the strike zone.

Signs can be tipped off from just about any position on the field. If the outfielders move too soon on a certain count, they may tip the next pitch. It is a hitter's count: two balls, no strikes. *Hmmm*, the lefty at the plate muses, *why did the right fielder just move three steps toward center? They don't expect me to turn on the ball. Must be a fastball coming. Probably outer third of the plate, too.*

These advantages become even more important when you are facing a pitcher that owns you. When you haven't found a way to beat him conventionally, it's time to predict the future. It may be the only chance you have of getting on base. Just as Greg Maddux figured out how to quick-pitch me because I looked down as I got into the batter's box, I eventually figured out when he liked to throw that backup slider to jam me inside with a runner in scoring position or that 3–2 change-up that he hoped I'd chase in the dirt because I was overanxious.

This day-to-day gamesmanship can mean the difference between a base hit and a foul out to the catcher, a stolen base and a caught stealing, a hit in the gap or a line drive out. The best at masking old habits have an instant advantage, while those who telegraph their every move are in for a long day and a short career.

Fool me once, I was just learning; fool me twice, lose my starting job; fool me a third time, welcome back to the minors.

The inability to hit a curveball—whether or not the pitcher has tipped it—has sent a lot of players back to the minors. So how do you learn to hit a pitch that seems to defy the laws of physics and drop down or move sideways as it approaches home plate? The gifted baseball writer Roger Angell said it best when the St. Louis Cardinals' Adam Wainwright threw a nasty curveball that froze the New York Mets' Carlos Beltran to end the 2006 National League Championship Series. Angell said that the pitch fell "like a bat in an elevator shaft."

I am probably not the most qualified commentator on this subject. For me, the curveball often prompted a bad and premature hack at the ball. I survived in the majors by hitting the flat, predictable, and minimally breaking fastball. But I can impart some curveball wisdom that might improve the mental part of your game, even though I make no such promises for your swing.

As a hitter, you have about two-tenths of a second to decide what pitch you are actually seeing, all the while attempting to put a round bat on a round ball that is bending and breaking in three dimensions. Needless to say, it took me my entire professional career to develop a halfway decent approach to hitting a curveball.

The curveball reality hit me all at once. I thought I could race through the minor league system on quick hands and exceptional coordination. That was until I ran into Gregg Olson, a pitcher who at one time was a dominant force in the Baltimore Orioles bullpen. He was known for his knee-buckling curveball, and he didn't disappoint. The first time I saw his Thor-like hammer, I thought, *This is not good.* That was the moment I became determined to learn how to hit a curveball for fear of ever again feeling like a frozen popsicle.

During an off-season instructional camp with the Cubs, I set up a pitching machine to send me the meanest curveballs it could throw. It took me a while, but eventually I was able to carve the ball into right field.

What I found was that your approach doesn't have to be any different from the one you use when dealing with any other curveball that life throws at you. We spend so much time cruising along, looking to hit the straight and dependable fastball, that the audacity of something different can cause us to forget the tactics that once gave us comfort and success.

In my fifteen seasons of professional baseball, there were a lot of off-the-field curveballs to go with in-game curveballs. On paper, a player's ascension to the majors looks straightforward: you go from Single-A to Double-A to Triple-A to the big time. But in actuality, you can wake up and be traded away to another team at the drop of a hat, as I was in December 1997.

Or you could actually go the wrong way on that highway. While I was in Double-A, my roommate, Paul Torres, got called into the office by our manager, Dave Trembley, for his demotion to a Class A club. He was leading our team in home runs and runs batted in and was the best offensive player we had, but he had to go down a level. The powers that be had ordained someone else "the best offensive player we have," so our actual batting leader's success was somehow unacceptable.

The biggest curveball of my life came when my father began his descent into chronic illness one spring training while I was playing for Philadelphia. He would remain sick and in and out of emergency rooms over the next three years. There was no machine I could set up to throw me that simulated nasty curveball; I had to learn to approach this one with no bat and with a blindfold on. This I accomplished by trying to focus on the few things I could control about getting my father healthier. I did what I could, and left the rest to forces bigger than myself. Even though I didn't hit a home run on this particular curveball, at least I recognized that it was outside my power to do much else, and so, in a sense, I didn't chase a bad pitch.

There is a constant debate among baseball hitters who deal with the question "If you could know what pitch was coming, would you want to know?" Since there are all kinds of tricks to figuring that out, it is a very real possibility that you can, at times, know what is coming.

You could take a page out of Bobby Abreu's repertoire and study a pitcher like Randy Johnson, who changed his glove position on certain pitches, or you could work out some secret key with a runner standing at second base who can see the catcher giving signs to the pitcher. Or maybe use Mark Grace's tactic, taking note of the shadow cast by a catcher during a day game to know where he was setting up behind the plate.

But do you still want to know?

Many players don't. Because as the hitter, you might try to hit the ball to the moon from the excitement of knowing what's coming, and end up destroying your mechanically sound swing in the process. My Phillies teammate Scott Rolen wasn't a big fan of any kind of tips. He wanted to zone in on the pitcher with his full attention, even to the point that if you were the runner on second base, he didn't want you dancing around trying to get a good jump (or faking a steal of third) because it distracted him. Probably not the best situation for someone like me, who lived and died by speed, but I knew that if I was thinking about stealing third with Rolen at the plate, I made sure I was going.

On the other side, some players definitely did want to know. My teammates on the Texas Rangers, particularly Alex Rodriguez, wanted every hitting advantage and plotted how to relay the catcher's signs they could see when standing on second base. We talked about sending signals by kicking the bag or making particular hand gestures. Eventually I tuned this out. All this talk was foreign to me, and since I was a base stealer, new to the American League, the idea of trying to relay signs and steal third base at the same time was overwhelming. The team seemed to agree, as the idea fell to the wayside.

It's one thing to share information with a teammate and quite another to let an opponent in on the secret. The news that Bobby Abreu had figured out what Jeff D'Amico of the Brewers was doing to tip his curveball spread to other teams. After we finished playing Milwaukee, our next in-league series was against the Cubs at Wrigley. As I was running sprints before the game, a player on the Cubs came over to me and said, "I heard D'Amico is tipping his pitches. We play the Brewers next series, what's he doing?" That is not how it works, you don't help some random other team, and besides, something didn't feel right about betraying D'Amico like this. So in effect, I told the player that, yes, D'Amico is tipping and you'll have to figure it out for yourself. Turned out he didn't pitch against the Cubs anyway.

So, no curveball is easy to handle, even when it is expected. We can practice all we want, but there will inevitably be times when it will shock us by its mere arrival. The curveball becomes that rude awakening that often derails us from our tried-and-true plan to go from A to B.

Even so, I kept working on hitting that curveball. I finally figured out that most of the time it was better when I didn't swing at it. Because, as in life, the curveball is often just a test—most times thrown to see if you will chase something out of your zone—and not the final pitch that will get you out. So take it from a dead-red fastball hitter: once you master your strike zone, you can win your battle with that curveball by just taking it in stride.

Ballplayers like to be in control. So when the official scorer throws you a curve, "taking it in stride" ain't so easy. It should come as no surprise that we are in no hurry to put those in charge of the scorecard on our holiday mailing list. The league-appointed official scorers, who decide whether a batted ball will be deemed a hit or an error, can't change the outcome of a game, but they do have the power to affect your batting average or fielding percentage, and, in some cases, your shot at making it into the record books. And there's not much you can do about it.

On one occasion my Phillies were playing the Pirates in Pittsburgh, where the scorer was notorious for being stingy in flashing the *H* for hit. Any ball that so much as touched a fielder was scored an error, even when it almost took his hand off.

Kris Benson, who always gave me a lot of trouble, was on the mound for the Pirates. He had a mean "slurve," a violently dropping curveball with a slider's speed. Somehow, with an 0–2 count, I smashed a hard one-hop ground ball that hit Benson's knee before he could get his glove down. If he were a ninja, he would have made that play easily, but there aren't too many of those in the majors. The ball caromed toward our dugout with some serious speed, so I felt good that I had myself a hit.

Now there is an art to looking up at the scoreboard to see what the scorer has decided. You can't be obvious about it. First of all, you don't want to look selfish. And second, you may miss the next pitch if the scorer takes a while to rule. So you glance as you take your lead or hope the chatty first baseman or middle infielder will give you a heads-up.

In the case of Benson vs. Glanville, the scorer remained his true Scrooge-like self, deeming my knee replacement shot an E-1. When you hit against pitchers you dread, you need every break you can get. I was happy to be on base, but would have been even happier to see my batting average go up instead of down thanks to the error-happy eye in the sky.

Because the rules of the game allow a scorer to reverse his decision within twenty-four hours, the second-guessing and lobbying often begin immediately. Protests come in waves. First, the beat reporters covering your team, who are sitting near the scorer in the press box, weigh in: "Oh come on! You're gonna score that an error?" Then the phone rings from the dugout, and the bench coach makes his case. Yes, in the middle of the game!

Players themselves think twice before taking action. While many might like to argue a scorer's decision, the etiquette of baseball frowns upon any outward signs of selfishness. If you fight too hard and have someone call up to the press box to debate the worthiness of your hit, you come across as caring more about your batting average than the team. And if you make the call yourself? Ask shortstop Orlando Cabrera how his White Sox teammates, the press, and the fans regarded him in 2008 after word got out he'd phoned the scorer during the game to protest an error call.

In 1998, the Rangers' Juan Gonzalez didn't even wait to get into the dugout to make clear his feelings. "Igor," as we called him, was on pace for a remarkable achievement—driving in one hundred runs before the All-Star break. He hit a line drive at Chuck Knoblauch, the Yankees' second baseman, who misjudged it. The ball hit off his glove and ended up in the outfield, allowing two runs to score. If it was scored a hit, Juan would get two more RBIs; if it was an error—nada. E-4 was posted.

The idealistic, "rah rah" baseball devotee might look at this and say, "Didn't two runs score anyway?" But it doesn't always work that way. Idealism be damned, Igor took the unusual step of debating the call while he was still on the field. He gestured with disgust toward the press box from first base.

The demonstration worked. Later, the scorer changed his call from error to hit and Juan got his RBIs. Juan did show remorse, stating, "I'm sorry I did it, but at the same time, I'm trying to do my job, get RBIs."

My own final stat sheet shows fifty-nine career home runs. Maybe there should be an asterisk, because if not for a scorer's error, I'd have reached the magic sixty (albeit in nine seasons). When the Phillies were playing the Colorado Rockies in 1998, I hit a ball on the ground down the left field line that ricocheted off the side wall. The Rockies' Dante Bichette overran the ball as it kicked back into fair territory, and I circled the bases for what I thought was surely an inside-the-park home run. Bichette never even touched the ball, and it didn't go through his legs.

The scorer ruled: "Double and an error LF."

What?

After taking heat from the Phillies media staff and just about everyone else up there, the scorer agreed to change the double to a home run. But more than twenty-four hours had passed (I think he had gone on a weekend vacation), and it wasn't earth-shattering enough for the team to file a formal dispute. As a result, I'm forever stuck at fifty-nine dingers.

You'll note I haven't identified any scorers by name. That's because the vast majority of those in that position lay low and remain anonymous. Smart move. No hitter in a slump would take too kindly to meeting the person who could have made his life easier by flashing an *H* on the scoreboard. There is a big difference between going oh-for-four while reaching base on an error and going one-for-four, especially when you are oh for your last fifteen.

I suspect scorers also aren't anxious to run into Gold Glovers whom they charge with errors. These defensive studs rarely screw up in the field, so the bar is high for an *E*. If Mr. Gold Glove dropped it, *no one* would have caught it. So give the batter a hit. It was always nice to hit ground balls to Ozzie Smith or Omar Vizquel that landed in that gray area between *H* and *E*. More than likely, I had myself a hit.

I don't know how much money official scorers make, but it can't be enough to compensate them for the grief they take. I confronted just one scorer in nine major league seasons, picking a fight because he refused to give me a hit on a hard ground ball that Mets pitcher Scott Strickland had no time to react to. The ball didn't hit Strickland's leg like the ball I had hit against Benson. Rather, the pitcher used his glove more like a shield than a tool to catch a ball.

When I saw the scorer, he gave me some song and dance about the ball having hit the pitcher's glove. But if the ball is coming in to the plate at ninety-two miles per hour, it is going back up the middle with some hair on it. Hitting the grass first may slow it down. So what is the difference between having 0.2 seconds to react and having 0.25 seconds? It's a tough play and ought to be scored a hit. Or so I rationalized.

This isn't to say scorers don't take their jobs seriously. When a ball is caught and then dropped after a collision, the play can be scored a lot of ways. After one mishap, a scorer tracked me down to ask what had happened on a play when Phillies shortstop Jimmy Rollins and I ran into each other in short center field. I told him that I had caught the ball and then Jimmy ran into me and knocked it out of my glove. He gave Jimmy the error since he broke up an already caught ball.

Many times a ruling is clear as day, but just as often it can be subjective. It's not the same when a big power hitter who can't run hits a ground ball and the shortstop drops it versus when a speed demon hits it and the shortstop knows he has a microsecond to get the ball to first. Hit or error? Tough decision.

If the man in the press box has to make two or three tough calls a game, he's had a busy night. Compare that to the four men in blue on the field, who have to make scores of bang-bang calls without shooting themselves in the feet—on the spot, without benefit of replay (at least while I was playing), unprotected from tens of thousands of screaming partisans. So, how about a little love for the umps?

When I first started playing professional baseball, my Single-A manager, Bill Hayes, told me that I was being too formal in addressing the powers that be of the game. I called him (and others) "Coach," and on the field I referred to all umpires as "Blue." No one seemed to like such formality, so eventually I accepted that I would have to use first names. I treaded lightly because I knew my southern-raised mom would cringe at the idea. But during my first full season in the minors, 1992, I began dropping *Mr.* and *Mrs.* from my conversation—ironically, in Winston-Salem, in my mother's home state of North Carolina.

The formality came from a place of respect. Umpires were the judges on the field; their job was to uphold the law. Sure, it was more like "uphold the rules," but during a game, in the midst of the exploding sliders, thirty-four-inch bats, and high-octane fastballs, it was the law to me. Every pitch was in the hands of these arbiters, so to me it was no different from addressing a police officer, an elder in church, or a schoolteacher.

Unfortunately, I learned very quickly that umpires and school cafeteria food have a common problem. No matter how good they are, we will always find something to complain about.

It must be tough to be measured constantly against perfection, as the umps are day in and night out. If you get every call right, you are invisible, but if you miss a call, you have tarnished the purity of the game. There is no in-between. It is either-or in its rawest form. You are doing what you are supposed to be doing, or you are flat-out wrong and ruining everyone's dream.

My one attempt at umpiring occurred when I was in high school. I somehow got roped into officiating a game and thankfully had the bases, not balls and strikes. Still, I had no idea where to stand. My instincts kept telling me that I should be in a good place to catch the ball, not where I would be invisible. I worried about blocking the second baseman's view, or getting hit by a line drive the pitcher had stabbed at, never mind making the right call on a close play.

At one point, a ground ball was hit to the shortstop, culminating in a "bang-bang," whisker-close play at first, where the runner's foot hit the base just as the first baseman caught the ball. I was still a full ninety feet away, acting more like a spectator than anything else. I called the runner out, only to learn between innings from the first base coach that the first baseman didn't have his foot on the bag. There was no way I could tell because I didn't know how to get into the right position to make the call. It takes a lot of training to move around like a panther, always be in position, and then go back to stealth.

By the time I became a major league player, I knew (at least by name) a few umpires from my minor league days. Andy Fletcher, C. B. Bucknor, and Bruce Dreckman had matured and learned their craft right alongside us in the farm levels. Long travel, bad motels, getting yelled at by upset booster club members—they had paid their dues.

Outside of this trio, I barely knew any of the umpires who oversaw major league games. After being up just over a month, I was greeted by the famously edgy Joe West. No one knew the rule book better than Joe, so even when he was checking you with that poker face, you understood that he just loved messing with you.

When I got to second base, Joe came up to me and asked, "Who the heck are you?"

I told him, "I don't know, but I guess we'll find out."

Umpires don't have a lot of latitude to be warm and fuzzy. They have to maintain objectivity; they can't really shake your hand on the field or make any connection that appears partial. So, for years, I'd learn their names, chit-chat a little on my way to center field, or maybe see them in the hotel lobby, but it was hard to get close. I was able to brush past that line in the sand for a moment with the umpire Jim Wolf, whose brother Randy was my teammate in Philadelphia. I sat with Jim once in a hotel in San Juan, Puerto Rico, briefly, on a day off. We talked about life, baseball, travel schedules, the future, like two guys having a couple of drinks. It was the longest conversation I would ever have with an umpire. And I almost felt like I was cheating.

While the men in blue might seem like a mystery, it's not reciprocal; they know you. One day during spring training with the Rangers in Arizona in 2003, I went to a Phoenix Suns basketball game. I was sitting courtside when a ball bounced into my lap. The referee came over, got the ball from me, and then paused for ten seconds to say hello and tell me how much he enjoyed watching me play. It turned out he was Joe Crawford, the brother of the umpire Jerry Crawford. How did he even recognize me? Jerry apparently shared with his brother stories he couldn't share with others—stories that showed a connection he may have made with a player or two.

I can proudly claim that I never got ejected from a major league game in my career. The most I ever argued a call was on a close play at first base during a game in Florida against the Marlins when I was with the Phillies. Frustrated—with my playing time, with the team's poor record, and with my batting average—I needed bang-bang plays to go my way. The first base umpire called me out. I argued, and to this day I feel bad about it, especially after I looked at the replay later on and realized he was right.

Only a machine could approach the accuracy we expect and demand from umpires. Super slo-mo replays might show what happened on a given play, but in real time, it is a roadrunner blur. I wish I'd had the luxury of slowing a few pitchers' fastballs to super slo-mo; I would have waltzed into the Hall of Fame.

Sometimes you hear talk about how umpires are getting more confrontational, but I am amazed at how calm they stay over the course of a season. For the most part, they keep on an even keel, even when coaches are in their face and players are yapping at them and fans are booing them out of the stadium. I'm surprised they don't snap more often, because they take a beating all year long. The Atlanta Braves manager Bobby Cox ranks first in ejections year in and year out, as he tries to win a battle of attrition with the home plate umpire every night. Hearing him all game long would drive anyone to the brink.

Once, I took the time before a game in Philadelphia to tell the home plate umpire from the night before, Greg Gibson, that he had called the best game I'd ever seen. He didn't miss a pitch; no one argued anything the entire night. It was as if he had bowled a 300 and no one had a clue. It wasn't on SportsCenter; it just fell into that bucket of how it is supposed to be every night. The exchange clearly was important to Greg; he thanked me, with a surprised look on his face. I just thought, *Everyone always voices their displeasure. What's wrong with voicing a compliment?*

Next time you go to a game, take a few innings and watch the umpires move on the field. On a fly ball deep into the outfield, you will see the choreography of base umpires moving into position. It is like some sort of judges' ballet. One is sprinting toward the play to see whether the catch was good; one is moving toward third base to anticipate the runner tagging up; the catcher's mask is being moved out of the way by the home plate ump. I certainly wouldn't want to run in their special protective shoes.

These guys are the best in the world, hands down, and, like us all, they make mistakes—which, unfortunately, is the only time they ever get noticed. I saw them every single day, and there is no other group of professionals in the world I would want to uphold the rules. Even if, once in a while, it tastes like cafeteria food going down.

When the skies open up before the first pitch or in the middle of the fourth or fifth inning, "calling a game" has nothing to do with balls and strikes. After another round of the card game of choice, pluck, we couldn't take it anymore. Were we going to play or what? It was nearing 9 p.m. It had been raining for over an hour. Our eyes were heavy. How could we play at this hour when we felt like we should be in bed?

During a rain delay, everyone thunders on what should be done. Each player has his own interpretation of the rules, none of which is based on the actual rule book. We rant about how the umpires are not being responsible or the front office doesn't care about us because it is all about the money made at the gate.

Consigned to the clubhouse, we bark and grumble through a tenth replay of SportsCenter; we watch Christopher Walken ask for more "Cowbell" in the classic *Saturday Night Live* skit; we make more turkey sandwiches; we whip out our meteorology degrees from the University of Google.

One teammate: "Did you see the radar? No way will we play."

Five minutes later, from another, teammate: "Did you see the radar? There is a window."

Ah, the infamous window.

The window is what we call the space within all that nasty green on the Doppler that gives us hope (or fear) that we are going to play that day. Its size is proportional to possibility; its speed measures the time we have to hope Cole Hamels can get five innings in and make the game official.

On one trip to Colorado, the Phillies saw the possibility of picking up ground on the division-leading Mets. We had a three-game set with the Rockies, but the weather was not looking good.

Before the completion of the fifth inning of game one on Friday night, the rains came down. We waited and waited. As the clock raced toward the wee hours, the umps finally announced that the game had been canceled. I was thankful, not only because it was past my bedtime, but also because I had dropped an easy fly ball, ending a long personal errorless streak. Because the game wasn't official, the error evaporated.

As we changed into our street clothes, it was discussion time. We learned that the Rockies had put in a request for a dreaded "split" doubleheader—one game in the afternoon, one in the evening, with three hours in between. Of course, the home team owners prefer split doubleheaders when rescheduling rainouts because each game gets its own gate. But all the players want to do is pull their hair out. There's no time to go back to the hotel—even though you can walk to the Westin from Coors Field. So pack your iPod or PS3 or bring along a good read because you're going to be at the ballpark from 9 a.m. to 11 p.m. When I was with the Cubs, Brian McRae preferred staying at the ballpark instead of going back to our hotel after a midnight-hour postponement; he traded his hotel room to the equipment manager for a spot in the guy's office in the clubhouse.

There are a lot of rules governing the decision to play a day-night doubleheader, most of which involve the understanding that such a decision will pass through the Players Association. On this particular occasion, since it was the last series of the season between the two teams, a clause kicked in that gave the home team the authority to make close to a unilateral decision about playing a split doubleheader. This didn't stop us from seeing what concessions the Rockies would make. Curt Schilling and I were the player reps, but Curt begin negotiations to barter for the day-night split doubleheader without consulting the team, much to the dismay of a few players who wanted to vote on the matter. He ended up exchanging our services for a generous contribution by the Rockies owner, Jerry McMorris, to the local ALS chapter. (ALS, aka Lou Gehrig's disease, is a cause to which Curt was deeply devoted; he even named his oldest son Gehrig.) Curt read us the agreed-upon terms and then declared it done. Then it hit us: Curt was on the disabled list—he wasn't going to be playing anyway!

Thanks to the Friday night washout, we played three games in twenty-four hours. To make matters worse, the Rockies swept us, precipitating a stretch in which we lost fifteen of sixteen games and fell fatally out of playoff contention. Talk about raining on a parade.

During my final season in Philadelphia in 2004, the weather forecast rarely mattered. There was a 90 percent chance that Glanville would be on the bench, with less than a sunny disposition. And on those days that I was in the lineup, there was almost a 100 percent chance that I'd be facing one of the league's toughest pitchers.

For the bulk of my career, my playing weight hovered around 175 pounds. If you saw me in person, you would not have mistaken me for a bodyguard. Yet in my twilight years in the big leagues, I was just that. My job was to ride the bench and protect the up-and-coming young player who had replaced me in the lineup.

I wouldn't have gone so far as to take a bullet for my Phillies teammate Marlon Byrd, but I did do a lot to help him become a better baseball player. Some of that help came in the form of direct advice, but a lot of it came indirectly—by taking Marlon's place as a starter when our opponent's best pitcher was on the mound.

Many teams are reluctant to pencil in their rising stars against the game's top hurlers. Recognizing that an oh-for-four day with a couple of strikeouts is a real possibility, management doesn't want to damage a young player's fragile ego. Similar sympathy does not extend to the veterans on the bench. If someone is going to wear the collar, it might as well be the guy whose psyche or batting average is of little, or at least less, concern. My diet as a starter-slash-bodyguard in 2004 consisted of past Cy Young Award winners and perennial All Stars. In baseball, as in poker, it's no fun to be staring at aces all the time. (At least in poker you can bluff.)

The aces I faced included Randy Johnson, Tom Glavine, Brad Radke, Dontrelle Willis, Brandon Webb, and seemingly anyone else who had finished in the top five in Cy Young voting over the last decade. On the days they pitched, Marlon often gave way to me, the crafty wise man. This wasn't necessarily Marlon's wish; he was a competitor coming off a stellar 2003 campaign. But this was how the Phillies' plan unfolded after Marlon struggled early in the season. My experience supposedly put me in a position to know how to prepare for the best in the business even if I hadn't played in three weeks.

Generally, playing bodyguard hurts your batting average and your ego along with it. My batting average that season was a whopping thirty-one points lower than my previous worst, my rookie year. It is one thing not to play for long stretches at a time, hoping your work in the batting cage is enough to still compete against the best. It is another to take that hope and make it work in a game situation when Radke has his sinker going or Johnson throws a one-hundred-mile-per-hour fastball.

As tough as it is to start under these conditions, it's tougher to know that even if you defy the odds and trump the ace by getting a few hits, you're still going to be back on the bench until the next superstar takes the mound against you. And so, if it hasn't already happened, you now have certainly lost all faith that baseball is a meritocracy.

As much as I like my friend and former Phillies bench coach, Gary Varsho, I used to dread when he would creep over to my locker after batting practice to tell me something like "Burrell can't go today; you may need to start." All of a sudden you were the ER doctor with a pager on your hip, the break-glass-in-case-of-emergency guy facing the best. Just like the time I found out that I was starting against Radke on the road, *after* I got to the stadium that day. So much for a heads-up. Out of sync and on call. A long way from those cushy days as a starter.

As a role player instead of an everyday player, you have to be prepared for more than just the "spot" start. You might be the pinch runner, the pinch hitter, and any other pinch person necessary, so you have to learn how to be "pinch ready." You watch the game differently, trying to develop a sense of what is about to happen and when you might be needed. This requires a kind of "Being John Malkovich" state of being—getting inside the head of your manager and the opposing manager. (You think being John Malkovich is crazy; try following the emotional ride with Larry Bowa!)

By the middle innings, a bench player starts getting ready. If your starting pitcher is getting knocked around, you may be the guy called on to hit for him in the fourth or fifth. If he is cruising along, you may be part of a double switch in the eighth. Should your team be on the losing side of the equation, it could be pinch running for a slow catcher or hitting against a tough reliever. If you are the righty on the bench, you will see a lot of the specialist left-handed relievers whose sole job is to get out lefties, provided the opposing manager doesn't switch to a righty specialist.

I made up the term *scares* to define the time when you get called in to pinch hit only to have the opposing manager take out his pitcher. If you are a righty and the pitcher is a lefty and the opposing manager brings in a righty to face you, it is likely your manager will bring in a left-handed hitter to pinch hit for you, the pinch hitter. I thought a word reflecting such intimidation would make pinch hitters who were pinch hit for feel better. As baseball becomes more and more statistic-oriented, perhaps we'll see the day when a wily agent demands more money for a role player because of his high number of scares the previous season.

On a typical day when you are getting prepared to enter the game in some capacity, you go back into the locker room and start a routine. This may involve warming up on the treadmill, using hot packs, getting on a stationary bike, watching video of the pitcher you may face, and hitting off the tee to get some swings in.

Just like a relief pitcher, you have to anticipate the game situation and how you may be used. It's easy to see how players who spent a lot of time coming off the bench often become managers; after a while you start to manage in your own mind.

Of course, there are moments when as a veteran player in this situation you question everything. Moments when you think you should have veto power. After Marlon Byrd was sent down to the minors due to early struggles, I was bypassed to be the regular starter in favor of another younger player, Jason Michaels, and Ricky Ledee. It was a great opportunity for Michaels, and it made me think back to when I finally got to play everyday center field for the Cubs when Brian McRae sprained his ankle.

One day Michaels hurt his leg and had to come out of the game after the first inning. A replacement was quickly needed. There was no way anyone would be ready to enter the game at that moment; I had hardly even opened my bag of sunflower seeds. If I could, I would have exercised my veto then. *Can't put me in; I just vetoed it!* But Michaels couldn't go on, and a veto was a figment of my imagination, so I got ready in a Superman minute. I use the word *ready* loosely. An oh-for-four later, I probably could have helped the team more by just eating more sunflower seeds instead of entering that game.

There have been legendary pinch hitters who have defied the practical realities of trying to be physically ready at any time, especially with age working against them. Rusty Staub, Lenny Harris, Dave Hansen, and Marlon Anderson all found ways to make pitchers and managers uncomfortable even when they had hardly any time to stretch. They somehow found a way to thrive in those all-or-nothing moments. These old pros often teach the young players how to go about their business. I tip my cap to them.

I didn't see some of the great pinch hitters of all time play, guys like Dusty Rhodes and Smoky Burgess, but I know about them. When you make it to the big leagues you develop a sixth sense—a sense of history. While the frenetic pace of a season sometimes makes it difficult to appreciate the historical import of a particular moment, we're pretty good at keeping track of milestones. When Mariano Rivera recorded his five hundredth save in a 2009 game against the Mets, his Yankee teammates mobbed him on the mound as if he had clinched the pennant.

I wouldn't be surprised if some of those teammates—and perhaps even some of the Mets—asked him to sign something to show that they were there when history was made. True, some players don't want to lose cool points for breaking out a camera in the locker room or approaching a guy in the opposite dugout with an autograph pen and his baseball card. But many players—whether they consider themselves students of the game or are looking for memorabilia to show off in their basement—are avid collectors.

I didn't like to bother anyone during the season with cameras and Sharpies, but as my career reached its end, I did get a lot of bats and balls sent over from their dugout to ours, from guys like Jeff Bagwell, Mike Piazza, Alex Rodriguez, Rafael Palmeiro, Mickey Morandini, Sammy Sosa, and Tom Glavine. Most of the time, you catch your opponent out at the batting cage during a rainy day when both teams have to hit inside, or you just send a clubhouse assistant over with a message to the player you seek.

There was the one moment when I reached third base in a game against the Baltimore Orioles, and Cal Ripken Jr. came over from his third base position to say hello during a break in play. I saw his cool black and orange spikes with the initials *C.R.* and a big number

8 on them. I asked him if he could send over a signed pair after the game, not really thinking he would do it. The magic shoebox arrived shortly after the final out was recorded. I had broken the autograph ice, ignoring any macho sensibility that would have told me to never ask an opponent for anything.

My collection isn't bad, but there was something about asking for memorabilia that was an admission that my career was ending and that I was becoming more of a fan than a guy who was supposed to be there.

4
...
RESPECTING THE GAME

Baseball is a game of rules. Three strikes and you're out. *Unless* the catcher drops the ball, in which case you must be tagged out or thrown out at first base. *Unless* there is runner on first base. *Unless* there are two outs. Wait a minute; maybe it's a game of exceptions.

Rules or exceptions, the game is governed by a book that spans ten sections (plus an index). The laws are interpreted and enforced by knowledgeable, impartial judges—the umpires, who have their own five-section manual including an ever-evolving eighty-eight-page section called "Procedures and Interpretations." You can plead your case to them and expect a fair and speedy verdict.

These rules of baseball apply to what goes on between the white lines, not between a ballplayer's ears. What if a player forgets to set his watch for daylight savings time and misses the team bus? What if he forgets how many outs there are after catching a fly ball with runners on first and third and tosses the ball into the stands, allowing each runner to advance?

No book governs such personal misconduct. No umpire determines how to deal with the offender. But justice will be served. Ladies and gentlemen, please rise. The kangaroo court is now in session.

The kangaroo courts of baseball have ruled on some of the greatest crimes of our era. And not just crimes committed on the field. Many a player with a bad sense of etiquette, a problem with authority, an issue with being on time, or a predilection for making bonehead decisions has been brought before this forum by his peers.

The court serves the public well. It keeps players from violating in-house codes for fear of being ignominiously "called out." Fans, you have no idea how this supreme gavel makes a player less likely to ask someone to buy him a hamburger, and to eat it in the bullpen during a game (as my Phillies teammate Mike Grace was caught doing) or go out to batting practice accidentally wearing the bat boy's jersey.

Clubhouse justice makes everyone aware of the possible consequences of brain freezes. Of course, there are some legends of the court who, despite extensive fines and constant trips to the docket, are just absentminded professors dressed in baseball uniforms. These repeat offenders cannot be helped by any system of justice, but they serve the team well by providing comic relief during the marathon of a long season.

Kangaroo court justice can be swift. But do not assume the judges are going to be fair or even know the law. Precedent doesn't matter, logic is out the window, and political leanings have absolutely nothing to do with anything. It is kangaroo law at its finest.

The rules of these courts vary from jurisdiction to jurisdiction. When I played in Philadelphia, players could drop a note with the alleged infraction into a secret box. Cases were heard once a month, with the person who was making the allegation stating his case in front of a panel of three judges. Should the defendant be declared guilty, he would be fined anywhere from twenty-five to fifty dollars, although the docket holder had the authority to determine such amounts. I don't recall any fine going over the hundred-dollar mark, but then again, anything too high would have made serial offenders bankrupt by the All-Star break.

If you were going to put something in that drop box, you better be sure. Should the defendant be found innocent, the accuser had to pay double the fine of the citation. Over a season, thousands of dollars in fines might be collected, usually ending up in the hands of a charity or to bankroll a team party.

One season in Philly, we appointed Rob Ducey, José Mesa, and Rheal Cormier to wear the robes, as they were senior players on the team. Seniority, however, does not equal objectivity. We had no illusions that their decisions would be even remotely connected to the rule of law.

Case in point was my complaint in *Glanville v. Lewis*. Our second baseman Mark Lewis had an endless repertoire of one-liners, but he rarely got caught on the other side of the joke. He kept his nose clean by kangaroo standards—other than a previous incident when we played the Reds in his hometown and his drunk buddy fell into our dugout in the middle of the game. Found guilty by association, Mark coughed up a few bucks for that.

I rarely brought complaints, but after a game in Boston, I felt I had a surefire case against Mark. In our Fenway Park locker room, the hot water went out. Any player who has logged time in winter baseball knows a little something about cold showers. I had my share in Hormigueros, Puerto Rico. You jump into the cold shower at an angle and figure out how to get clean in less than three minutes.

After my chilly wash in Beantown, I noticed that our resident comedian had improvised. Mark had avoided the shower by turning the whirlpool, which was for water therapy only, into his personal spa. Worse, he even had the nerve to stand up to lather up—an image that took years to erase from my mind. I immediately filed the infraction, which fell under the category of "Nastiness." My case was a slam dunk, I thought, so I didn't bother to prepare a formal argument. No need to explain why our second baseman should be punished for the indefensible act of misappropriating a whirlpool.

Upon reading my accusation aloud, the judges had some questions. I scored points by explaining that all Mark had been missing was a rubber ducky. Defending himself, Mark argued that he was utilizing all available tools and resources to deal with an unpleasant situation.

To my surprise, the judges ruled in his favor, explaining that he had displayed "ingenuity" and "quick thinking" in avoiding the freezing shower. What a travesty! I had to pay double the fine. Fifty bucks.

I know what you're thinking. Fifty bucks is hardly a deterrent for wealthy baseball players, unless of course you are Wayne Gomes and constantly in need of a good attorney. Wayne was our resident repeat offender. He was fined for getting caught on camera peeking out the door of the bullpen Porta-Potty *during a game* at Jack Murphy Stadium against the Padres, and he got nailed again for expressing confusion (within earshot of a teammate, Matt Beech) as to why our defensive meetings hadn't covered a player who had retired two years earlier—the Hall of Fame first baseman Eddie Murray. It's a good thing the kangaroo court was there to teach Wayne and others like him to be a little more observant. Fans can rest assured that justice is indeed being served in the clubhouse, even if sometimes it belongs inside a Porta-Potty.

But sometimes players decide to forgo the kangaroo court and take matters into their own hands. Or fists. The results aren't pretty.

Most professional players are accustomed to success. They broke Little League records, won high school MVP awards and All-State honors, challenged for college championships, and were anointed All-Americans. Legends in their home ponds, they often find themselves at the bottom of the food chain when they get to the big leagues. Winning can go a long way to making this unfamiliar status palatable. Losing, on the other hand, leaves a bad taste in the mouth. And when the *L*s pile up day after day, life can be hard to stomach.

This was the case in 1997, when I played with the Chicago Cubs; we lost our first fourteen games of the season. Even after we got our first win under our belt, it was clear that it was going to be a long season. The frustration in the clubhouse grew with each passing week.

Paranoia spreads throughout a locker room as if someone planted the losses there. Soon you start to look at your teammates in a strange way. Fingers point. Words follow. Almost every conversation begins: "We would have won if..." Rarely does the analysis that follows involve blaming oneself. Selfishness rears its ugly head as self-preservation starts to kick in. *What is my batting average again?*

That frustration finally turned into fisticuffs on a bus ride to our hotel after a game in San Francisco. It began, as fights often do, over something seemingly harmless. A seat.

Some background: rookies understand that, unlike veterans, they should never expect to have a row of seats to themselves on the team bus. If a senior player comes along and wants a row for himself, the rook occupying the coveted space must move and "double up" with a fellow newcomer.

Coming back from Candlestick Park, sparks flew when Kevin Orie, a rookie, anticipated being kicked out of his seat. Proactively, he went to "double up" in a row with rookie pitcher Ramon Tatis. Already on edge following another loss, Ramon made it clear that, etiquette be damned, he was going to have his own row. After three attempts and three rebuffs, Orie pounced. As he later told me, "I gave him three chances to move; three strikes and you're out."

It's one thing to let off steam. It's another thing to let the steam injure a teammate. Mark Grace, who'd seen it all by that point in his career, didn't bat an eye and said, "If they are going to kill each other over a seat, let them." The rest of us were less nonchalant. Fearing that two of the young guns were about to put themselves on the disabled list, we peeled Orie from the neck of Tatis.

Superstars, too, are not immune to the virus that losing creates. On the flight from San Francisco to our next destination, we had to separate Sammy Sosa from the personal space of a flight attendant over a misunderstood drink order. Both were right, both were mis-heard, both were victims of a long and arduous April. Sammy should have ordered a win.

The book of unwritten rules gains a special power when a team is losing profusely. Rookies dare not cross certain lines when the team is on the verge of elimination in the first month of the season. Players tiptoe around one another, the music volume gets softer, the phone calls after the game turn to whispers. My former coach John Vukovich used to go ballistic when we had just lost a game and a player was talking loud or laughing on a cell phone. In theory, you are supposed to keep an even keel in this oscillating game of emotions.

One thing that separates players from fans is how each group responds to a heartbreaking loss. Most players take defeats in stride—even when the fans may be lying on the floor in a fetal position. By the time most players are established in the major leagues, the number of helmet breakers or wall punchers goes down significantly. It may be a function of maturity; it may be because we can't risk hurting ourselves or knocking out the ace of the team's rotation with a ricocheting bat shard. We also begin to catch on that there is always tomorrow, or next week for that matter.

We have to keep moving because long before we ever put on a major league uniform, we fought, scrapped, and clawed our way through the minors. Most of us learned quite a bit about humility and about how to manage our reactions. Games come at you so quickly that you don't have time to curl up in a ball.

The guy who showed you up last week, which would have caused a war between rival high schools back when you were eighteen years old, is now the same guy who is pitching against you next week. In fact you are playing his team fifteen more times before the end of the season. You can wait. You will see him again. No need to overreact.

Our memories are long, and our patience is longer.

I recall hitting against Tim Wakefield when the Pittsburgh Pirates demoted him to the minors in 1993 after he lost his feel for his knuckleball. Here he was, back in Double-A, pitching against a bunch of kids. I managed to get a couple of hits against him, and after a triple, he backed up third base. He walked back to the mound and stared at me, so I asked him, "What are you looking at?" He shot back, "What are *you* looking at?" A tense moment, but it soon passed.

I would face him nine years later in Texas, when he was with the Red Sox. In fact, in my last at-bat as a Ranger before the team traded me to the Cubs in 2003 (my one thousandth game played as a major leaguer), I hit a home run off Tim. Kind of a sweet full circle for me, if not for him.

Don't get me wrong, players are not unaffected by losing. If you played for Larry Bowa and John Vukovich, losing was not an option, and complacency was not tolerated. So occasionally you yell a little; once in a while that helmet looks like something you want to break into a million pieces. But there's a problem. What do you do tomorrow for an encore when you lose again? Because it is going to happen—a lot.

That stone-faced third baseman being interviewed after he bare-handed a bunt and threw the ball into the stands allowing the winning run to score is not quite so stoic on the inside. He has merely learned to stay in control when he needs to. Even though every big-league player is a breath away from losing his job to another, he has learned a thing or two about not rocking the boat with unnecessary drama, especially when he is struggling or in the lineup for someone else.

There are other options when coolness isn't your thing. The nightlife helps out; I picked a few people off the floor from time to time. Having a few brews after the game was common for Bowa's Phillies between 2001 and 2004.

No matter how you take it, you usually have the luxury of digging in the next day. Even for the most hotheaded player on the planet, the notion that there's almost always a tomorrow offers some peace of mind.

So we care. We want to win all of the time, but we also know that those days of dominance, when your high school team only lost once in four years, are gone. So are the days of throwing three no-hitters in a season and waiting a week to play your next game. You have to spread out your emotion a little and rechannel it for tomorrow or risk being burned out and finding some illicit way to stay intense.

Part of preparing for that next game is knowing that you will be back to make amends and to take advantage of a second chance tomorrow. And if tomorrow never comes, you will keep waiting until it does.

Baseball invites superstition. Playing a game in which you are considered a success if you hit safely 30 percent of the time begs for the knock on wood, the salt over the shoulder, the lucky socks. You need something beyond your own body and mind to help you survive if not prevail. So it was no surprise that when the future Hall of Famer Ken Griffey Jr. came to the Chicago White Sox in a midseason trade in 2008, he expected to wear the uniform number that had served him well: 30. A number, the reasoning goes, carries with it a special weight that can be tipped in the wrong direction if you become separated from it.

Unfortunately, Nick Swisher was already wearing Griffey's precious number 30. Sometimes deals can be reached, numbers traded. But here Nick had an entire fan club called "the Dirty 30." What to do?

Nick was in a quandary that I understood well. In the middle of my first full season with the Chicago Cubs, the veteran Lance "One Dog" Johnson was traded to my team. He was one of the top center fielders in the National League and I was a young center fielder looking for my first shot, so I knew I had a career-advancement problem. The problem was even bigger than it had first seemed. In addition to having obviously been passed over as the Cubs' next starting center fielder, I was also wearing the number 1 on the back of my jersey. Anyone with the nickname "One Dog" would presumably come sniffing around for it.

I spent the next few days consulting teammates on how to handle the situation. After a little research, I understood that the option of my keeping number 1 was completely off the table. Young players have a duty to give veterans their choice of numbers, even when they are asking you to peel it off your back in the middle of a season. If a young fan had picked up a Glanville T-shirt with 1 on the back, it was too bad; the best he could hope for was a favorable return policy.

The silver lining to all this is that the veteran player who would take your number is expected to compensate you for your troubles. I heard that I might be showered with gifts ranging from a personalized Rolex watch to a shopping spree at Hugo Boss.

I could work with that.

I told the press that I would certainly give up my number, and when asked about what I expected in return I responded, "We'll see."

Well, One Dog arrived, and the cameras filmed our first encounter. We talked, we bonded, and I turned over my number 1 to him. There was no pomp and circumstance.

Eventually, a window opened up for us to discuss the compensation for my act of deference. One Dog told me, "I will give you something more valuable than money. I will teach you how to play this game. I will give you advice."

Advice? Then it hit me. He was going to leave a check in my locker with *Advice* written on the signature line. Yeah, that's it. If not, One Dog had clearly spent too much time in the junkyard barking at hubcaps.

He was true to his word; my cash compensation never materialized, but he did show me the ropes over the next few months. Even though I was a center fielder, I had earned my way to being the starting left fielder after a few young teammates struggled. One Dog kept me sharp and nipped at me whenever I showed frustration or exhaustion.

"Are you tired?" he asked me once.

"No."

"So why didn't you run hard on that last ground ball?"

Even though his wisdom was helpful, I was still a little bitter about having to give up my lean and singular 1 for the big fat 8 now covering my back.

I never did get that 1 back. When I was traded to the Philadelphia Phillies during the off-season, I chose to wear number 6. I didn't have many choices anyway, since I wanted a low number, so 6 it became and that is how it stayed for the remainder of my career.

In Philadelphia, I did have a chance to pass on the legacy of the number hierarchy by repaying the favor to a young shortstop named Jimmy Rollins. He was a rising star when we teamed together for a few years on the Phillies. Then, after the 2002 season, I left to play for the Texas Rangers, and Jimmy took my precious 6, a number he wore in high school.

When I came back to Philadelphia in 2004, I called Jimmy and asked if he would be willing to give up his number to an "old vet." It was hard for him, but he agreed. He knew the rules about the base-ball pecking order, and he respected them. He has worn number 11 ever since.

Griffey ultimately didn't press Swisher to give up his number, something a veteran player can graciously elect to do. "I don't want to be a disruption to the team going in there," Griffey said with his usual class. "I heard Nick is a little out there, something about some 'Dirty 30,' so I'm going to stick with 17 and be happy with it."

For my part, I didn't leave Rollins empty-handed. I picked him up a Sony VAIO laptop for his sacrifice. I gave him advice, too. And considering that he has since been voted the National League Most Valuable Player and has a World Series ring, maybe I should ask for that laptop back.

When I was in Triple-A with the Iowa Cubs, my superstition had nothing to do with my uniform number. I stumbled across a 3-D book called *The Magic Eye*. When you stared at an illustration, an image in the background seemed to pop right out at you. After starting the book, I noticed something magical was indeed happening: no one could get me out. Not wanting to spoil a good thing, I stared at this book every day. My hitting streak reached ten games, fifteen, twenty.

Was the book the reason for my success at the plate? I wasn't sure. But I knew I didn't want to jinx my good fortune by departing from my new pregame ritual. Only after the streak ended could I rest my eyes. When I returned to earth, my teammate Matt Franco told me, "You used up all the hits in that book."

On a scale of one to ten, I was probably a two or a three when it came to superstition. The pitcher Turk Wendell, on the other hand, was off the charts. When I first read about Turk's tics in *Baseball America*, I certainly thought his approach was strange. Little did I know I would play with him and see superstition in 3-D every day. Among other things: he demanded that the umpire roll the ball to him on the mound instead of throw it; he began games he started by waving to his center fielder—at times, me—and wouldn't pitch until the center fielder had waved back; and he would brush his teeth between innings after chewing a mouthful of black licorice on the mound, driving veteran catchers bananas, since he was trying to avoid cavities instead of planning how to get the next three hitters out.

Turk, a nice guy behind all the shark-tooth necklaces and homemade venison sausage, was one of a kind. So what does that make Ugueth Urbina?

I had played against Urbina for years while he was pitching for the Montreal Expos, and he led the National League in saves in 1999. We became teammates in Texas in 2003, where he was the closer. Early in the season at the Ballpark at Arlington, I came into the locker room in the middle of the game. We had these sweet reclining black leather office chairs in the clubhouse, and Urbina was kicking back in his. Nothing unusual about that. Closers have their own routines.

It was, however, odd that Urbina didn't have his uniform on. He was wearing all his blue and white undergarments capped off with shower shoes. He looked as if he was getting ready to smoke a pipe, not close out the ninth inning.

As it turned out, Urbina wasn't needed that day. But he would repeat this ritual day in and day out. After one game when he had entered as our closer, we did our usual postgame routines, culminating in a roster of humanity in the showers. Something was strange, however—not because Urbina was in the shower, but because he was in the shower wearing that same pipe smoker's outfit he had been wearing in the sixth inning.

Remember the Tom Hanks line from the movie *A League of Their Own*: "There's no crying in baseball"? Well, there's no privacy in baseball, either. You have to shower in the same area as twenty-four other guys. If nothing else, this does teach you to maintain eye contact when someone is talking to you. Here's a rule: never stare in the shower, even if someone wants to show off his new tattoo.

After years of doing tricks with my eyes from all these Turkish bath experiences, I had a lot of staring time accumulated in my system. Urbina allowed me to use all of it in one striking moment because he proceeded to shower while in his outlandish outfit. Socks, shirts, long sleeves, turtleneck, whatever else he had on was rinsed like it was his first wash cycle.

Several thoughts ran through my mind when I saw Urbina in the shower. *Was he trying to save the team some money on laundry? Maybe he was just very shy in the shower. Perhaps he was a germaphobe.* Nothing made sense, so I kept staring.

Since there was only one item in the ensemble that made any semblance of sense, I eventually went with the changeup: "You might want to take off your shower shoes," I suggested.

He explained in no uncertain terms that this was his cleansing ritual. That was the last time I bothered to understand or ask.

In 2007, Urbina was convicted of attempted murder in his native

Venezuela, a sad story for all involved, and one that haunts those of us who played with him. I never thought that he might be reckless with human life as opposed to just unusual in how he coped with his own life.

Licorice on the mound. Clothes in the shower. Ritual remains our feeble attempt to find comfort in the face of so many days of disappointment, of oh-for-fours or blown saves. It is our way of trying to control the uncontrollable, to find an answer in the unanswerable, or maybe just have something that is routine in a life of new hotel rooms, new girlfriends, and new lockers. Maybe it has no quantitative impact on our performance, but at least when we come out of that locker room, even if it is after the sixth inning, we feel like we are going to make a difference. Even if in the end, all it does is save the team from buying one more box of Tide.

Ugueth Urbina was also known for rolling up his sleeve to flex his bicep while on the mound as if he was entered in a Mr. Universe competition. If he struck you out, he would prance off the mound in a forearm pose that was forever burned into your consciousness.

That's also against baseball's unwritten rules. Under no circumstances should you show up an opposing baseball player. We hold grudges forever, and we will find a way to throw it back in your face. It could take a week, it could take twenty-five years; in fact, just like any other debt, your heirs may have to pay if we don't get you while you are alive. Still, we will get you.

Sure, it seems petty, but it's what makes this game go round. Beat me with your fastball or with your timely bunt with two outs in the ninth, and I will tip my cap to you. But do not ever, ever, ever show me up.

Showing someone up can take many forms. It could be a self-admiring gesture you make on the field—pretending your hands are six-shooters and firing them off after striking someone out. It could be the way you record an out—you're pitching, and you field a ball, but instead of throwing to the first baseman, you sprint over and step on first base unassisted. You could even show up your own teammate—say, you're playing outfield, an opponent hits a mammoth home run against your pitcher, and you don't even turn and make a courtesy run after the ball, even though you know it's probably going to break someone's windshield in the parking lot.

Once, when I was playing with the Phillies, my teammate Wayne Gomes was pitching after some bad blood had developed over a few days with the San Francisco Giants. We had intentionally hit Barry Bonds with a pitch earlier that game, and there was some glaring and jawing.

Gomes threw a pitch that J. T. Snow deposited into the right field stands. Snow stared at his handiwork for a second, threw the bat around his back as if he was Magic Johnson (it rolled farther than the "show up" rules allow), and then took a nice slow trot around the bases. I am sure Snow felt vindicated on behalf of his team, since we had kind of started it. But Gomes was fuming, and after the game, he told any teammate who would listen that if he ever got a chance to face Snow again and struck him out, watch what he would do.

Ah, the beauty of baseball. The next night, Gomes got his wish and he delivered, striking out Snow. All the way in center field I could hear Gomes yelling at him—"Sit down! Get out of here!"—as Snow walked toward the dugout. Of course, I am leaving out a few words, but you get the picture.

It was one of the few times a brawl almost started over showing someone up where no one was hit by a pitch, no one was spiked, there was no contact whatsoever.

It is important to note that there is little latitude in the world of showing someone up. Players tend to understand that it's permissible to point to the sky to acknowledge the loss of a loved one, as Bobby Abreu has done after each hit, in homage to his father. But even those gestures have slim room for interpretation, and depend on when, and how emphatically, you exhibit them. It is one thing to get a base hit in the fourth inning and make a quick gesture as you go back to first after making your turn; it's another to hit a home run and point to the sky all the way around the bases while glaring at the pitcher as if he was the one who put your loved one six feet under.

I tried to respect my opponents, but there was one time I slipped up. After hitting a home run against the Toronto Blue Jays during the first week of spring training, I got caught in the moment and flipped the bat a little farther than was necessary. I can't tell you who the pitcher was; most of the time you barely know who you are hitting against in spring training. My punishment for showing up this nameless hurler was paranoia. From that day forward, should we play Toronto, I had to look over my shoulder, waiting for that fastball in the back. Recognizing that the fellow I couldn't recognize may have moved on to another organization, I had to be prepared any time I faced a pitcher with an unfamiliar name.

That's a lot of paranoia to manage. It's best to know the names of those whom you have shown up and those who have shown you up. Lesson learned.

In 1999, I posted a .325 batting average on 204 hits, quite a few of which were against the New York Mets. A few years later, having never matched those numbers again, I ran into the Mets' fine pitcher Al Leiter at a meeting of the Executive Subcommittee of the Major League Baseball Players Association. "What happened to you?" he asked. "You used to be a tough out."

Since then, I've gotten to know Al better, and I realize now that he meant the line more as a compliment than an indictment. But at the time I saw red. His words became fuel for the fire to try and be a near impossible out from that day forward. I wish more pitchers had challenged me in that way, for in the end, my numbers against Leiter were among the best I had against any starting pitcher.

If I'd have wanted to be uncharacteristically nasty, I suppose I could have spiked Leiter's foot when he covered first base as I tried to leg out a bunt for a base hit, or I could have waited until he was backing up a base that I was running toward and thrown that forearm shiver from my Nerf football days. But that wasn't my style. Revenge is a dish best served cold.

But still, some prefer it hot and spicy. If the Guinness people ever publish a list of baseball's most intense grudges, my Phillies teammate José Mesa would be near the top. As the Cleveland Indians' closer in 1997, José, you might remember, blew a save opportunity against the Florida Marlins in the ninth inning of Game Seven of the World Series. Two innings later, the Fish were world champs. It doesn't get much worse for a pitcher than that.

José's teammate from that Indians team, Omar Vizquel, reminded the world of that inglorious moment in an autobiography that was published at the beginning of the 2002 season. Vizquel opined that José had choked or was scared. "The eyes of the world were focused on every move we made," he wrote. "Unfortunately, José's own eyes were vacant. Completely empty. Nobody home. You could almost see right through him. Not long after I looked into his vacant eyes, he blew the save and the Marlins tied the game."

Okay, I can see how that could be taken badly. Your move, José.

"If I face him ten more times, I'll hit him ten times! I want to kill him," the pitcher said.

Problem was, José and Omar played in different leagues. Opportunity did not knock until June, when the interleague schedule pitted us against the Indians in Cleveland. José made no secret about his desire to pitch in a situation where he could get Vizquel and not blow a save at the same time. You can't, or at least shouldn't, hit an opponent—not even a mortal enemy—and put him on base if it's going to jeopardize a win.

We managed to take one game into the ninth inning with a nice four-run lead. Sure enough, José was put in the game. Omar was due to hit second in the inning. Cue the theme from *Jaws*.

After a quick out was recorded, Omar got in the batter's box. Most of the Phillies knew something ugly was going to happen, but still we were curious to see what José would do. At the same time, we were wary of giving a runner a free pass to first base.

I watched from center field when, with a 1–0 count, José reared back and fired. It may have been my imagination, but instead of stepping straight toward home plate, he seemed to be throwing at an angle in order to get a direct line to Omar. All his momentum was toward the man in the batter's box. The catcher's glove was just a rumor.

As the ball popped Omar in the arm, José called out, "Cómo se siente?"—How does it feel? José, no doubt, felt a sense of relief. I didn't, because the Indians eventually got the tying run to the plate. But we still won the game.

So why is this grudge Guinness-worthy? Because José hit his nemesis the next three times they met! *Is it over*, I wondered, *or is he really counting to ten?*

You need a good memory to succeed at baseball. You want to remember pitch sequences, hitter tendencies, and in some cases, when you have been wronged. There is no statute of limitations, no expiration date for when the grudge is declared null and void.

The grudge follows you to bed, follows you in a trade. It stalks you right into that blank moment when all you can think about is getting back at its cause. You fill in the blanks by plotting the dream encounter so that you can bury the hatchet and get some rest. But first, you need to taste the sweet flavor of revenge. Apology not accepted.

Although Omar Vizquel did not charge the mound after José Mesa plunked him, I wouldn't have blamed him if he had. I once went after a pitcher—and he hadn't even hit me.

I had watched from the dugout as yet another home run by my Double-A team, the Orlando Cubs, sailed over the left field fence to turn an already one-sided game against the Greenville Braves into a complete blowout. My instincts told me that my opponent was going to retaliate out of frustration, and I had vowed to my teammates that I would defend our honor by charging the mound if he did.

After a ninety-mile-per-hour fastball barely missed my head, I lunged into a dead sprint toward the pitcher and managed to push him off the mound. For the rest of what became a bench-clearing brawl I saw virtually nothing. The opposing catcher had me face-down in a full nelson near the pitching rubber.

That was the first of four fights in that series—one more than Ali-Frazier. But ours weren't championship caliber. They devolved into the realm of the strangely humorous with each subsequent round.

One fight started because our pitcher threw his bat at the oppos-ing pitcher. Another because our manager literally jumped on the neck of the opposing manager. A third when both managers were discussing the ground rules with the umpire before the game and then started rushing each other. (The two were banned from coach-ing against each other for the rest of the season.)

Such outlandishness is not the sole province of the minor leagues. Take the fight I was in against the Atlanta Braves. Over the course of a week, my Phillies teammate Paul Byrd, a pitcher, had unintentionally hit Braves catcher Eddie Perez in the back not once, but twice. Perez and Byrd had once been teammates (and Bible study partners), but Perez had apparently left forgiveness at the door. When Byrd stepped up to the plate for his next at-bat, Perez popped him and then jumped him. Since I was on deck and the closest player to the fray, I ran over to pry them apart.

The next thing I knew, I was at the bottom of a pile of players, my legs trapped, spikes barely missing my various body parts. The Braves' Ozzie Guillen evidently decided that the best way to get out of the pile was to pull me out by the head. I had a stiff neck for three days.

What I found surprising was that instead of Perez and Byrd ripping each other's hair out, they were locked together in a protective embrace, apologizing and praying to get out of this mass of humanity. Everyone within earshot was wondering why we had all risked physical harm for these now spiritual pacifists. To add injury to absurdity, when our bullpen coach came running in from left field to join the fight, he pulled a hamstring halfway to the pile.

When a fight is on national television, as this one was, no one can tell tall stories about what they did; it is all on tape. Supermen can be reduced to mere mortals when the PLAY button is hit. So—perhaps for the benefit of the cameras—we puff out our chests, stare one another down, and occasionally bear-hug someone to make sure they don't escalate things. But I am confident that only a few players really know how to fight. I certainly never took any martial-arts classes. I am even more confident that hardly any of them really want to fight. After all, our bodies are the instruments with which we make our living, and if they become damaged, there goes our livelihood.

The year that my Orlando Cubs team got into those four fights, minor league officials wanted to crack down, so they instituted a strict fine system with suspensions for anyone who left the bench to join in. This put quite a damper on the retaliation protocol, to the point where when one of my teammates, Brooks Kieschnick, charged the mound after being hit by a pitch, he stopped halfway and started scolding the pitcher. That was a first: intimidation by lecture.

Since in the minor leagues most players are living paycheck to paycheck, the new fine system worked like a charm. During that same on-field berating, I looked into our dugout and noticed that one of my teammates, Mike Carter, was breaking yet another unwritten rule by not joining his teammates in the rumble on the field. Raising his violation status from plain wrong to egregious, he was the *only one* who did not join his teammates. I asked him about this later. "Mike Carter has to pay his bills," he replied.

The irony of these on-field altercations is that the fans are often much more likely to engage in a real fight than the players. When they fight in the stands to defend their teams (or for other reasons), they often go for the knockout. Players just go to send the message, "We will not be intimidated!" while whispering, "Watch my right arm, I need that."

5
...

THE STRESSES OF THE GAME

I made my major league debut on June 9, 1996, in Chicago. It was a cold and rainy day at Wrigley Field, but I didn't care. After years toiling away in the minor leagues on a dream and a prayer, I had finally made it.

But had I truly arrived?

"Arriving" implies longevity and a deep-rooted understanding that you belong somewhere, that you're not just passing through. The amazing thing about arriving in the big leagues is that it only starts to feel valid when you get a stamp of approval from your childhood.

Give me a minute to explain.

I was playing for the Cubs' Triple-A affiliate in Des Moines, Iowa. Having played center field the entire season, I knew something was up when I started one game in left field. When it comes to helping the major league team, you have to be ready to play anywhere just to get in the door. Although I was a center fielder by nature, if the Cubs needed a left fielder, I would be a left fielder.

After the game, I got called into manager Ron Clark's office. He and I weren't always on the best of terms, so I usually rued these meetings. But when I saw two of my teammates, Mike Hubbard and Terry Shumpert, were also in Clark's office, I sensed that the big call-up was about to happen.

"Congratulations, you earned it," Clark said to Mike. He told Terry, "You've been there before; you know what to do." Then he turned to me: "If you make the same mistakes up there as you did down here, you will be back here."

Obviously, he wasn't my biggest fan. But he couldn't stop me from getting on that plane to Chicago. I spent all night packing and calling friends and family, and then I caught a crack-of-dawn flight to the big leagues.

Six hours later, when the Cubs took the field against the Montreal Expos in front of thirty-thousand-plus fans, I sprinted out to left. It was like floating on air with two tons of butterflies in my stomach. Here I was in a lineup that included Ryne Sandberg, Sammy Sosa, and Mark Grace. How did I get here?

In my first at-bat—against Kirk Rueter—I got good wood on the ball and lined out to left fielder Henry Rodriguez. I didn't get a hit in my next three trips to the plate, but I did make a nice diving catch on a ball hit by Mark Grudzielanek.

Surreal. Clark had been brutal in his send-off, but his words had a ring of truth. As I survived each day on a major league roster, I slid further into disbelief: I was still trying to figure out whether it had actually happened. I kept looking at the newspaper wondering, *Who is this new guy Glanville?*

This "Glanville" only truly became me when I was able to match the expectations I had as a young kid in Teaneck, New Jersey. Basically, it meant that I had to have enough major league service to be included in a Strat-O-Matic baseball set; to see my name written in script on the side of a Rawlings baseball glove; and to gain sufficient influence to meet my favorite band, Hall and Oates.

Ultimately, all these things would happen. And that, in effect, is when "Doug Glanville" finally became real, too. Only then did the childhood version of me nod his head and say, "Okay, now you have made it."

———

At each level of the staircase from the minors to the majors, the amenities improve. You begin in peaceful Small Town, USA, in cities like Pasco, Washington, or Huntington, West Virginia, and end up in major urban centers like Miami or Los Angeles. After starting in Geneva, New York, I went to Winston-Salem, North Carolina, then Daytona Beach, Florida, then Orlando, Florida, then Des Moines, Iowa, and, finally, Chicago. As I moved closer to the majors, the cities got bigger, the hotels got a little nicer, our seat options on the plane no longer included the dreaded "middle" seat, and the clubhouse food tasted a little better.

When you're rising up through the ranks, it is impossible to avoid exposure to the culture—and the stresses—of the upgrade. You go from Single-A to Double-A, and that studio apartment becomes a one-bedroom, or you decide to pick up that new Xbox 360 so you can compete with your roommates. From Double-A to Triple-A, you scoop up that first car you had your eye on, or maybe you can get rid of roommates once and for all. But there is nothing like going to the major leagues, no telling what you might upgrade to there.

What you covet as you advance is determined in part by the people ahead of you on the staircase. Professional baseball is a hyper-competitive environment, and everyone is obsessed with what is happening in front of him. In spring training you cross paths with players at all levels in the organization, so you get to see what the next level looks like: "Oh, *that's* what Greg Vaughn is driving." Or, "I didn't know you could get that kind of jewelry on a Triple-A salary." Or, "When did he start dating Jessica Biel? What happened to his high school sweetheart?" Guess she needed to be upgraded, too.

No one sets the tone for social climbing better than major leaguers. To a young and impressionable rising minor leaguer, it is tempting to do exactly what the big leaguers are doing. After all, these are the players you idolized as a kid.

And so, all of a sudden, whatever you have is not enough. In fact, what you *thought* you wanted is not enough. It was fine in Single-A ball, but it's not going to pass the test in Triple-A. It is an internal battle to keep up with the Joneses, and it can play out in any area of your life if you are not careful.

Living on "Temptation Island" makes every player susceptible to these material cravings. Those that don't fall prey (and there aren't many) are usually seen as having dedicated their lives to some pseudomonastic pursuit. It is much easier to jump in and accept the "island," and then try to extricate yourself from its siren call. Of course, jumping in makes getting out even harder, because it is kind of fun.

My first car was a Toyota Camry (despite my older brother's efforts to sell me on a Porsche). It was a practical and well-researched pick, and it drove like a charm. When I reached the highest level of A-ball in Winston-Salem, I had three roommates, one of whom was the first-round draft pick from two years before, Earl Cunningham. He was a super talent, ran like a linebacker with size and power. One of his prized possessions was a white Mercedes-Benz he'd picked up from major leaguer Matt Williams. It even had this alarm system that said, "VIPER! Stand back!" All in all, there was no way my Camry could hold a candle to his car—until one of our other roommates told Earl that my car rode more smoothly. Earl was crestfallen.

When I played in Chicago, it seemed like every time Sammy Sosa bought something, my friend José Hernandez picked up the same thing in another color. I don't know if they were competing with each other or just teammates taking advantage of some bulk discount deal while shopping together on off days.

A big-league ballplayer will purchase just about anything. Player A knows someone who is selling something and vouches for him to Player B. So Player B buys from that someone. Pretty soon, the entire locker room is buying from this someone. It could be jewelry, houses, cars, cigars, whatever. A person who becomes a preferred vendor can start to influence the consumer culture of a whole team.

After a while, this attitude can take over just about everything. You start to notice your living quarters are getting nicer, more expensive, bigger, and emptier. Single players usually ride this path right into enormous homes with no one living there except themselves and a dog, if they even have a dog. You have more services than you have socks.

The walls around your home also get higher—gated communities to protect privacy. Maybe you get that security system you thought was cool. For part of my career in Philadelphia, I lived directly across the street from Randy Wolf, a teammate and friend. I didn't see him for almost two years unless it was at the ballpark.

Soon you are getting further away from your original tastes and closer to what you think a major leaguer is supposed to live like. It takes a lot of introspection to realize that as you are "upgrading," you hit an invisible peak and then hit this precipitous downhill slope of declining benefits—because this particular home plate keeps moving, teasing you into needing to go just a little further. Sure, you could date actresses and supermodels until you pry Angelina Jolie away from Brad Pitt, but you forget that when your career is over, the people whose approval you've been seeking stop paying attention.

These diminishing returns are reflected in lost time or lost opportunity. Maybe you spend so much time chasing Halle Berry through her agent that you forget about the girlfriend who was there for you when you had back surgery in the minor leagues. Maybe you get on a two-year waiting list for a car that only three people in the world have, only to miss driving your first car, the one with the sticky windshield wipers. Or maybe that McMansion going up on the waterfront for you and your posse (so that you can get on *MTV Cribs*) takes so long to build that when your grandmother passes away you realize you spent more time looking at floor plans than sharing her last moments.

At spring training with the New York Yankees in 2005, Gary Sheffield offered me this financial advice: "Get a chef, you'll save on groceries." Sure, why not? But it's a shame when, deep down, you really love to cook.

We call it advancement, the act of getting closer to something ahead or in front of us. But when we lock in on that target as the next step, sometimes we forget what got us here. The need to demonstrate success, the show, and the glitter all play into why we can end up chasing illusions that take us away from our true selves.

All players battle with this in some form, and most get lost for at least a moment or two. (If you are lucky, that's the worst of it.) But when you get disoriented, you just have to be courageous enough to turn around, regroup, and look for home. That place where you can look closer at the matchup of needs versus wants.

Even if you have to go back down those stairs for a while.

My baseball card listed my height as six-foot-two and my weight as 175 pounds. Needless to say, I wasn't drafted for my bulk. Forget about adding pounds to my slender frame; I had trouble keeping the meat on the bones.

My first full season as a starter in the major leagues was a shock, as it is to virtually all young players. Besides the microscope you are under to produce every day, it is the first time you are playing a 162-game schedule—a full month longer than the minor league season. And that extra month is a bear. Jimmy Piersall, my outfield coach in the Cubs system, put it plain and simple: "This game will bring you to your knees."

I ended up on my knees as the 1998 season wound down. It was my first year in Philadelphia, but it was as enervating as it was energizing. The spotlight of being in my college town shone bright. A plethora of interviews and charity requests and tickets for everyone who ever knew me was what I would term a "difficult positive."

By the end of August, I was approaching six hundred at-bats, more than enough for an entire season. My manager, Terry Francona, kept running me out there, a wonderful vote of confidence. I dared not ask for a day off. I didn't want to miss a single moment and leave even the slightest crack to let someone take my job. So I carried on.

As our final games approached, the bat was swinging me. My

hitting coach, Hal McRae, appreciated my tenacity, but the numbers didn't lie. Going into September, I had needed twenty-nine hits to get to two hundred and be the first Phillie since Pete Rose in 1979 to do so. This seemed achievable, as my lowest monthly total all year had been twenty-eight.

I was consistent throughout September. Consistently bad. I ended up with only eighteen hits over 102 at-bats (.176, one walk, twenty-two strikeouts), and my average plummeted from over .300 to .279.

During my precipitous decline, *The Record*, the local paper where I grew up in New Jersey, ran a story titled "The Skinny on Glanville." I had never thought my weight was worth a full article, but welcome to the world of being an everyday starter. The reporter, T. J. Quinn, drew a connection between my fragile frame and my falloff in productivity during the closing months of the season. This was an understandable conclusion, and it was nice that he was at least trying to find a reason why I was so terrible. But he also implied that my body couldn't sustain the grind of 162 games, even though a couple of years earlier I had been consistently productive over a two-year run of winter leagues, spring trainings, and regular seasons.

Then again, I also thought, *That may be true, but at least I played clean.*

I wasn't the first and certainly would not be the last player to have weight become an issue. When you produce, it doesn't really matter what you look like, but when you don't, that weight issue stands front and center. The Cubs catcher Hector Villanueva put it so well: "When I am hitting, I'm big. When I'm not, I'm fat." I turned Hector's statement upside down: "When I am hitting, I'm lean. When I'm not, I'm skinny."

Even so, I brooded about my weight during the off-season—drinking shakes, working out, going to spring training early. I had done these things before, but this time, I wasn't going to let my body weight stop me from producing. *I can handle it—no, I have already handled it*, I told myself.

And I was right. In 1999, I couldn't wait for September to roll around. One year after my swoon, I had another shot at two hundred hits—especially after I racked up a five-hit game against the Astros in the Astrodome. On September 29, I had my cake and ate it, too: my two hundredth hit of the season was a home run against the team that had traded me, the Cubs. Trumping the assumptions made about skinny people was sweet. So was the realization that no one would talk about my weight again.

If I had been scheduled to become a free agent after that successful 1999 season, I could have scored a nice fat contract. But, as everyone knows, in baseball timing is everything. For better or worse, I had signed a long-term contract after the 1998 season, the one when I cooled off at the end.

We actually began discussing that contract in the middle of the season when I was still on fire. The Phillies' general manager, Ed Wade, approached my agent, Arn Tellem, about a multiyear deal. The numbers were mind-blowing.

Thinking about money like that for too long makes playing a stressful ordeal. You can't help but worry about getting hurt. Will this windfall go away if I break my leg in a freak collision with the shortstop? I wanted to find a hermetically sealed case to play in.

The distraction became too much. After Arn recited the blow-by-blow details of the negotiations, I asked him to tell me only the big moves. Let's wait until we have a full counteroffer, I told Arn and his right-hand man, Joel Wolfe.

They obliged, but the cat was out of the bag. Knowing what was at stake made each day seem like a month to me. Will the Phillies get tired of all the back-and-forth? Would they still have nice things to say about me if this drags on into the off-season?

If I sound slightly paranoid or at least distrustful, it's for a reason. I'd been through this before. Most players have.

On draft day, the phone rings, and the team tells you and the world how smart they are to have chosen you because you are the cream of the crop. You can hardly contain yourself. Then the media goes away, and it is time to negotiate your first contract. All of a sudden, you hear all the things you *can't* do.

Welcome to Baseball Business 101. "We like you," the team says to you, while thinking to themselves, *We want you to stay cheap for as long as possible. But hey, you get to play baseball for a living.*

As you scrape through the minor leagues making peanuts, a touch of resentment gains momentum. You match the long bus rides with your $850 monthly paycheck, and something doesn't quite add up. The excitement of being chosen to play professional baseball stays with you, but as the dream meets the reality, you wonder if the team's treatment of you and your fellow minor leaguers should be ruled fair or foul.

When you finally make it to the big leagues, something interesting happens on the balance-of-power sheet. Six-figure salaries kick in just as a clock resets to zero. Your major league service counter is now at "0000" and ready to inch up each day, racing against Father Time and your bad knees.

If you can survive long enough—three years—you reach arbitration. You're not a free agent who can pick and choose your team, but you can go to "court" for an impartial judgment on your market value. In effect, you are compared to other players with the same amount of service time who have performed like you.

If you weren't curious before about how your fellow third-year men were performing, this is quite an incentive. I paid particular attention to Brian Hunter and any other leadoff hitter who was playing.

If you are an everyday player with strong statistics, arbitration is your ticket to a big payday. Salaries go up manyfold. The process is straightforward: you submit a price tag, the team submits a price tag, and the arbitrator picks one or the other. There's no in between, so good luck.

Though straightforward, the process isn't always pretty. Each side plays the numbers game. Shawon Dunston talked about how in one of his arbitration cases his agent and the Cubs went at each other furiously. He couldn't help but be offended by some of the arguments the team made in presenting its case. Mark Grace advised Shawon, "You can't take it personally." To which he replied, "Of course I am going to take it personally; they were talking about me!"

Brian Hunter told me that when he was up for arbitration one year, he was amazed to hear the team's attorneys bring up the history of the union-owners dispute. After that he just got out of the way and listened to the debate. The two sides debated not only the merits of his stolen base totals and his solid defense, but also topics from the long-standing battle between the owners and the Players Association. Everyone has a very long memory, it seems.

Hearing stories like these, some players go for the gusto, reasoning that they'll receive a substantial pay increase even if the team wins. Other players, figuring better safe than sorry, opt to compromise before the hearing begins, as I did a few years later, in 2002. A lot of the will to fight stems from the lack of power a player has over his value all the years before becoming arbitration eligible. You just had to accept any salary offer that came your way. Now you finally hold a hammer in your hand.

Have you picked up on the fact that the Phillies approached me about a long-term contract in the middle of the season before I was arbitration eligible? Welcome to Baseball Business 201. The Phillies made a decision that teams make from time to time in a rising baseball economy. They didn't want to go to arbitration, where they might have to return the next year. They also knew that if a player performed at the same level year in and year out, he would make more money negotiating year by year than if he took a multiyear contract that predetermined his pay increase in the future. (Granted that's a risk for the team, too. Consistently improving performance is not a sure thing, and the security of a multiyear deal can create complacency, leaving the team on the hook for more than the player is worth.)

From time to time, I wonder how things might have gone differently. What if I played a little bit better that September? What if I had waited a little longer to sign? Then again, what if I slipped on my driveway?

But, even then, it was surreal to look at the final terms and think that at such a young age I could make in a year what my parents may have made in a lifetime. A little guilt crept in, but then the real game began. *There's no more talk of "potential," Glanville*, I told myself. *Now you have to produce.*

Every player feels overwhelmed at one time or another, by one thing or another. The stress maker can be the illness of a loved one or the strain of maintaining a marriage when you spend half your time on the road. It can be your plummeting batting average during a free-agent season, drying up the pool of teams interested in you. Or maybe it's the cumulative effect of performing every day, center stage.

All the little requests players receive during any given week can really build up. Can you meet with this wonderful charity before the game? Can you do this photo shoot in the concourse? Can you do this interview with Comcast? Can you find time to read a few lines for a commercial? Nothing nefarious; in fact, often it's for a good cause or simply part of your responsibility to promote the team. You are happy to be in the big leagues, and you welcome any opportunity to do more while you have the gift of being at that level.

So why can it become such a struggle?

For one thing, thoughts can escalate if they are not managed. And the pressure of fulfilling all those requests can start to follow you out of the locker room. Suddenly it's hard to deal with all the ticket requests in your hometown, whereas before you couldn't wait to have twenty-five people at the game. Or you can't commit beyond a few hours in advance because you don't even know whether you'll still be on the team tomorrow. Or you feel clammy because your girlfriend wants to know if she can visit you six weeks from now and you can't begin to imagine what might interfere unexpectedly that day, despite the fact that your schedule is posted in every media outlet on the planet.

In 2009, the Cincinnati Reds first baseman Joey Votto spent weeks on the disabled list. One minute he was dominating the National League with a sizzling .357 batting average (to go with being runner-up for the Rookie of the Year in 2008), and the next he had disappeared. The team announced that he was struggling with an ear infection, but lurking behind it was something Votto later explained: he was totally overwhelmed with grief and anxiety.

Votto publicly attributed his anxiety to the death of his father the previous August. He had been frequently coming out of games because of the stress, and on two occasions, it drove him to call 911. The death of his father left a huge void in his family that he felt the responsibility to fill. His three younger brothers and his mother were in Toronto without him.

I am not an expert, but I understand that there are many types of anxiety. Some relate to general situations, others to social settings; performance can be a cause, and panic attacks can creep into the mix. Anxiety can seem like a silent disabler to those on the outside, but to those affected by it, it is active and dynamic.

And there are other stories, like the Royals ace pitcher Zack Greinke, who was in the big leagues by age twenty and in 2006 was diagnosed with social anxiety disorder; or Khalil Greene of the Cardinals, who has been working through the challenges of social anxiety disorder, which caused him to go on the disabled list for the second time at the end of June 2009; or Dontrelle Willis, the former Florida Marlins ace now with the Detroit Tigers, who threw only twenty-four innings in 2008 and in March 2009 was diagnosed with an anxiety disorder that had affected him throughout that season.

I remember when Mark Wohlers, the Atlanta Braves closer, suddenly could not find home plate. A guy who normally was lights-out whenever he came into a game, he just lost all sense of the strike zone. During the period when he was fighting his way back, the Phillies played against him in Atlanta.

I was asked to lay down a bunt, which was not exactly a comfortable thing to do against a pitcher throwing ninety-five miles per hour who was having issues finding the plate. The first pitch missed the catcher's target entirely. He then threw one I could bunt, resulting in a slow roller right back to him. Cruelly, he now had to throw the ball again, to first base. I had my head down, trying to beat it out when I heard the crowd give a collective groan. Wohlers had lobbed the ball, as if throwing a timing pattern to a wide receiver; it sailed over the first baseman's head by a substantial margin.

After going on the disabled list for anxiety disorder with the Reds in 1999, Wohlers eventually made a comeback, not quite regaining his old form, but still putting in some quality time before he stopped pitching. He had found a way to turn himself around, even though the window for his dominance had closed.

I remember the constant stress of trying to navigate my emotions after my father suffered his stroke. Eventually, it became tangible, creeping out of my head and manifesting itself through my body. I started having trouble focusing on the pitcher as well as I needed to; it seemed like my eyes were darting all over the place. When I would view the video, everything looked normal. But I certainly didn't feel that way.

Since you have only a microsecond to react to a ninety-five-mile-per-hour fastball, that little bit of doubt—*Am I seeing what I think I am seeing?*—can turn into an exponential miscalculation in the space between home and the pitcher's mound.

Then the snowball effect kicks in, and you become more and more conscious of what was not even there six months ago. The routine and mundane become next to impossible.

So I had to learn a little bit about anxiety and its roots. I began to understand that even though you can recognize that the anxiety is unreasonable, irrational, or even ridiculous, it can still consume you.

Thankfully, it can be addressed. But many baseball players are conditioned to resist help until it is very late. They don't want to give in because that would be admitting something a professional athlete is never supposed to admit: "I have vulnerabilities."

I was thankful to see Votto take time out and share with the world that he is human and needed help. He was able to get back on the field and instantly contribute to his team. Willis came back feeling very optimistic, had a setback, but says he is committed to getting through it. The once-troubled Greinke has become an American League All Star and Cy Young Award winner.

It may not be a torn tendon or a broken bone, but what put these talented athletes and others on the disabled list was much more challenging to overcome—a condition they may have to manage for the rest of their lives. But it can be done, especially if they don't suffer in silence.

July is probably the month during the season when the collective anxiety of major league ballplayers reaches its height. And so when I fielded a call in July 2003 from John Hart, my general manager in Texas, my heart skipped a few beats. Knowing that the trade deadline was approaching, I figured that there was a good chance my life was about to change—or at least my address.

"I have some news you may have expected," Hart said. "I have traded you back to your old team." When he said "old team," my heart stopped. I had signed with the Texas Rangers in the off-season as a free agent because they were the only team that had assured me I would be a starter. I had declined an offer from the Phillies, for whom I had played for the previous five years, because they wouldn't make that commitment. As my Rangers contract was less lucrative than the one the Phillies had offered me, it seemed crazy that when all was said and done, I could be traded back to Philadelphia after accepting a contract inferior to the one they originally offered me.

"As you know, we have underperformed as a team," Hart continued. "It isn't your fault; you are doing your job, but with the trade deadline upon us, we wanted to make some moves. So, I traded you back to Chicago."

Chicago! I was to be a Cub again. Back to where it all began.

As I sat in my apartment in Texas, I realized I'd come full circle, going back to the mother ship that had once jettisoned me. There was much to do before returning. I had an apartment lease to cancel. (Royce Clayton was very understanding.) I somehow had to move everything I had to Chicago—including a car—and be in uniform the next day. And of course I needed to say good-bye to my teammates and pack up my baseball equipment.

When I arrived at the Ballpark at Arlington, my stuff was neatly packed for me (a page out of the disgruntled employee handbook). All that was left for me to do was say parting words to A-Rod, Juan Gone, Hammer, Raffy, Tex, El Indio, and every other teammate with or without a nickname.

I had my moving plan: I would pack as much as I could carry on the flight to Chicago, then clear out my apartment and jam everything I could into my car. Then, on the Cubs' next trip to Houston, I would catch a plane to Dallas, meet up with an auto shipping company, and have my car shipped to Chicago. Amazingly, it all went off without a glitch.

In the end, my trade from Texas back to Chicago produced my only postseason experience as a major league player. For that I was grateful, but at the time of the trade, it was a tough pill to swallow. Before the trade, I was playing the best baseball I had played in a long time (maybe that's why the Cubs noticed). I hit close to .400 in July and was poised to finish strong in the fall. Since I would be a free agent again at the end of the season, it was important for my long-term future to be in a good position at year's end.

The Cubs were in a playoff race, neck and neck with St. Louis and Houston. So it appeared I was moving into a good situation, except that the Cubs used the trade deadline to stack their team with veteran players. As a result, my position in Chicago was vastly different from my everyday role in Texas. I went from starter to bench player in a flash. This, for my long-term prognosis, was hardly the best situation from which to go into free agency, even with a division title at stake. But I could do nothing about it.

One team's trash is another's treasure. I can say I have been both, and either way you slice it, you can't help but feel like property, even if only for a moment.

Jimmy Rollins, my Phillies teammate and protégé, once gave me a poignant piece of wisdom that normally should flow from mentor to mentee, not the other way around. "Do it afraid" was his advice.

A healthy amount of fear can lead to great results, to people pushing themselves to the brink of their capabilities. I can recall an Opening Day when I was a Chicago Cub getting set to face the Florida Marlins and hearing Mark Grace explain to the young players how he still got butterflies even after all his years in the majors.

Yes, baseball players are afraid. A player's career is always a blink in a stare. I retired at the ripe old age of thirty-four following a season of sunflower seeds and only 162 at-bats. I had been a starter the year before. In this game, change happens fast.

Human nature wants to put the brakes on that rate of change. While your clock is ticking, players who are faster, stronger, and younger are setting up their lockers next to yours. They usually have better sound bites and lower salaries, too. In 1998, I was the new kid in Philadelphia, battling Lenny Dykstra for the center field job. Five years later, I was mentoring another new kid, Marlon Byrd, so he could replace me. Faced with that rate of career atrophy, players are capable of rash, self-serving, and often irresponsible decisions.

There is a tipping point in a player's career where he goes from chasing the dream to running from a nightmare. At that point, ambition is replaced with anxiety; passion is replaced with survival. It is a downhill run, and it spares no one.

For me, it started with my first trip to the disabled list after tearing a tendon early in the 2003 season. I realized I couldn't just roll out of bed and play anymore. All of a sudden, I felt old. It was the moment when a player is faced with the choice between aging naturally or aging artificially. I chose door number one, and two years later it was Triple-A or bust. Those who chose door number two— well, you know the rest.

To explain the ice water in his veins, Michael Jordan once declared, "Fear is an illusion." But I think fear is real and every bit as much a part of baseball as popcorn and peanuts. I remember learning on my first trip to Dodger Stadium that "no one wants to strike out here because it is a long walk to the dugout."

We're scared of failure, aging, vulnerability, leaving too soon, being passed up; and in the quest to conquer these fears, we are inspired by those who do whatever it takes to rise above and beat these odds. We call it "drive" or "ambition," but when doing "whatever it takes" leads us down the wrong road, it can erode our humanity.

The game ends up playing us.

6

...

RELATIONSHIPS IN THE GAME

The window of opportunity in baseball is the size of a hailstone. Even if you kick that window down and announce your presence with authority, you will be lucky to be in the game until you are forty. So it takes all-out focus, dedication, and commitment just to get the chance, much less succeed. As Joe Tanner, one of my base-running instructors in the minor leagues, told me, "You have to give up the best years of your life to make it in this game." All players come to understand advancement has a lot to do with not getting distracted with anything that can derail them—and at the top of the list are women.

There's only so much room to love yourself, love a jealous game like baseball, and then love someone else who wants love back. The significant others who travel the road—metaphorically, not literally—with the players during these years often play second fiddle to the game, at least during the season. They provide support and comfort and, yes, they often look the other way. They may be selfless, or they may be as self-absorbed as their man. Either way, it's a tough role to play.

No one keeps statistics for DFP (Depressed Former Players) or DAR (Divorces After Retirement), but I assure you they are plentiful. Players know this. Behind the bluster and bravado, they are as uncertain and fragile as any other human beings. If you hear enough stories of fellow players losing half their wealth, of wives sleeping with the strength coach, of mistresses gone bonkers, you can become fatalistic. You begin to anticipate your own unhappy ending. And so you shun all possible love connections, or you find any excuse to fortify the wall around your heart.

Dormant heart does not translate to dormant libido. The soundtrack of your life isn't a love song, but you are playing a game of musical chairs. In every port there is a companion, and you start to play one person off another so you don't get close to anyone. As soon as Suzy gets on your nerves, you call Kim, but then Kim is demanding too much time that you don't have, so you call Linda. At no time do you figure out that you are practicing bad habits no different than when you work on your swing repeatedly by holding the bat with your hands backward.

You may not be able to cope with any challenge that comes up in a relationship, but the fantasy world you are living in keeps telling you that a goddess will drop from the sky and magically you will know what to do with her. But, like baseball, it is hard to know how to do much of anything well or consistently when you never practice doing so.

It's also hard just to keep track of everyone. The invention of caller ID was a relief to many players. (I remember thinking how I would make a boatload of money if I could provide a way to tell where an incoming call was coming from.) Who is calling? When one of our teammates received a call showing just a phone number with an unrecognizable area code on caller ID, we would put our heads together to try to pair it with a city and state. Then we'd collectively ask our teammate, "Who do you know in Milwaukee, Wisconsin?" It is really bad when you can't answer the question, as well as the phone.

At a game in Puerto Rico, the girlfriend of one of my teammates was outside waiting for him. She waited and waited and waited. Eventually, I offered to check on him since I was in no rush to go home—a rookie mistake on my part by getting involved. He was in the clubhouse waiting for the girlfriend to leave because he had another woman at the game.

It was now a war of attrition. Eventually the other woman left. It had to be over an hour later. (My teammate married the woman who won the waiting game, but a divorce was right around the corner.)

In the back of my mind, I was worried that I couldn't sustain a loving relationship while I was in uniform. As I got older, particularly in my last few seasons, I was open to it. But after fifteen years of buses, bad hamstrings, and sacrifice, I was finally reaping the benefits, and, at that point, it was hard for me to share them with someone else.

The fear of vulnerability that comes with relationships creates a problem for many players. If you care too much about someone, their actions and moods can affect you and quite possibly ruin your game. We heard too many stories of players having bad years because a spouse skipped out on them (although I am sure that was only half the story). Yet the oversimplified response of becoming an island unto oneself is not necessarily a better option.

I think our hardwiring and our culture point us to needing and wanting some sort of base, some stability. Some players manage positive romantic relationships while in the game, but they seem to be the exception rather than the rule. If your reasons for getting involved with someone are selfish, you are bound to end up by yourself.

Seeking terra firma in a marriage to avoid Temptation Island, as some players do, is not the best foundation for a "till death do us part" union. A player may have known his wife for a long time, yet even with the stability of having a history together, their relationship can be tearing apart at the seams. We know that loyalty is wonderful—just as we expect our manager or our organization to stick by us during a slump—but we don't always have the confidence to embrace that expectation for ourselves. The exciting life of baseball thrives on elements that can destroy even the most dedicated of partners, if you get caught up in the luster.

In a culture of upgrading, it is tough to stop trying to go higher. The ladder of professional baseball makes you believe everything has steps to the next level. Soon you apply this philosophy to your dating scene. The longer you wait, the more you have; the more stable your career, the more tired you are of the flings, the more you know what you want. In theory you are ready for a deeper relationship. The women get more beautiful, and you get more points with the team peanut gallery. You forget about the excuses for why you can't let someone in, and see yourself sliding into the "happily ever after" home plate.

But then something unexpected happens. You slide down that sharp slope of diminishing returns. You get older, have more baggage, become more set in your ways. Sure, the younger women look good, but they are, well, *young*, and how they will mature is a big unknown. Time is passing you by, and you still can't make a commitment. Suddenly the count is 0–2, not 2–0, and the fastball you were sure is coming could now be one of five pitches.

I've heard (and used) so many excuses for holding back. I'll settle down when I get to the big leagues, when I finally get to be a starter, when I get some financial security, when I get off the disabled list, when I get settled in with this new team, when I make it to the playoffs, when I get the ring, when she proves to me she isn't in it for the money.

When implies you have full control over the next step. This is part of the arrogance that comes with the territory. And it ain't true. It is more like *when I can commit*, and it may be a long time before that can happen.

In the meantime, love is waiting; all is not lost. But will you know what to do with it?

The beginning days of a young player's life in the majors are full of obsessive focus. You may be pinch hitting; you may be going in for defense; you may be called into the office to go back to the minor leagues. Every time you hear your name, an alarm goes off.

Eventually there is a defining moment in your career when you can finally take one eye off the game and see what else is going on during the three-plus hours you are competing. This isn't a moment that arises because you feel like you have made it for good. It is more like the moment when you figure out that you can slip that piece of gum into your mouth during class. It is more about knowing how to do things without getting caught than about any sense of permanence.

The scenery at a major league park is busy and lush. There's a sea of people responsible for making sure everything goes smoothly—from the grounds crew to the guy who takes care of the umpires. And there is even more going on in the stands. Thousands of people moving and shaking, all at the same time. It can actually be quite intimidating at first.

Baseball players, by design, have eagle eyes. As a hitter, such vision is a prerequisite for being able to track a ball moving at close to one hundred miles per hour. Once you gain the freedom to look beyond the action between pitches, innings, or visits to the mound, a whole new world opens up.

All of a sudden that date you put on the pass list can be spotted in a sold-out stadium. After the game, when you meet up with her, she is shocked that you knew when she got up to get a hot dog in the third inning or that you saw she was wearing that pink team hat after the seventh-inning stretch. A woman dressed to kill is spotted instantly by everyone in both dugouts.

You develop a sixth sense of sorts. Once you nail the timing down, you don't miss a single phone call to the bullpen or that nasty fastball José Valverde just ran in on Ryan Howard's hands while you see what is happening in the mezzanine level. This terminator scan just needs a few snapshots to put the entire landscape together.

As might be expected, when I reached the big leagues, my scanning ability was also at rookie level. It took a dramatic moment to break in my virgin eyes and send me off on the path to the superpowers enjoyed by those who have been in the game for a while.

During a day game at Wrigley, I was playing left field, a fish out of water. Because my natural position was center field and I had little experience in the corners, each pitch was an adventure. You see the ball from a totally different angle in left. What's more, you are exceptionally close to the fans down the line and behind the wall. For a center fielder, this is like being in a foreign country. I was afraid to take my eyes off the game for even a split second.

Finally, there was a rare break in the action when I could allow myself to sightsee. I scanned the stands. My eyes landed on a blue silhouette down the left field line. Stunning brilliance, almost blinding, and somewhere within this mini-sun I saw a wave of the hand, so I waved back. I'd lost my virginity, made my first bold gesture, demonstrated that I had enough confidence to look away and sneak in the chewing gum.

The moment passed. The Lady in Blue disappeared from sight if not mind.

After a few more weeks of major league life, my eyes kept getting better—although I still had a ways to go. It was easy to spot the actress Alyssa Milano cheering on Carl Pavano in Florida, but I hadn't reached the point where I could see the tattoo on the back of a woman in the third deck sitting next to a left-handed ten-year-old who chose ketchup over mustard. Only a select few reach that level, but we all try.

No matter how good my eyes would get, they never liked to be interrupted right after they were closed for the night. The phone rang just as I had fallen off into dreamland in my hotel room in St. Louis. An unrecognizable female voice was on the line.

"Who is this?" I grumbled.

The caller explained that this was unusual behavior for her. *Sure*, I thought. How many times have we heard someone say, "I don't ordinarily do this, but . . ." She went on to tell me that she was the Lady in Blue.

Oh. I had no idea how she got the hotel number, but then again, how many luxury hotels are there near Busch Stadium? I suppose

I could have been excited—*a beautiful woman was calling my room!*—but I was exhausted. In that moment I understood why many players use aliases on the road: they prevent surprises in the middle of the night. But for my entire career I would fight the choice to have an alter ego for my hotel name. As a result, I had to field calls like this from time to time. I guess this was better than a ticket request.

Thankfully, she was calling from somewhere near Chicago, so there was no chance of her waiting in the lobby and being a stalker, I told myself. She seemed to just want to make an introduction based on the fact that in an unrookie-like fashion, I chose to wave back and spark a connection.

Sleep is golden before an afternoon game. As intrigued as I had been when she had waved, I was now more concerned about keeping my day job. I muttered something to the effect that now was not the best time to talk, and rushed her off the phone.

Because my disposition had been less than sunny, I assumed that this was the end of the saga. But when I related the curt conversation to my friend and mentor Shawon Dunston, he scolded me for being rude. It turned out he knew the Lady in Blue and her work with children with learning disorders and emotional challenges. "She's a respected educator," he said. "You have to go out with her."

I tried to explain the "booty call" hour of our first conversation and how I was sleeping in preparation for the nasty Cardinals. He didn't care. I had offended his sensibilities and his friend.

When Shawon spoke, I listened. So he saved me the clichéd approach of sending a phone number to an attractive admirer. I did not have to put my number on a baseball and give it to some naive batboy to bring to her, nor would I have to master the art of tossing a baseball softly into the waiting arms of an admirer with my phone number on it. Here, Shawon was trying to save me a step and make the love connection for me. I also realized that he was the one who had encouraged her to call me.

Shawon later passed me her phone number, demanding that I

call my wave partner and take her out. We ended up going to an Italian restaurant in Chicago to break the ice and match a face with the dress. She turned out to be very nice—nothing like the stories I had heard about people who call ballplayers near midnight.

This would, however, not be a love connection. I wasn't particularly looking for one since I was in survival mode to keep my job. I also was still smitten by a woman I had met in my first year in winter ball in Puerto Rico. As with many careers that absorb you into the world of single focus, relationships are necessary collateral damage. Still, I learned a few things that most young players figure out sooner or later. First off, throwing a ball with your phone number on it is out of the question from left field; this works much better for a pitcher in the bullpen. Second, I came to understand that you never know who may call your hotel room in the middle of the night. Despite the inclination to expect a shady "opportunist" to knock on your door five minutes later, it may be a great citizen of the city, so be nice. Third, even though your elders have been around the block and have better scanners than you do, when it comes to relationships, you have to be ready for one—even for a Lady in Blue.

While I refused to use an alias, many of my teammates and other players were walking aka's. Tony Montana, Burl Ives, Fyodor Wiggins, various characters from *Star Wars*. Whatever your fancy.

Why didn't I? In part because I remembered that when I was twenty years old and trying to decide upon a sports agent right before the amateur draft, I had a chance to talk to one of the finalist's clients. I called the front desk of his hotel, asked for "Cal Ripken Jr.," and Cal answered. First he asked who was calling and why, and then, satisfied with my answer, he let his guard down.

That stuck with me. If Cal didn't need an alias, I certainly didn't. So I thought.

For 99 percent of the days on the road, that was a good approach.

But when I went to Atlanta, I questioned my decision and seriously thought about using an alias I had tucked away for emergencies, "Dante McWhat."

The Atlanta difficulties began with a call to my room my rookie year. Since in many ways rookies are like raw meat to a seasoned carnivore, this self-proclaimed attractive woman apparently assumed I would jump at the opportunity to have her take me out to lunch and kindly "drive me to the stadium."

As a rookie, there was no way I could ask other teammates for advice. I suspected that most would have laughed me out of the locker room. This would have been the easiest hookup ever engineered. So what was the problem?

Momma told me not to talk to strangers. That was the problem. I knew this advice she had given me when I was in preschool was still relevant at twenty-six years old. And so I politely stayed on the line for a little while before ending the conversation with a "thanks, but no thanks."

She called again the next night and the night after that. (Red flag number one.) Then she claimed she had seen my picture on the Jumbo-Tron at Turner Field and had been told by someone in our bullpen where we were staying. (Red flag number two; this was unlikely.)

She went on to explain that her father had a reputable business in the city and her credibility could be verified. For the most part, she was persistent but cordial. I wanted to get off the phone, but I didn't think being rude and hanging up on her was a good option—especially if she was not wrapped too tightly.

I gave her very little information about myself. I just talked in platitudes and generalities, but she was pesky and left me disconcerted. Eventually, there would be a window to get off the phone, and I would take it; nevertheless, I acknowledged that the loneliness of the road, especially for a rookie, could almost make this exchange comforting.

After hearing a few conversations in the locker room that sounded an awful like what was happening to me, I concluded that several other teammates were getting the same calls from the same woman. Was she calling everyone on the roster? I came to find out that there was one common denominator: her targets were all African American, and they were usually young and vulnerable players. Interesting.

To my horror, one of my teammates did accept that ride, and, worse yet, she left a picture at the front desk to showcase her good looks. It reminded me of a scene from the Police's "Wrapped Around Your Finger" video when Sting was running around a bunch of candles as if he was related to Dracula. (Red Flag number three—now even a bullfighter would have walked away.)

My teammate claimed it was an uncomfortable ride and that he wasn't all that blown away by her beauty. I just told him he was lucky he made it to the stadium and didn't end up in a landfill somewhere. I meant it.

The Stalker called regularly when I came to Atlanta. MLB Security provides a plastic card with a list of personnel in each city that you can call if you have trouble. Whenever we visited the Braves, I kept it nearby.

(MLB also provided the best entertainment each spring training by playing a video that warned us of a different deadly sin a year. The videos hit on gambling, drugs, stalkers, infidelity, violence. My favorite was about a player's wife who surprises her husband by showing up while he's on a road trip. She gets the key from the front desk and goes up to his room. The husband has only a few seconds to whisk his mistress behind a curtain. In response to his wife's declaration of "Surprise!" he says, "You know I don't like surprises!" Everyone loved that one.)

Still thinking it better to placate rather than provoke, I continued to take the Stalker's calls. One night she started getting antagonistic because I had repeatedly refused to see her anywhere, anytime. She began to rattle off a list of players who she claimed were gay, citing verifiable evidence from people working at gay establishments in Atlanta. I assumed she was implying the same about me since I would not succumb to her advances. She was escalating her behavior, and despite not caring to clarify my sexual orientation out of ego, I worried about where these conversations were going.

I had heard stories about players getting stalked. One former National League All Star, who prefers to remain anonymous, had some random fan follow him home over the course of time in his home city. Her persistent nature was impressive since she rode a bicycle while chasing his car. His mistake was that he took the same route home every day.

She would pedal as far as she could until she lost him, and then the next day, she would start at that very spot until he would pass her. Then she would go as far as she could until she lost him again. And repeat and repeat and repeat.

Hearing that story made me part nauseated, part amazed at her tenacity. She eventually made it to his home. Needless to say, he pulled out that security card and got some professional help to quell the situation. No one got hurt, but his family lost any feeling of comfort.

I didn't have a family or a home in Atlanta, but I knew how easy it was for people to get to players at the hotel. I started to look over my shoulder a little bit and ignore the phone when it rang. I could always check for messages later. Once cell phones became the preferred method of communication, it got even easier to avoid the room phone.

For a couple of years, my trips to Atlanta became quiet again and Dante McWhat would remain a name I didn't need. But the playoffs are another animal. The Atlanta woman called again when my Cubs came to town for the National League Division Series in 2003. I exchanged pleasantries. Then, older and wiser, I told her never to call me again and hung up.

She never called again. As usual, Momma had been right all along.

My momma, who played a major role in making diversity a strength for the school system in my hometown, never told me to avoid being seen with white women. But during my rookie year one of my

African American teammates on the Cubs did. I knew he was looking out for me. Since I'd been seen with white women before and
had survived quite nicely, I was surprised and disturbed by his
words of caution. Also, the woman in question wasn't even a girlfriend; she was a pal from college.

"Ms. San Diego," as I'll call her, had lived next door to me in a
coed dorm at Penn. My roommate and I hung out quite a bit with
her and her roommate, a young freshman of Jamaican descent who
became our protégé as we helped her adjust to college life. I enjoyed
assisting her particularly since my father had come to America
from another Caribbean island, Trinidad.

I stayed friends with Ms. San Diego over the years. She had
returned to her home area of Southern California after graduation,
and when I made it to the big leagues, I invited her to a game when
we played the Padres. First we planned to go to lunch, and I asked
her to pick me up at the hotel.

I learned as a rookie that it's better not to be seen or heard, especially after midnight when you might run into a coach. Don't hover
in the lobby too long after the game ends, don't be seen getting into
a cab after hours.

But what harm could possibly come in the middle of the day?

Ms. San Diego parked in the hotel lot and met me in the lobby.
By happenstance, a few veteran players and coaches were checking
out at the front desk since it was "Getaway Day," so they saw us. It
was a little awkward because no young player wants any of his personal business out there, but I didn't think it was worth high alarm.
We had our lunch, and she came to the game that night.

Not too long after this, I heard a couple of comments about
her visit. A few players noted that she was an attractive woman and
seemed genuinely impressed.

One teammate, however, had a wholly different take, one that
was new to me at the big-league level. With a somberness suggesting
that someone had just died and a tone that was meant to protect

another member of the African American club plagued with high rates of attrition, he took me aside and said, "Never let them see you with a white woman."

My minor league experience, like that of many players, had been less than ideal. I lost close to a year buried in an oil-and-water relationship with my Triple-A manager, and that is to put it mildly. As a result, when I was first up in the big leagues I needed to impress or face losing my window of opportunity. If you aren't cracking that starting lineup regularly by the time you are twenty-six or twenty-seven, you can easily end up as a role player in perpetuity. I had arrived with the "now or never" weight on my shoulders, but it had never occurred to me that never might come because my lunch date was white.

It's not as if I didn't know about the fraught nature of love across the color line. My mom had grown up in the South at a time when there was real and genuine concern about interracial dating. And my older brother had strange things happen to him—including losing his starting job—when he brought his white girlfriend to his summer league games. (To his credit, he never backed down from a good relationship because of race, but it was trying for him.) My parents spoke about the challenges and the lack of readiness our society has in this area of socialization, but more as a warning, not as a stop sign. I came along a little later than my brother and witnessed firsthand the power of diversity in high school and college. Still, even in the 1990s, a good many Americans still considered it taboo for a black man to date a white woman or even to be seen with one.

I could see where my teammate was coming from. But since this wasn't my girlfriend and, in theory, adults should be able to lead their own lives, I wasn't sure what to do with his suggestion. I did think back to a story one of my older teammates in the minor leagues had told me. He was a white player who was dating a black woman. An administrator called him into the office to encourage him to end this relationship, threatening to call his mother. I wish that guy had tried to call my mother. She would have set him straight.

This was the reality of the generation of those who played before me. The African American players who came up in the 1970s and '80s had a rough time and could not do anything that they thought would scare off the coaches and executives who controlled their fate. Real or imagined, if a date can wreck your future, maybe you should think about finding someone else to share a midday taco.

I remained friends with Ms. San Diego, and she would come to all my games when we played the Padres. But I looked over my shoulder from time to time, thinking about the persistence of this interracial question—even in baseball, where a smorgasbord of cultures mixed relatively easily.

Sure, there were coaches and players who were in interracial marriages, which seemed to go over better in the community than casual flings. I just found it overly simplistic to box someone in based on race. You miss out on a lot of wonderful lessons and experiences, including our shared challenges. That box also seemed antithetical to a game that had rapidly expanded worldwide with people of all cultures trying to find a way to win together.

Despite my respect for my teammate's experience, I did not pass down his wisdom to the next generation of players. I know he was trying to help me in an area that was touchy and potentially dangerous, even in the 1990s, but I chose to move past it. Instead, I decided to challenge everyone else to learn the lesson of understanding across historically divisive lines. Thankfully, an entire generation turned the page and allowed for lunch dates that spanned the cultural spectrum, not to mention getting down to what really counts.

For some ballplayers, just as for some in every other walk of life, what really counts is beauty.

My good friend and former teammate Marlon Anderson used to say, "Major League Baseball is like a big high school." In pro baseball you certainly have all the cliques and groups from those teenage years: the squares, the nerds, the popular crowd, the users, the bad boys, the jocks, the militants, the out-of-towners. The insecurity about fitting in or achieving your goals also remains. But one thing is different in the big leagues: it's a lot easier to get the girl.

When I was a teenager, I walked the halls of my high school representing a little part of just about every group. Unfortunately (or maybe fortunately), with my mother teaching math under the same roof, I also had to think twice about how much of a bad boy I wanted to be. The answer? Not much. As one of my crushes told me, "I couldn't date you now; you are marriage material." Apparently I would have to wait until she was ready to wed, or I would have to become nonmarriage material. Kind of complicated for an adolescent.

Most people assume that the star athletes in such an arena automatically attract the coolest girls and possess the confidence to know what to do after they've connected. That may be true of some football and basketball players, but in my high school, members of the baseball team were as anonymous as members of the electronics club. (Yes, I was on that team, too.) If we got twelve people to watch one of my high school games, we were shocked. As a result, we baseball players had to work a little bit more to leverage that "star power" to get the girl. One of my female friends signed my yearbook "see you in the pros." That was the only reference to my potential baseball future from anyone I thought was cute.

Evaluating your own attractiveness is out the window once you turn pro. It is sort of like a real-life Bud Light commercial: average guy gets stunning glamour girl. Although your mediocrity in certain areas can lazily be masked in fine suits, dark shades, or by picking up that shiny new Benz you had your eyes on, somewhere inside is still that kid from the electronics club. When I met Sammy Sosa's wife, Sonia, for the first time, I thought, *Wow. I guess in the big leagues, you don't have to run from women who are that striking.*

One night during my first spring training, I went out to a club in Tempe, Arizona. I saw this attractive woman from afar and eventually worked up the courage to ask her to dance. She said, "Ask again if we run into each other later." Nice move. So I ran into her again, and we ended up dancing.

While on the floor, we exchanged the usual questions. What is your name? Where are you from? When I answered that I was from New Jersey, I didn't make the connection that being in Arizona for six weeks was unusual—unless of course, you were a baseball player. She did. Her next question was "What round were you drafted in?" Wow, straight for the jugular.

You don't have to be a math teacher to figure out that signing a professional sports contract changes the social equation for young men. It is an opportunity to take who you were inside those high school walls and make him null and void. Suddenly you have a free pass to social acceptance. It gets you into those inner circles; it most certainly will get you into the good graces of the girls who once seemed out of your league. They may have been unapproachable because they didn't think you were cool enough, but more than likely you struck out or never even took a swing because of your own insecurity, your conclusion that you had no chance.

Slap on those pinstripes sporting your name on the back, and all of a sudden you have instant courage. As you climb the ladder of pro baseball, the word *unapproachable* falls to the ground. Sure, it may be because you have an entourage approaching someone on your behalf or because you can now afford to buy enough drinks to drown your anxiety, but however you do it, you can now talk to the women who used to fill you with fear.

Let's be honest. Those girls who once left you tongue-tied and staring at your navel were the high school beauties. And the women you now feel comfortable approaching are just as gorgeous if not "off the charts." You're still as shallow. You're just not in over your head anymore. You quickly learn that beauty and baseball have a no-trade clause. You have to play well, but you have to look good, too, and so do the people surrounding you.

This is a heady realization for guys who weren't Don Juans in high school. Even though my wonderful momma told me that you should want to spend time with people who see past the glitz and the hype and love you for who you are, still there was something that was exciting about this new life. Now you can finally get a date with women who would have left you speechless in high school and probably wouldn't have spoken to you anyway.

All those indirect rejections for dates, all those moments when you couldn't muster up the courage to ask her out, all those frozen spines stopping you from bending over and kissing her fly out the window once you hit the big time. I had come a long way from tripping over words to ask Christine Saunders to the prom. You can now flash the MLB card and cut through all the inconvenient fear that used to tie you up in knots. Better yet, maybe you have your agent or a member of your entourage flash the card for you.

Getting on this road to make up for all the social slights from high school can be addictive. Some sort of "notch in the belt" syndrome takes over as players revert to their high school years while in the big leagues. In an environment where youth is king and the key to major league longevity, it is easy to fall prey to its illusions by embracing all the ways to stay young. You can therefore go back in time and turn the table on all of those "could'ves, should'ves, and might'ves"—even if you have to stay in high school for a ten-year major league career.

It doesn't help that most of your teammates egg you on. It becomes a topic of conversation that someone saw you coming in late with a blond bombshell or the actress from a popular TV show on your arm. You gain street cred as you cause jealous teammates to break their necks to catch a glimpse of your date. Then you have to live up to the hype and do it all over again.

I never got more inquiries about my relationships than when I dated Lisa Harrison from the WNBA's Phoenix Mercury. On top of that fact, my cred points increased exponentially once the word got out that *Playboy* had asked her to pose. One day in Milwaukee, my Cubs teammate Tony Womack greeted me with an interesting hello: "How are you doing today? Oh, why am I bothering to ask? I know you're happy. You're dating Lisa Harrison!"

When the model-actress K. D. Aubert came to one of our games, many of my teammates spent a good part of the game looking backward into the stands, staring at her. I had seen her in a movie and reached out to her through her professional network in good fun, figuring nothing would come of it. (Wait a minute, now I'm the stalker!) To my shock, I received an instant response, and I also found out that she had played some softball in college and shared a passion for salsa music. That common ground led her to accept an invitation to bring her friends to a game to see me play. When my teammates figured out that she was a guest on my pass list, I was etched in locker room lore. The members of the team staff who sat next to her practically begged me to get her to come to the next game. I had no way to reach her directly, but it turned out that she enjoyed the game and got in touch with me the following day to request tickets for the next game, for her and another group of friends, thereby granting the staff's wish. Amazing how it all works.

Peer pressure drives the social circle in Major League Baseball. Much of your time is spent conquering and burying that old self, that high school kid with braces or acne, so that he can now fit in, be accepted, be desired. Too bad all you end up doing is bringing him back to life, desperate to be cool, years after you could have just outgrown him.

Dating a beauty might earn you cred points for a while, but no matter how good-looking your girlfriend is, she'll eventually have to pass muster with your family. Your baseball family, that is.

In 1979, the world champion Pittsburgh Pirates were known as "the family"—a tip of the black and gold cap to the team's omniblaring (at least to this nine-year-old Phillies fan) theme song, "We Are Family," sung by the aptly named Sister Sledge. Truth be told, every baseball team is a family—not necessarily a functional one, but a family nonetheless. This can give birth to problems: namely, how to balance your kin on the roster with those on the family tree and in the extended circle, most notably girlfriends. If a player or a team can't achieve that balance, it will be a long season.

Every stadium has a "family room," a place where the players' relatives can congregate. Its location varies from stadium to stadium, but it is always top secret to everyone outside the inner circle. It may be upstairs, downstairs, near the locker room, on the concourse; only an elite few have access.

Inside, most family rooms have space for kids to play or retreat to during a game—a must at the Rangers' park in Arlington, Texas, where caretakers needed a place to take young ones who were melting in the smoldering heat. TVs adorn the room so that everyone can monitor what Dad (or son, brother, husband, etc.) is doing on the field.

Before a game starts and after it ends, the family room fills with wives, children, brothers, sisters, mothers, fathers, and the occasional extended family member and whoever accompanied them to the game. It can be an incubator of great ideas for charitable causes or a safe place for a player's family to bond with other families similarly situated. But just as there are a lot of rules that govern the game on the field and in the locker room, in this sacred space there is also a code of conduct, most of it unwritten. Once you get settled in, you are expected to know how to behave. Year in and year out, however, there is never a clear-cut way of dealing with girlfriends in the pre- and postgame sanctuary.

A girlfriend's appearance in the family room is a privilege, not a right. Whether to grant that privilege is often the subject of hotly contested debate involving the boyfriend, the families, and the team's community relations officials. Girlfriends are seen by all of the above as having ticking clocks strapped on their backs. Time will eventually expire, and the player will in all likelihood replace rather than reset until proven otherwise. But until that seemingly inevitable expiration date arrives, a player's girl has the ability to sour a room. The way she dresses or walks or talks can easily offend a wife or a mom or upset a kid. (In general, the dads and brothers want no part of this dynamic.) So if the girlfriends are wise, they tread lightly.

Once an outsider gains admittance, a Queen Bee sets the standard for behavior. She is usually the wife of a senior player. Mess with the Queen Bee, and you'll get stung, especially if you're a rookie.

My introduction to this phenomenon came during my first year in Chicago. I had a guest at the game and hadn't made clear where she should wait for me after the game. I just left the tickets and figured that I would run into her near the team parking lot. She ended up in the family room, probably by following the crowd around her, as she was sitting in the VIP section with the guests of other players.

After the game, I strolled toward the family room. When I got there, our Queen Bee, Margaret Sandberg (wife of Ryne), stopped me at the door and began her interrogation. *Was that woman inside the room my guest?* I was speechless and must have had a quizzical look on my face because I genuinely could not see past her. In fact, I am not even sure I had ever even been in the family room at that point. I had no wife, and my parents were back in New Jersey. Peeking inside, I immediately understood the problem with bringing "random" people into the family room. My date was wearing a skintight white body suit with PRECIOUS stenciled across the front written over a set of red lips—a fashion ensemble that understandably made a lot of people in that room uncomfortable.

Since I was a rookie player who was single and free-flowing, I could not fathom the importance of protecting the nuclear family as the Queen Bee needed to do, but I understand it now as a father and a husband. Girlfriends could be interacting with your children in an intimate setting, and you would certainly want to screen them. You also have to be sure these girlfriends aren't opportunists and wearing skintight bunny suits for everyone else's husband. Even as a young prospect, I immediately understood that I needed to promise Mrs. Sandberg that I'd be a little more careful in the future.

Precious's onetime fashion faux pas was nothing compared to

the constant havoc created by the girlfriend of my Phillies teammate Mike Lieberthal, whom I'll call Rita. From the first day she
strode into our world, Rita refused to learn the rules of the room.
She came in firing from the hip, daring anyone to keep her out. And
each time thereafter she seemed to be making a conscious effort to
surpass her personal worst. On one occasion, she entered the room
wearing pants that were, in the words of my schoolteacher mother,
"transparent."

It's not pretty when a girlfriend, especially one who has broken so many rules as Rita did, manages to get more privileges than
a player's wife. After the 9/11 attacks in 2001, security went up ten-
fold. A player and anyone in his circle had to get a special ID to go to
the family room or any other restricted area. Girlfriends were also
allowed to get this identification. Somehow, the rebellious Rita was
able to secure her ID well before everyone else. She then flaunted
that fact to the wives, one of whom had been denied admittance to
the family room because she hadn't yet received her credentials.
(She had to wait in the stands while pregnant.) The fallout was dramatic; the issue made it all the way down to the players at batting
practice.

The single player with a Precious or a Rita on his arm must navigate dangerous waters. You don't want to sell out your girlfriend.
But at the same time you don't want to upset your teammates, who
are going to hear it from their wives if you bring a snake into their
pre- and postgame Eden.

Players are aware of the importance of team chemistry and cog-
nizant that the introduction of unstable elements can cause a devas-
tating explosion. So, despite family pressure or personal distaste, it
takes the most egregious of violations for a teammate to confront
another teammate about his significant other. Most players bite their
tongues, hopeful if not confident that time is on their side.

When Rita stopped me in the parking lot after a game in New
York to tell me that she thought my guest was too "flashy" for me, I
didn't react. I decided to wait, knowing her timer was going to hit

zero and that Lieberthal would, fingers crossed, choose not to reset it. That's what happened, and all was well in the family room again—at least for the time being.

This is not to say that family room dysfunction never disrupts the clubhouse. Sometimes a girlfriend's over-the-top behavior cannot be overlooked. Before Rita was out of the circle, her repeated antics actually caused teammates to caucus before several games to figure out how to approach Lieberthal. Nothing transpired of substance other than to keep whispering in Mike's ear that there were other fish in the sea. But just reaching that level is like DEFCON 5 for a baseball team.

Going to the family room after each game is a little like having Thanksgiving dinner day after day for six straight months. You can't choose your teammates any more than you can choose your kinfolk to share this special day with. So you laugh at your uncle's or second baseman's eccentricities, ignore your cousin's or catcher's obnoxious kids, and for the sake of self-preservation if not unity, you definitely do not bring a girl in a skintight white getup with THANKS stenciled across the top.

After all, we are family.

Why have so many members of my baseball family felt compelled to honor their history and the people they knew before their careers exploded, even when it's to their own detriment?

Locker room talk suggests that "keeping it real" is a noble effort. It is thought to show that sudden success is not going to change your stripes: you are that same coal miner's son from West Virginia, and your one-million-dollar signing bonus has had no impact on the company you keep. You still like to fish at the crack of dawn with a transistor radio blaring. You still like extra hot sauce on your chicken-fried steak.

But is it real?

"Realness" is relative. Something is real only when you feel it in your bones, and so only you really know how genuine your behavior is. Contrived realness isn't real at all, and that soon becomes apparent.

For a baseball player, it is a long road to prominence. Even the best of the best stay mired in the minor leagues for at least a couple of years. To most of my friends and family, I got drafted by the Cubs and then disappeared into a minor league vortex. I made only $850 a month that first year, and despite the fact that there are probably ten times as many minor leaguers getting paid to play as there are major leaguers, most people hear the word *pro* and think only of the majors. But I had a signed contract with the Cubs. And even though I was in Geneva, New York, and not Chicago, I was, legitimately, a pro.

But I was also a bonus baby. A first-round draft pick with a six-figure payoff for signing.

Today, six figures is out the window, and seven figures is your new ID. But one issue doesn't change: what happens to those relationships with friends and family from your past—your contemporaries who haven't left the neighborhood or who are just getting going at their accounting firm or beginning their mechanic apprenticeship—while you're pulling into the team parking lot at Yankee Stadium in your new Ferrari at the age of twenty-five? Can we still be friends?

By the time I got my first pro contract I had already forged some of my closest and (still) longest-lasting friendships. In fact, two college friends, Bruce Brasser and Jeff Miller, had promised to be at my first major league game, no matter what. When the time came and I called them at the crack of dawn before heading to the airport, they made arrangements to see me at Wrigley that same day. Jeff came all the way from Washington, D.C.

Over time, I felt that my experience navigating social settings and relationships was strengthened by having taken the extra years to attend college, something that is shared by only a portion of major league players. If you were drafted out of high school and then shot through the minor league system, you might not have had the chance to socialize beyond high school before becoming another Manny Ramirez. I played against Manny when he was nineteen, in the Carolina League, and he was already on his meteoric rise—a lot of responsibility for a young man.

College or not, it can feel safer to rely completely on old friendships, or blindly trust your handlers, than to invest in the possibility of new encounters. Everyone still has to work through the unprecedented amount of new friends that pop up on the scene once you're established.

Most of my teammates who made money in a relatively short period of time struggled with this balancing act. There's a lot of work involved in "making it." As a result, you might not see those old friends often, changing your dynamic forever. On the other hand, once you're a highly paid athlete you don't want people to think you've let the money go to your head and become a snob.

Scott Rolen, my Phillies teammate for many years, was the pride of Jasper, Indiana, and kept the friendships he had when he was growing up. (He married his hometown sweetheart.) I remember all the hurt teammates who didn't get invited to his wedding, or even know about it until it happened. But he kept his circle tight as part of his survival strategy; just because you were teammates didn't mean you got a free pass inside.

Scott's approach is something all players use at one time or another. Even friendships between teammates of many years can still be placed in that "new friend" category, not on par with the original core group that you know and trust. Sure, you spend an inordinate amount of time together during the season, but when that off-season bell rings, as the Cubs' minor league head trainer Dick Cummings would say, "Now you can choose your own friends."

It's natural to want the world to know you haven't changed, but the fact is that to endure and produce at a high level, you have to change or at least adapt. Making that change a positive one may depend on whether you learn to handle your new surroundings and circumstances maturely. Maybe you tipped a few cows after a couple of brews in between junior year and senior year of high school, evading the authorities for a few days. But try the equivalent of that as, say, the starting shortstop of the Los Angeles Dodgers, and that video you made is going to be looped through cyberspace. Same act, different reaction.

If you stay stuck and don't reevaluate your relationships (including the one with yourself) over time, you will make the same decisions you would have made as a teenager, because you're surrounded by the people who were there for you then. Some of those friends don't necessarily want you to grow—not for any malicious reasons but because they're afraid they will lose you, and you are afraid of the same thing.

As my mom told me once, when she was quietly recommending that I move on from a relationship that was dead in the water, "You want the person to add to your life. In my relationship with your father, it was an exponential increase. So why would you accept subtraction?" Spoken like a true math teacher.

Keeping it real can be a good thing. It allows us to stay grounded; it reminds us of where we came from, who we are; it keeps us centered. Jobs come and go, money and fame can disappear, so changing everything to try to fit into something that's fleeting will create problems. But when you keep it real just because it's the easiest route, whether out of insecurity, peer pressure, or maybe denial, you end up missing an opportunity to enrich your life with new experiences.

It doesn't even have to be all or nothing: you can be grounded and fly. And part of that balance comes from understanding that doing the same things as a twenty-eight-year-old star first baseman that you did when you were seventeen and reckless doesn't mean you're "grounded"; it means you've crashed and don't know it.

One thing that will really keep things real is having a baby.

No one will dare say it, but there is a clock ticking when you leave your team for the birth of your child. Granted, it isn't twenty-four hours, but it isn't a week, either. And once you cross that threshold of acceptable leave of absence, people start grumbling.

Now that I'm retired, I do miss baseball in some ways, but what I don't miss are the sacrifices you're expected to make in the face of life-changing events. There is a game pretty much every day, and to be absent from one is unheard of. You have to be dead, or someone else has to be dead, and after a day or two any excuse short of that is frowned upon.

Come to think of it, in baseball it is understood that you shouldn't even plan to have a child during the season. Childbirth is an off-season event, and anyone not taking that into consideration is not making a wise choice—as if we have this level of control over the timing.

I recall a Philadelphia Phillies teammate, Ron Gant, discussing his battle with one of his previous managers on another team over spending too many days at his wife's bedside after the birth of their child. Disgust over his taking too long made it into the papers, and the local disapproval spread, as comments flew back and forth about the inappropriateness of Gant's return timeline. He had failed to remember that the moment it was clear that his wife was okay and his premature daughter was okay, he was supposed to be back in uniform.

When my son was born, three years after my retirement, I was able to ask questions of the medical staff, learn how to feed and change him (didn't have a clue before), and just be there. The high-octane world of baseball does not allow much room for these things; someone else is always trying to take your job, and too many optional days off equals a lack of commitment, no matter what the reason. And people are making too much money to have paid vacation days.

These issues came into play when my father was chronically ill for three years while I was still playing. The Phillies did what they could to accommodate my need to be with him—they even offered to let me leave the team for a few days—but I also understood that my career could change if I were to take too much time off. Either the competition would gain on me, because I'd lose the edge and focus, or there'd be a league-wide question mark regarding my "commitment."

There's a premium put on players who do "whatever it takes" to be productive. So in the end, it falls into the lap of the player. No one is forcing you to not be there for events that are important to you. No one is twisting your arm to get back to the stadium even though in your heart you know you need to be there a little while longer to make sure your newborn son is okay. No one is suggesting any of that, but the message is being delivered just the same, albeit from a dark corner of the game's culture.

7

...

BRIDGING DIFFERENCES
IN THE GAME

When people ask me what I miss the most about playing professional baseball, my answer usually surprises them. Fame, fortune, performing, and world travel had its perks, but what I really miss is the diversity.

Take a close look at the World Baseball Classic, and you'll see how far the sport has come in a short period of time. It is no longer a homogeneous, closed circle of local athletes, but rather an entire world of cultures.

Only sixty years ago, Jackie Robinson broke through the color barrier that excluded African American ballplayers. Since then, there's been a quiet inflow of players from many other cultures who have also changed the game dramatically. The impact of Latino players is clear; they now represent about 27 percent of all major leaguers. In the last decade there have also been icons like Japan's Ichiro Suzuki (who has a type of sushi, the "Ichiroll," named after him at Safeco Field in Seattle) and Hideki Matsui, who became a one-man movement in Japan after signing with the Yankees. I witnessed firsthand the paparazzi following him around during spring training in 2005.

There is tremendous new talent to be found all over the world. Recently, a player named Gift Ngoepe became the first black South African to sign a professional baseball contract. Soon baseball scouts will have to cover the entire planet or risk missing a superstar who not only might help an organization win games, but also might open up a whole new market. The fact that we can now watch teams like the Netherlands make a run at the World Baseball Classic title— which Japan has won two times in a row—makes it clear that the game has grown in ways that once seemed unimaginable.

The game also grows and changes when its doors open up to the world. Each culture adds its own flavor. Jackie Robinson, for example, arrived with elbows flying and spikes high—aggressive play that was more of a hallmark of the old Negro Leagues. And in our day, we recognize that great players come from all over. Pedro, Jeter, and Pudge are all names that in five letters apiece evoke something powerful about baseball, yet in the World Baseball Classic they played for three different countries.

This challenges everyone to see the game through new eyes.

When I played, I was always inspired by the fact that my teammates of nearly all walks of life prayed together, won together, lived together, traveled together, cried together (yes, there is crying in baseball), rose above together—and we did it every single day. If you want to survive as a unit, you have to figure out how to work in harmony. Once you taste the power of pooling geographic, cultural, and economic diversity—religious diversity and sexual orientation still need some work (a baseball clubhouse is a hard place to be "out")—it is almost impossible not to have a new understanding of how much people really have in common and how much further we can go together when we respect that power.

I have had the pleasure of speaking to many players from the Negro Leagues, like Buck O'Neil and Mahlon Duckett, and without exception they were humbled and thankful for their trials and tribulations— something I found to be amazing. They maintained their faith in a better day for all of America, when the game of baseball would no longer exclude them.

In Teaneck, New Jersey, I grew up in a community committed to learning how to communicate across cultural and religious lines. Cottage parties would fill up a neighbor's basement to discuss Jewish and African American relations, meet-up groups would form to decide how to celebrate various cultures at Teaneck High School, dialogues and community sessions were constantly challenging people to learn outside the box. The town decided that it was stronger as a cohesive unit than as a scapegoating machine that fell back upon stereotyping. It took control of its destiny and found a way.

My baseball team in high school was ethnically diverse. Unfortunately, it was not uncommon for us, when traveling to some nearby towns, to hear from opposing fans exactly how uncomfortable our smorgasbord of cultures made them feel. Once, one of my teammates got tired of the verbal abuse from a spectator who had gone on for an entire game, and yelled back at the offender. After the game, this fan's husband (who happened to be dressed in business attire) waited near our bus and kicked a different player in the chest. He capped that off with some racially inappropriate comments.

Every player banded together and stood firmly behind our teammate in support. We did this not because he was black, or because he happened to be our captain, but because he was our teammate.

After I left high school, I didn't see quite that kind of commitment— people working together unyieldingly to make diversity a strength— until I put on the major league uniform. I still believe it is the best lesson baseball can give us.

Baseball has the ability to unite people and transcend stereotypes and, most important, to teach young people the importance of understanding and inclusion. This is what opens up our world; this is what allows us to see how much more potential there is in cooperation.

Not long ago, I received an e-mail from a writer who had interviewed me a couple of years before for Black History Month. We'd kept in touch, and he was writing to inform me of the promotion to the major leagues of Will Venable, a rookie outfielder for the San Diego Padres.

The reporter also told me that Venable was the second African American Ivy Leaguer to make it to the big leagues. And he confirmed something I had suspected but had never fully explored: I was the first.

Throughout my career, I knew that being an Ivy League graduate in Major League Baseball made me something of an anomaly. There have been only a handful of Ivy League baseball players of any race, though our ranks included some of the greats: Lou Gehrig, Eddie Collins, Ron Darling, and Red Rolfe. In the minor leagues, that pedigree wasn't considered a badge of honor or even much of an asset. Quite the opposite. The fact that I'd gone to a school like Penn caused question marks to swirl about my "focus" and my "commitment" to the game. After all, I was seen as someone who could walk away at any time, as one of my teammates who'd gone to Stanford did after a demotion.

I had critics say in print that I was "too smart for my own good" or that I "spent more time philosophizing than working." I recognized that I often asked a lot of questions to get a deeper understanding of some techniques, but I always found it curious that I was accused of thinking I had all the answers and asking too many questions at the same time. A writer friend of mine, Alan Schwarz, describing how my Ivy League degree was perceived, referred to my experience coming up in minor league baseball as "Poison Ivy."

When I was feeling alone in the minors, I focused on what all the players had in common: a love for playing this game and a dream of the major leagues. And despite everything, there was a lot more that brought us together as players than not. I also needed to believe that performing well can trump everything.

In some ways, embarking on a baseball career is a lonely walk for all players—young men who are often leaving home for the first time— but I knew from the moment I showed up for my first professional game, in Niagara Falls, New York, that there weren't a lot of people who shared my particular experience. I was fortunate to have been raised in a town that embraced ethnic, religious, and economic diversity. Otherwise it would have been much more challenging for me to find common ground with my teammates and coaches.

My minor league outfield instructor was the retired major leaguer Jimmy Piersall, and it took the two of us years to figure out how to deal with each other. He wore his edgy history on his sleeve while referring to college graduates like me with a word I'd rather not put in print. But we found a space where we could connect: in the work ethic required to make it to the top of the profession we both loved. In the end, he became my number-one advocate, despite our diametrically opposed experiences.

I also spent a lot of my minor league career shaking off the exhausted "black athlete" labels of laziness, natural talent, and nonchalance. I could only turn to mentors, my family, and history to find my path, because there was no one else around who had my specific kind of challenge: bridging both the racial and educational divides. So I adopted the same mind-set that helped get my mother and father out of bed every day: they expected a degree of unfairness in life, but they knew that the people who had paved the way carried bigger burdens in much more difficult circumstances, enduring challenges just to find a job or to be able to vote.

It was a lot to juggle, but the saving grace was that, in the end, we all had to try to hit that baseball. We all had to perform. In some ways, that is what makes the game so great; it forces people to look beyond certain things because when they don't, they miss some of its beauty.

I also thought about my Negro League predecessors, who set the stage, turned on the lights, and paid the bill, and now I was able to enjoy performing in the theater they constructed. They represent everything baseball should want to be, everything America should want to be: sacrifice and humility, patience and faith, forgiveness and perseverance.

———

It's fair to say that in the big leagues, what you drive defines you. Car dealers seem more than happy to be part of your world, so the odds are you'll end up scoring a deal on a luxury auto unavailable to the average fan who puts down his or her hard-earned money to see you play.

I haven't heard too many players complain about this state of affairs—or about getting comped at restaurants or clubs or concerts. But it does take some getting used to. One minute you're broke in the minors, needing freebies to help stay afloat. The next minute you're flush in the majors, expecting something free just for being you.

If you're uncomfortable with the special treatment, you can always put on your humble hat when you enter an establishment. Losing the swagger and adding your favorite sweatshirt with the hole in the armpit and some dark shades to cover the bags under your eyes from that late-night arrival from the West Coast should ensure anonymity and guarantee that you pay everyman prices.

Most players seem to prefer the entitlement hat. They stride into a store or showroom wearing a desire for a quick transaction and an expectation of a bargain even when they can pay more. I wasn't immune.

When I was a rookie, Shawon Dunston introduced me to the art of the deal. Soon I was able to rent a spanking-new Ford Taurus in spring training for seven dollars a day. Who has ever seen those rates (even when adjusting for cost of living in today's dollars)? Then again some players didn't have to pay at all.

After leaving the Cubs and becoming a Phillies regular, I drove a Lexus GS 300. With the lease on that car expiring, I decided to move on up.

I arrived at a Mercedes-Benz dealership in one of my Nike sweat suits that I had obtained via an endorsement contract. But, I suppose, I was wearing my humble hat—one that I believed in anyway, because good service should be good service no matter who is walking in the door.

I will never forget my first experience at a North Carolina Lexus showroom, after I had only a "cup of coffee" in the majors; the salesman pretended to lose the keys to the car I wanted to test-drive in the hope that I would go away. Ditto my experience after celebrating my first-round draft pick status, when a Honda salesman told me that he wasn't going to show me any car because "you couldn't pay for it anyway."

From those experiences, I concluded that something irrational was in play. I was sure it had something to do with race or, as I was told, my "baby face." Either way, it was unacceptable, and now that I was in another kind of driver's seat as the Phillies' center fielder, I was curious to see how these dealers would respond. Would I still be treated as the "Invisible Man"?

My eyes were on the newly designed S-Class Mercedes. This beauty was sporting a seventy-thousand-dollar sticker price. It was a large car for just one person, but at the very least I wanted to test-drive it after measuring the performances of a Lexus and a BMW earlier in the week.

The salesman—who had no idea that I was a Phillie (not that it should matter)—insisted that the S-Class was a near impossibility to buy. Its new design created such demand, he said, that there was no way I could get this car within my required timetable. The waiting list was close to two years.

No problem, I said, but when the salesman moved on to the other models, all of them seemed to have the same limitation. High demand and a long wait. All models, that is, except for one: the C-Class Benz—the smallest and most inexpensive model—was available immediately. The sales rep seemed to believe this was the car for me, even though my head scraped the ceiling when I got in. No thanks. Despite my lack of interest, he sent me on my way with a C-Class brochure, something I was ready to throw in the trash—before someone came sprinting out of the dealership.

This other salesman caught up with me in the parking lot, and the first words out of his mouth were "Are you Doug Glanville of the Phillies?" His tone suggested that he already knew the answer was yes. And it was clear that he deduced that I was not thrilled with my experience.

I mentioned that the other representative insisted that the waiting list for the S-Class and all other models save the C was lengthy. I needed something in three months. Not to worry, he said. He assured me there had been a "miscommunication" and assigned me the dealership's top sales rep to bring me into the Mercedes family.

Despite the positive outreach, the damage had been done.

So, was it a sweat suit thing? I would love to chalk this one up as a salesman's snooty notion that Mercedes-Benz drivers would never come to a dealership in Nikes. But I had been down this road before when I didn't identify myself as a ballplayer. I couldn't see into that salesman's heart, but his behavior suggested my sweat suit was not the only factor that led him to jump to conclusions about me.

Based on the second rep's "makeup call," it's apparent that if I had walked into the dealership flashing my Phillies credentials the result would have been different. I could have bypassed any waiting list and probably gotten a deal to boot. For better or worse, the baseball card trumps the race card.

I know plenty of other ballplayers who have felt invisible or worse when wearing the humble hat. Now that feeling could be a wake-up call to reality, where you finally share an experience that most consumers have when looking to make a purchase or obtain a service. However, despite your confidence on the field or in a nightclub full of opportunists, when it comes to an experience that brings in a question of prejudice, you can't help but recall the vulnerability and anger you felt as a kid when that convenience store owner singled you out and followed you around to make sure you didn't steal anything. Is it any wonder that anyone with this history chooses to wear the entitlement hat?

We have come a long way toward realizing Dr. Martin Luther

King's dream, as evidenced by the fact that I could live the dream of millions of Americans, in a country that now has an African American president. But humility was part of his dream, something that unfortunately doesn't always land you the best service. When I went to a restaurant and saw autographed headshots on the wall, I always wondered, *Do these people carry them around in their wallet?* I guess they worry about being forgotten or invisible, too.

It is expected that a baseball player will be treated differently in his experience outside the stadium. Players have a notable and unique profession with a following in the millions, which requires maturity to know how to navigate the off-the-field experience—an experience obtained by hard knocks and practice. But most players, after tasting the preferential treatment, don't know how to live without the expectation that this treatment can always be used to their advantage.

So they wear the entitlement hat at all times, a wardrobe choice that, quite frankly, looks ugly on most people.

Carl Everett would have responded differently than I did in that Mercedes showroom.

I played against Carl when he was with the Mets and Astros, and he deployed what seemed to be an endless arsenal of tools. Switch-hitter, great speed, power, good eye at the plate. But it wasn't until he became my teammate in Texas that I understood the complete Carl Everett.

From our first day in the outfield together in spring training in 2003, I realized that Carl was someone you could not overlook. He challenged the coaches on their choice of drills, he commented on how to improve teammates' technique, he took pride in every ball hit to him, and he expressed these thoughts in stentorian voice. There never seemed to be much room to chime in with another perspective.

Dallas, home of the Conspiracy Museum (yes, really), was the perfect city for Carl to pontificate in, and his theories extended well beyond the Kennedy assassination. He questioned whether the landing on the moon was legitimate, citing documentary films purporting to show the American flag waving in an environment where there was no wind and little gravity. Although he was not the only one to endorse this theory, many did not find his arguments persuasive. He eventually relented, explaining his doubts by stating, "There were many failed attempts before they got it right. Success doesn't happen without failures."

Carl also disputed the existence of dinosaurs. Fossils, he said, were man-made fakes. Off the wall, perhaps, but what got lost in translation was where he was coming from. His faith, like that of many others, compelled him to embrace the Bible's account of creation and its timeline. Whether you agree or disagree with such theology, there is no disputing that Carl was being Carl, open and real without apology.

As far-fetched as these notions may have seemed, you needed to bring your A-game if you were going to debate Carl. He had a lot of information, he was well-read, and probably a great candidate for *Jeopardy*. He was sure, so you better be sure, too.

As we got settled in with our new team (both of us were free-agent acquisitions), I realized that Carl's raw abilities had slowed a little (like all of us pushing deep into our thirties), mostly because of various injuries and other issues that come with playing baseball for a lifetime. But he competed with a fury. He was always looking for ways to improve his game or the game of other players, taking on everyone around him in the process.

His analysis spared no one. He loved being a mentor to young players. In fact, he made the effort to mentor anyone who was ready to talk shop. Age was never a criterion.

I realized that Carl and I were two very different people. I related to people with finesse, tact, and diplomacy. Carl related with his hands on the pulse and throat, with brawn and brute volume.

At times, Carl took me out of my debate game. The normal time I would take to digest information and then wait for the right moment to speak was constantly steamrolled by Carl's ramblings. But we were on good terms; I frequently told Carl that he was often misunderstood because he spoke with such definitive conviction. I saw that his passion and conviction walked the precarious line between strong dialogue and explosive disagreement, but he was authentic, for sure. If you engaged with Carl, you better have a sense of where the dynamite was hidden and where the safe zone of a conversation was located. This is true in all relationships. Everyone has dynamite hidden somewhere; Carl's just happened to be close to the surface.

On one defining day in March, our third base coach, Steve Smith, went over the verbal signals that he would relay to a runner leading off second base. He explained that he would clue the runner to the positioning of the shortstop or second baseman by saying three different words. One word was to let you know you were safe. Another was an alarm to get you to go back to second base right away. The final word, *careful*, was intended to urge caution.

Careful. Carl didn't care for this choice of a warning word. He felt it would compromise his aggressiveness in his possible attempts to steal third and would make all our runners tentative. As Carl explained: "It was about the timing of when to use this word, not the word itself. If a runner is in steal mode, a *careful* stops him if he has already expanded his lead. On top of that, no signal is needed when a runner hasn't expanded." His appraisal was reasonable. His delivery was not. Subtlety was clearly not one of the tools in Carl's arsenal, just as "in your face" passion was not in mine. Frustration was bubbling as Coach Smith made futile attempts to move on to another topic. Carl sought resolution. But I could sense it was about to get ugly.

And it did. To advance the conversation that had circled the drain many times, Smith tried to defuse the conversation with a one-liner, but by then both he and Carl were standing up, separated only by the rules of engagement between staff and players and a paper-light folding table.

Smitty basically told Carl that he didn't consider him a threat to steal third anyway, so he shouldn't worry about it.

Uh-oh.

Player and coach seemed like two hyenas circling the tables where we were sitting. At the crescendo, Carl turned one of them over, and it ended up partly on top of some teammates. It took a handful of the strongest Texas Rangers to calm Carl.

This was the moment I realized that Carl represented the "Angry Black Man" that everyone was afraid of—including other black men who saw their survival in the game as contingent on following Jackie Robinson's example (in which he had no choice anyway). Dignity with a stiff upper lip.

At one point in the 1970s, about 25 percent of Major League Baseball players were black. By the time I hung up my spikes in 2005, we constituted fewer than 8 percent. There have been numerous theories—most of them guesswork—as to why there has been this sharp decline. But my challenges rising up the minor league ranks only confirmed what my parents had admonished: that race mattered and that to some decision makers it can be the deciding factor.

My parents preached that it was more effective to speak softly and carry a big stick. Boisterous personalities, they noted, seemed to always end up on the side of the road by bringing an inordinate amount of attention to their already apparent skin tone. To be threatening and scary, to live and die by conviction, carried a great deal of risk and little reward unless you were "can't miss." And in baseball, as opposed to, say, basketball or even football, "can't miss" is a rare description of anyone on Draft Day.

Jerry Manuel, who was my manager in the Arizona Fall League, called me into his office after I lost a ball in the sun during practice. Knowing my reputation for being overly cerebral and nonchalant, he advised, "You need to be the type of person that they want you to be to get to where you want to go. Once you get there, you can be whoever you want." I filled in what was implied: that my personal style was threatening to the status quo. The game was still adapting to men of color who asked a lot of questions, not to mention the anomalous nature of my having an Ivy League degree. It was practical advice even though it was also frightening advice. Would there be anything left when I did get there? Would I recognize myself?

This was an age-old survival approach that many black families had employed. Don't rock the boat, stay under the radar, work with your head down. My mother's southern upbringing and my father's Caribbean laid-back approach united in my personality so that I would just stay the course and be unfazed. Carl, on the other hand, seemed to leave a trail of turned-over tables and tears.

Still, he survived. Head up on the field and head up off, the Angry Black Man was able to make it to the top of the game, becoming a world champion with the Chicago White Sox in 2005, complete with long-term contracts and patience, if not forgiveness, from the front office when he almost took a few heads with him. It appeared that the game had come a long way to be able to embrace this personality, which would have most likely imploded in the previous generation of players.

I didn't understand Carl at first, maybe because of our diametrically opposed approaches, but a bridge of understanding and respect developed from watching each other play the game. Seeing how we went about our business trumped our differences, and soon we could wink to each other that we were misunderstood in different ways. I had fielded criticism about my alleged nonchalance, laziness, and questioning of authority, so I knew all about surface labels, too. As all players learn, shaking these off is part of the process.

Carl shared with me his frustration by explaining, "I get goose bumps down my spine when I look back and see how many people I've helped. That's one thing they can never take from me." He was disheartened by people who made judgments based on hearsay rather than face-to-face contact. "You've never met me, and you only heard what another person said about me who also has never met me!" he wanted to tell his critics.

When I spoke to Carl recently, he conceded that he had made his share of mistakes, but he lamented that many in the game didn't take the time to go deeper to know him. "Was I really that bad, angry black man?" he rhetorically asked me.

Carl showed a lot of young players, black and white alike, what was possible in a game that gradually allowed them to be themselves—aggressive or careful—as they matured and rose to the highest level. Later I was able to thank Carl for that. It wasn't the way Jackie Robinson would have done it, but in his own way, he liberated a lot of people.

Sometimes, what separates you from your teammates is not the color of your skin but what is happening beneath the surface. One sunny April day in Arlington, Texas, I hit my fourth ground ball to the Anaheim Angels' infield. I ran down the first base line to try to beat the throw to the first baseman. Taking my first step out of the batter's box, I hoped my reputation for speed would force the second baseman, Chone Figgins, to rush the play and make a mistake.

Head down, dirt, grass, and white lime flying, I was oblivious to any sound. I started this sprint from home to first as I had done thousands of times before—in a vacuum of meditative concentration. And then I heard a *pop!* I felt it, too. Uh-oh. I kept running, but after a broken rhythm of uneven strides on one good leg and one bad leg, I knew my hamstring was not right.

For eleven straight seasons of professional baseball, I had fought the perception that I was too frail to survive in the game. I worked hard to stay in shape, and I had defied the conventional wisdom. I had never been seriously injured, and I had never been on the disabled list as a big leaguer.

I expected to be healthy enough to play at all times, even if no one else expected that of me. Now, on this April afternoon, I couldn't get off the field under my own power. I was somewhere between the first base line and the coach's box. My manager, Buck Showalter, and the head trainer, Jamie Reed, came out to check on me and, ultimately, assist me for the short walk to the dugout, which now felt like a ten-mile mountain trek with two career grim reapers propping me up.

When I told Buck where I hurt, he immediately opined that my recovery would be fast. I say this with great affection: Buck never met a question he couldn't answer. Google was the twenty-sixth man on his roster. Perhaps he had searched the Internet for a prognosis as soon as he had heard the pop.

I wasn't as upbeat. Ballplayers know their bodies. We are constantly checking ourselves out. *Is that twinge in my bicep something to worry about? Is that soreness in my groin going to materialize into something more?* I knew my body far better than Buck did. Being unable to walk off the field meant I was definitely in trouble.

I had seen injuries many times before. Every year, players are whisked on and off the disabled list, some for weeks, some for months, some for the rest of the season. A player depends on his body for his livelihood, so any change in its makeup can change his game and therefore his value. My game was speed, and I could only wonder if my leg was ever going to be the same again.

When I was just starting out in Chicago, my teammate Kevin Tapani went on the disabled list. Shawon Dunston pointed out in a team meeting that Kevin felt invisible. No one seemed to talk to him as much. He was on another schedule and barely noticeable. He was trying to stay out of everyone's way and work on getting healthy. He would come to the ballpark at hours very different than when he was active and healthy, do his physical therapy, and be out of the way before game time.

I came to understand his reality and all its effects after I elected to have surgery to repair the damage from that ill-fated run to first base: a torn semitendinosus tendon. I acquired new medical knowledge that I certainly didn't want: that the hamstring group has three major muscles to it, attached by various tendons to the bone. One of my tendons was now gone. The MRI looked like a rock guitar player had popped a string while reaching the crowd-pleasing crescendo in his favorite song.

After a second opinion confirmed the extent of the injury, I heard the famous prediction of "four to six weeks" to describe my timetable for recovery. This is a crossover moment for a player, a moment when invincibility fades to self-doubt and a cold stare in the mirror.

So how bad do you want to get back to full strength? If I were a person who didn't rely on his body to earn a living, a few months would have been a normal timetable. But my job was my body, and I would have to devote every waking moment that I could stand to getting back to full health. My career depended on it. This wasn't about just being able to walk; it was about being able to have the kind of speed that would make infielders rush and catchers jumpy. Was that going to be possible?

My rehab assignment was full of high-tech and low-tech methods to work on my legs—from the underwater treadmill to the ultrasound massage to break up scar tissue to the makeshift skateboard I used to crawl around on, using only the leg that was now missing a hamstring tendon. My mom came to town to drive me around, noting that I was moving like an old man.

I had to sleep for a few nights with a leg brace that was attached to a pump that would circulate ice water around my leg to keep it cool. It held such a minuscule amount of water that it had to be refilled all the time. Sleep was a figment of my imagination.

Many injuries are accompanied by pain, and the question of how to manage that pain. I was concerned about the slippery slope of escalating pain meds to hasten the recovery. We heard too often the story of players who, in their impatience, turn to something illicit while seeking that magic healing elixir.

Even postsurgery, I elected not to use the painkiller (I believe it was Percocet) that was a thumb push away, much to the annoyance of the attending nurse. Once the pain comes, it is hard to reverse it. I was given an anti-inflammatory drug, Vioxx, and after some over-the-counter pain meds didn't really float my boat, I just toughed it out. Fortunately for me, my pain was manageable. I doubt that is the case for everybody.

After three and a half weeks of following a schedule that had me at the stadium in the morning for about four hours of rehab, and, like Kevin Tapani, trying to stay out of the way during home games (I didn't travel with the team, which was very weird at first), I was declared healthy enough to go on a rehab assignment to the minor leagues. It would be the first time I would be back in the minors in eight years.

I headed off to Des Moines, Iowa, to meet our Triple-A affiliate, Oklahoma City. I limped my way around the field over the next four days but, most important, I didn't get hurt any worse. That was the first stop of my tour of the Rangers' farm system over the next two and a half weeks.

There is an etiquette that must be followed when major league players go down to the minors for a rehab assignment. For one, you must respect the culture of your new environment. My teammate Chan Ho Park also came down for rehab when we were both assigned to the Double-A affiliate in Frisco, Texas. He immediately took six bottles of water from the team's fridge. That's fine in the big leagues, but after hearing the grumbling among the players, I found out that they only had about two dozen bottles a day for the entire team.

Another rule: after the game, the rehabbing player is supposed to buy a nice dinner for his temporary teammates. I had Buca di Beppo picked up one night in Des Moines and delivered to break up the monotony of the postgame spread. But when I asked Chan Ho to splurge for our Triple-A Oklahoma City teammates a short time later, he balked. (We both went up to Triple-A during our rehab assignment.) It wasn't really out of cheapness; it was an etiquette he didn't subscribe to. But like that magazine you don't want, I gave him my subscription anyway. I ordered from Outback Steakhouse and put the bill in his locker. As I pointed out to him, for every minute he was on the training room table, he made more money than the minor league team's entire payroll. Sure, I was exaggerating, but the point was made. I wasn't bankrolling like that, but I knew that my annual salary was also of a different order of magnitude. Popping for a good meal is the least a major league player can do for the team that is generously hosting him.

After almost three more weeks of painstaking drills and limping around, I finally got some pep in my step. Back in Dallas, I was getting some heat from management that I was not doing all I could do to get back, an accusation I found offensive given that I had no incentive to stay on the shelf and miss a chance to return to the big leagues and be a viable free agent that off-season. So I called Jamie Reed and said I was ready, even though my leg was still feeling alien to my body.

And so I made it back and fought the invisibility of being on the disabled list. I battled the demons that tell you to do whatever it takes to get back, even if it is illegal. I returned on the back end of that "four to six weeks" that was predicted.

When you play for a decade without missing a game, a trip to the DL is a trip to another planet. After reentry, your body isn't the only thing that has changed. You enter the major league clubhouse with a new appreciation for the opportunity to live your passion day in and day out—and get paid for it.

I realized how much I missed directing my fellow outfielders to move, doing my quad stretch on a river of tobacco juice, wandering downtown Pittsburgh trying to find my favorite barber shop. And given what I had just gone through, it didn't even hurt that much to read less than flattering things about myself in the papers. *At least I'm back*, I told myself, *and they've got something to write about.*

The players and the press play a never-ending game of chess. Or maybe it is more like checkers, because many players try and hop over the questions they don't like. Chess or checkers, you have to remain alert and play wisely. One bad comment can make for a video or sound bite that goes viral in a nanosecond. From an iPhone to someone's blog to YouTube. No news is exempt.

Like hitting the curveball, fielding questions from the media is something all players have to learn to improve on as the baseball years go by.

After one spectacular game in which he hit two home runs at Wrigley Field off Jim Bullinger of the Montreal Expos, my Cubs teammate Brooks Kieschnick met the press. Asked about his approach at the plate, Brooks went into great detail about which pitch he looked for in certain situations. Afterward, Mark Grace, our All-Star first baseman, took the youngster aside to point out that he had committed an error.

"Don't let them know your secrets," Gracie advised.

Typically after a game, there is a cool-down period before reporters can enter the clubhouse. This allows each player time to decompress before he says something he may regret. Better to take ten minutes and do some deep breathing as well as some deep thinking about how quoteworthy you want to be. Do you really want to call that first base umpire who missed a call a "goon"?

Once the doors to the clubhouse open, players, especially young ones, are of two irreconcilable minds: *Why are the reporters bugging me? Why am I supposed to share these personal feelings with a world of people I haven't met before?* Or: *Why aren't they bugging me? Don't I matter even if I didn't get the game-winning hit?*

Ultimately most players learn to navigate these waters and come to regard reporters as individuals who, like us, have jobs to do. The beat writers are with the team from beginning to end, and you develop a bond of some sort with each one. It may be a friendship, or it may be a connection like two people handcuffed together. It just depends on the people involved.

Beat writers certainly have to be as careful about what they write as we players are about what we say. If they alienate a player, the manager, or the whole team by betraying a confidence, misquoting, or getting a story wrong, they risk losing the coin of their realm: access. So out of necessity and, one hopes, mutual respect, an unwritten contract exists between writers and the written-about. Treat me fairly, and I'll treat you fairly.

The most challenging interviews usually come from writers who are only in town to do a hot story or from gung ho reporters who are trying to make a name for themselves in their first week. One year when I was with the Phillies, I was on fire for two months. I hit in fifty-two of fifty-six games, and people were talking about how that was only four short of Joe DiMaggio's mind-blowing streak of fifty-six straight. (I understood that it wasn't the same, but I also understood why they thought it was worth a story.) *Sports Illustrated* sent a reporter to cover my run. Since he would get the story and most likely never see me again, he would have less concern about playing nice. Instead of getting feedback on my interview the next day or by the weekend, I had to wait a week or two for the issue of the magazine to come out. Fortunately, he played nice, but I would have had no recourse whatsoever had he not.

When my father became chronically ill in 2000, I fielded a lot of questions I did not want to answer about his health. That was bearable with the beat writers since I knew them well and many of them had met my father. But when my hometown paper came to town, despite that geographic connection, I didn't know the reporter as well, so I resented talking to him about my father. I asked him about his family too, just to be sure we both were sharing, and he actually opened up about his mother. I appreciated that.

Sometimes we also had to deal with unexpected midseason replacements. When a new reporter, Dennis Deitch, came on the scene one summer in Philadelphia, he arrived with guns a-blazin'. He might as well have had a column called "A Phillie a Day," because he chewed up one player every twenty-four hours. But his style was raw opinion with not much sugar coating. When Kevin Sefcik was buried in a column, he lamented, "I barely get a start. What does he have against me?"

After the writer lambasted first baseman Rico Brogna, who had returned from an injury and was still not quite back to old form, our All-Star third baseman Scott Rolen told Deitch to cool it, and he took that into consideration. To explain his edge, Deitch later said, "It is worse to be so chummy with players that you end up getting used. I'd rather be more the other way if I had to choose an extreme." Still, the sheer shock of his style caused players to talk about icing him for being too over-the-top in his criticism. But Dennis was consistent and eventually became a regular.

Another thing that players have to cope with as they climb their way to the major leagues is that the cities tend to get bigger. And the bigger the market, the larger the press contingent covering the team. In smaller markets there may be one writer. In Chicago, there are ten or more.

And some of these reporters are women! Rare is the young player who isn't thrown off his game that first time he comes out of the shower wearing only a towel and sees a female sportswriter near his locker. Your routine is no longer routine. Nothing like a testosterone-laced locker room touched with the scent of a woman.

Again, everyone eventually adjusts. When I saw my Cubs teammate Brian McRae wearing only a jockstrap for an interview with a female reporter, I thought wearing a towel wasn't half bad. Then again, Brian, who had a fan group called the "McCrazies," didn't let much faze him. He'd wear short sleeves if it was thirty-four degrees at game time, and spandex sleeves if it was ninety-eight degrees. So why not a jockstrap for females and a parka for males?

Many of the women were as unfazed as Brian. It was impressive to watch Carrie Muskat, then at USA Today, tactically maneuver around the Cubs locker room every day. She was a true pro, and I would guess she mapped out her route in advance before we got there.

The cute, rookie female reporters seemed to have bull's-eyes on their backs. I always felt for a woman in this position because, in addition to trying to do her job, she had to deal with the added pressure of navigating covert advances from players. The female reporters who did not enjoy this dynamic must have had nerves of steel to deal with that daily test. Either way, their presence changed the chemistry of our space, instantaneously.

Man or woman, the press is going to press. It isn't fun to answer a question as to why you lost that ball in the sun or why you hung that curveball to Albert Pujols. But if the press likes you, that hanging curveball will be discussed in the context of the great pitch sequence you threw the inning before. If they don't like you, that hanging curveball to Pujols will be mentioned in tandem with the five other hangers you threw last week.

The wisest among us learn to make peace with the voice of the people. My advice is simple: Give the press what they need. Wear a towel or wear a jock. But don't let them know your deepest secrets. Your opponent is reading.

If there was ever a city where you could enjoy a variety of major league experiences (many of which you would like to keep secret), it was Montreal. I was single my entire major league career, but I tried to keep my socializing within civilized bounds and out of the gossip columns—except whenever we crossed the border into Canada. After my teammates and I whipped out our passports, it was as if a chorus of werewolves just formed out of sports coats and ties. *Bonjour, Montréal.*

Before I get to the good part, a few words about the only downside of heading up north. Flying to and from Montreal—even before 9/11—was a royal Canadian pain in the butt. We prima donnas had to go through customs in the airport—a nightmare for any large group.

Toss Shawon Dunston into the mix, and you've got trouble. My good friend was so patriotic (and impish) that every time he dealt with Canadian customs he kept saying, "God Bless America." After all the dirty looks he received, I was surprised the Mounties weren't summoned to teach him a lesson.

Coming back into the United States was no better. Mark Grace told me that on one trip to Montreal years before, Shawon had bought enough suits to fill a closet. Unhappy with the new dress code of suits and ties that manager Jim Lefebvre had implemented, Shawon picked up a bevy of suits in Montreal in collaboration with his teammate Andre Dawson, who used to play there and knew all the best stores. As he approached customs, he felt compelled to be honest and declared them on his form, which caused the agents to check his bag and be suspicious of everyone thereafter. When I asked Dunston about it, he admitted that he did "hold up the plane for a while."

Since Montreal is much more of a hockey town, we didn't even need protection from excited fans (or maybe disgruntled fans) at the airport, something that was untrue when we had to go through customs back in the States. North of the border, we might as well have been a team of goat herders. And in many ways, that was the advantage of Montreal: anonymity.

Despite the travails with customs, players loved to go to Montreal. Our positive feelings certainly had nothing to do with playing in Stade Olympique, a domed stadium with turf that made your knees hurt after each series. Nor did it have anything to do with the crowd, or lack thereof. Most players like to perform in front of a large audience. But in Montreal attendance was meager. How meager? One day my brother came up to visit and sat behind me in the center field stands. We were virtually alone out there, so I talked to him the entire game during down time.

So why the love affair? Montreal is a cosmopolitan playhouse with people from all over the world, speaking many languages, out to have a great time. Some hermits will come out of their caves for that.

I enjoyed the sightseeing; cruising with teammates on a boat around the island was one thing I did an hour after getting to the hotel from the airport. I enjoyed the exposure to other cultures— watching and listening to the restaurant staff of La Queue de Cheval, right next to our hotel, who hailed from Egypt, Sri Lanka, Trinidad, Algeria, and Greece. I enjoyed the food—any cuisine you desired. I also enjoyed trying to speak French, after studying Spanish in high school and in winter ball. I even took up Greek for a month after meeting a Greek woman at a salsa dance club in Montreal. I enjoyed the shopping, mostly for music—particularly at the then-favorable exchange rate.

And yes, I enjoyed the clubbing and partying.

Montreal is a city where it's expected that people will stay out all night. (A popular strip club, Chez Paris, even serves breakfast.) When I was with the Phillies, we loved to go to a dance spot called the Jet Club. We became friends with the owner, Ray, and we would invite the entire staff to our games, drawing as many as forty (at that time it seemed to be about 10 percent of the crowd). When we were at the club, Ray would practically rope off a section so that we could all hang out. Drinks would flow; lips would get loose; flirting was at an all-time high.

Something about Montreal allowed us to bond off the field as a team. One weekend, the first of the new set of *Star Wars* movies (*Episode I*) was released. Curt Schilling bought every ticket in the theater so the Phillies could have a private screening. As Kevin Jordan said, "We are the most spoiled people in the world."

Of course, a team of Phillies in a movie theater in Philadelphia would have been a tough thing to pull off while maintaining secrecy, but going to Montreal was a relief. No one knew who we were, and even if they did, they more than likely wouldn't have batted an eye. It was a place to fade into the background, be low-key and part of the landscape. Something that players enjoy once in a while.

We used to relish the solitude of the locker room at Stade Olympique, which had a much lower number of beat writers and reporters. There were hardly any local Montreal journalists, so we just spoke with our familiar faces in the press. It was as if the game didn't happen.

Something about this anonymity was relaxing. Anything you did seemed like it was under the radar. I may have gone oh-for-five, but no one knew about it. You made a great play or an error, and no one said a word. The fans were more excited by the Guess Jeans fan contest, where the best dancer would win a gift certificate to the Guess store, than they were about a diving play by José Vidro.

To the single fellas, Montreal was like a never-ending bachelor party, so there was an unspoken rule: Never bring your girlfriend to Montreal. (By the way, I had my actual bachelor party there.) We reasoned that if everyone flew solo, no one else's girlfriend could get you in trouble with your own girlfriend and vice versa. In practice, there were a lot of holes in our thinking. We resembled a group of wayward lemmings, and our migration north of the border inevitably caused the occasional fall off a cliff into a violent ocean. In our case, the ocean of boncheaded plans. But when we totally lost our way, we found safety in the simple understanding that Montreal was the Canadian Las Vegas. What happens in Montreal stays in Montreal.

Montreal made sure you wouldn't run into any surprises. The actor Donald Sutherland attended one of the games, which I guess counted as a surprise, but I doubt he would have ratted you out if he was sitting next to your HGH supplier. Montreal lulled you into believing that you could be anything you wanted to be and hang with anyone you wanted to be around. I chose to be a party seeker for the three days we were in town, which was noted by my teammate Robert Person. "Everywhere else I have to call you to go out; in Montreal you call me," he noted. The city was rife with clandestine possibility, so if you wanted to run naked down the street, this was your chance. I'm not saying you wouldn't get arrested, but somehow it seemed it wouldn't be as big a deal.

Mike Lieberthal and I enjoyed a local Irish pub (and its great jukebox) down the street from our hotel, and we hung out with the award-winning bartenders there. This was our relaxation spot after a game until Mike once violated the unwritten bachelor rule and brought his girlfriend Rita to town. On that trip, those invited to our imaginary bachelor vacation had to tiptoe around for fear of any word getting back home. It was like bringing your fiancée to your bachelor party.

Even if you as the "bachelor" are okay with it, you ruin the experience for everyone else. Or as a friend of mine would say, "Don't people understand that the bachelor party is for the fellas, not the bachelor!"

I enjoyed inviting my buddies to visit me in Montreal. When my good pal Mark from Philadelphia came up to spend some time, we went out for breakfast at my favorite spot, Nickels, a diner chain owned by Céline Dion. The hostess was a good-natured, attractive woman named Dina. Over the years, she and her fellow employees had come to a few games courtesy of tickets I would leave at the gate. When Mark met her, he turned on his charm and asked if she was single. She said no, she had a boyfriend. Using what I'm sure was a well-rehearsed rejoinder, Mark said, "Wish you had a twin."

"I do," she said.

D'oh.

Even more shocking, her twin sister was just upstairs. Since Mark is also a twin, I was overwhelmed by the Doublemint Gum commercial I was witnessing. This never happened in other cities, not even Minneapolis/St. Paul.

Despite the playland flavor of the city, I can't say it changed our ability to win or lose. I suppose you could be so excited and fired up that you play the best baseball there, or you could be tired from coming in at 3 a.m. and play like garbage, but when you have a string of night games, there is plenty of time for you to recover from whatever happened the night before. And inside that dome, you don't have a clue what time it is anyway.

I performed fairly well in Montreal. I saw the ball clearly out of the pitcher's hand against the vacuous backdrop, and Astroturf was usually an advantage for my game of speed. In the end, I didn't see too many examples of an entire team partying themselves to the point of being completely ineffective. A day game after flying across the country was more likely to cause poor play than too many lobby arrivals with the sun peeking over the horizon.

When the Expos moved to Washington, D.C., and became the Nationals, a lot of baseball hearts were broken. No doubt some of those were the hearts of the loyal Expos fans who had lost their team. But just as crestfallen were the players—hermits, family guys, and playboys alike—who could no longer head to mini-Europe in the middle of the season for a significant amount of fun and shopping in a diverse culture. So for now, I say good-bye to Screamin' Rita; Djazia; Ray Ray; Gigi; Val Khan, the restaurant owner who sold me *pan doré* every day for breakfast; sore knees from that horrible Astroturf; the Expos' cool *Survivor* Opening Day ceremony; St. Catherine's Street; listening to two national anthems; Prince and his then-wife, Mayte, whom we met at "Dome"; Marc Anthony's timbale player; the Expos' ridiculous mascot, Youppi; Kyriakoula Kontolemos; the crazy currency (the "Loonie"), which was both gold- and silver-colored; the favorable exchange rate; Le Centre Sheraton; the completely inaudible PA announcer; and the train station Pie IX, where we would get off to play the game.

Vive la différence.

If I let my hair down figuratively in Montreal, I did other things to it in Texas.

A confession first: I have never been one to obsess about fashion and hair. When I was drafted and then reported to my first minor league assignment, I owned a pair of pants that was a cross between polyester and tissue paper. When it rained, they got several shades darker. My rotation of T-shirts—many of them dating from high school—were equally past their prime.

Even though the Cubs' minor league staff didn't question my attire, the Glanville look had somehow disturbed the sensibilities of my teammates. Eventually, my teammate Ozzie Timmons stepped in. "Let's go to the mall," he demanded. Thanks to Ozzie's intervention, I ramped up my wardrobe and started buying print color shirts from J Riggins and Structure.

Major league teams usually do have dress codes. Some are stricter than others. In Philadelphia our manager, Terry Francona, didn't really care much about our threads. Jeans were fine. Collared shirts worked. Terry wasn't going to win *GQ* manager of the year, but then again he has since won two World Series rings with the Boston Red Sox, so no one is arguing. Larry Bowa raised the ante, insisting we "look like winners." Collared shirts, nice pants, and dress shoes on the road—always. No sneakers!

My Cubs teammate Mark Grace certainly looked like a winner on the field, but he had no interest in being an off-field fashion billboard, and it showed. After a decade of major league play, he would waltz into the clubhouse in his favorite T-shirts. Once, maybe to just quiet the peanut gallery, he picked up some nice suits for a road trip. But the gallery was far from silent. Noting that Gracie's teal blue suit ensemble resembled that of the Florida mascot, Brian McRae began calling him "Billy the Marlin."

After I'd been in the league for a few years, the high-end clothing maker Élevée tried to get me to buy a custom suit collection. I resisted for several seasons. But during spring training of 2003, my eighth year, I was ready to take the plunge. I'd joined the Rangers during the off-season. Everything was first-class with the team, including our own jet, courtesy of the team's owner, Tom Hicks. The least I could do was step up to the fashion plate. I ordered a nice collection of suits that I could rotate for the rest of my career.

This was the year after my father died. My heart was still heavy. As a result, I had a new edge—a mix between spending more and caring less. To demonstrate just how little I cared, I embarked on a "hair gone wild" phase. My new goal was to match the legendary Phillies center fielder Garry Maddox in Afro volume. I shunned all barber shops.

I got the impression my manager, Buck Showalter, wanted to say something about my lack of hair care, but he just rolled with it. Maybe he understood that I was in an out-of-body place. Also, I still did use shampoo after games.

My mom came out to Texas for the opening homestand, and the Rangers graciously put me on the cover of the program for her. She never did say much about my new look; I think she was happy that I was making a fresh start in a new environment. Still, I suspected she was wondering if I was trying to trump my peaceful teenager years.

Eventually my hair was coming out of the sides of everything I put on my head. My helmet size went from 7⅜ to a whopping 8. For the first time in my life, I could make miniponytails on my own head. I didn't recognize the guy I saw in the mirror, but somewhere in there was a clean-cut engineer from the University of Pennsylvania.

Make no mistake about it, the hair had power. You would think that looking like a member of Earth, Wind, and Fire during their 1970s run would make dating next to impossible. But during this period, I also had a new girlfriend who actually agreed to a second date after I showed up on the first one looking like Dr. J without the sheen. Since she played in the WNBA, she may have even seen my hair as an asset.

My continent-sized Afro remained until I was traded to the Cubs that July. If I were negotiating that trade, I would have made the Rangers throw in extra batting helmets for my escalating hat size. But shortly after I arrived in Chicago, my new manager, Dusty Baker, pulled me aside. Apparently I had offended his sensibilities. He told me I had two choices: cut it or braid it.

In some ways I was surprised my long hair lasted so long. But Baker, who must have sported his own 'fro in the 1970s, was the last cat I expected to demand I change my stripes. In baseball, you never mess with a good luck charm. Then again, my mop wasn't exactly neatly kept.

I set up an appointment and got the Afro reduced to mini-'fro proportions. I heard later from the Houston Astros catcher Gregg Zaun that he was thoroughly disappointed. While we were stretching during pregame, he came over to tell me he had loved the rebellious look I had been sporting.

My teammate Juan Cruz kept staring at me after my hair was cut. *Who is this guy?* he wondered. I had a couple of conversations with other people who didn't have a clue they were talking to me, so it was a radical move.

I never took the time to figure out my statistics pre-'fro and post-'fro, but I certainly felt I had lost something when I saw my hair at the foot of the barbershop chair. The Samson Effect, circa 2003.

There are times when you are playing that you need to let go. You could be fighting the establishment; you could be letting your opponent know that you are wild enough to take their head off; or you could just be going through something that needs to flush itself out.

I could have responded to my father's death by engaging in truly destructive behavior. Fortunately, I found a way to act as edgy as possible without crossing too many big lines. The little lines always seem erasable, so why not?

I may not have surpassed my childhood hero Garry Maddox in Afro volume, width, or weight in 2003. Then again, this was an impossible goal since Garry probably spent a decade growing his hair. Still, for half a year, I let it all go. I didn't care about what people would say about my look, and in the end, it added color to my life.

Since I would have never been mistaken as a rebellious teenager back in the 1980s, I guess this was my opportunity to have some delayed gratification in "fighting the power." When my dad saw my first big-league car complete with chrome rims, black interior, and tinted windows that microwaves could not penetrate, he commented, "Looks like a drug dealer's car." So I wonder what he would have said about my hair.

He was one of the cleanest-cut men I have ever known, so he probably would have told me something similar to what Dusty told me. Instead of giving me a choice, however, he probably would have made me believe he would cut it himself if I didn't do it. (His haircuts were awful.) The point would have been made, and I would have looked back and known he was right.

8

...

GIANTS OF THE GAME

I have had the good fortune to play with and against some of the best players ever to swing a bat, throw a pitch, or catch a ball. But, as with so much else in life, you always remember the first. For me, that was the future Hall of Famer Ryne Sandberg.

In 1993 Sandberg broke his hand in spring training, and his rehabilitation assignment was to play with our Single-A team, the Daytona Beach Cubs, until he could move back up to the big club. For two whole games, we had a major league All Star in our locker room.

Crowds came out in droves as he graciously signed all autographs. One thing became clear to me during his stay: it takes all types of personalities for a team to succeed.

Sandberg said next to nothing the entire time. He whispered here, he mumbled there, but mostly he just worked and worked at getting himself back into major league form. He was hitting off a tee; he did rehab on his hand; he strategized. We younger players learned a lot from him, most of which was by example, not by loud talk. He killed you with silence.

Opposing team pitchers were so excited to face him that they made a lot of mistakes. And when they made those mistakes, Sandberg made them pay for it. On the rare occasion when he was unhappy with the result, he didn't punch a Gatorade cooler or kick the mascot in the back of the head. He calmly took his place on the bench, no doubt thinking about how he would do things differently the next time.

As I watched Sandberg carry himself on the field and off, I thought of something I had heard before from Rick Patterson, one of the Cubs' minor league directors. "Everyone on this team will eventually carry this team on his back," Patterson had said. "It doesn't matter if you are the leadoff hitter, the cleanup hitter, hitting ninth, or pinch hitting. You all will have your day."

From that wisdom and from watching Sandberg go about his business, I had the clarity to know that it is more than just the diversity of job descriptions that help a club succeed. You also need a spectrum of personalities that work together for a team to operate on all cylinders. You need the rah-rah cheerleader; you need the hothead; you need the spiritual guru; you need the quirky left-hander; you need the party animal; you need the "baseball or bust" guy; you need the quiet leader. Everyone has his role to play at different times in the season.

It isn't about right or wrong or louder or softer. When people can flourish by being who they are, something powerful happens. Everyone learns something new, everyone expands his capabilities by seeing many ways to approach a challenge, and certainly over the course of a long season, there will be a lot of challenges.

So I thank Ryne Sandberg for imparting advice that did not even come from his mouth. He showed me that you can be passionate, strong, intense, and dedicated without breaking a helmet or emoting every emotion. And he did it solely by action. This meant a lot to me because I was not the "fiery," helmet-throwing type. I was steady and unflappable, focused on my job, and passionate on the inside.

Years later, when I made my major league debut, Sandberg would be my teammate in Wrigley Field. There he was, quietly getting ready for the game, waving to the fans, and silently burying his opponents. I had to smile because my arrival validated what I felt inside all along. Sandberg showed me that you can make it to the top by being exactly who you are.

It's probably safe to say that a relatively skinny six-foot-ten-inch guy who unabashedly sports a mullet for millions to see knows exactly who he is. One morning I saw this fellow, the Arizona Diamondbacks' ace Randy Johnson, in downtown Philadelphia before a game he was to pitch against us. It was hard to miss him. He was towering in a booth at the International House of Pancakes.

Apparently Randy loved breakfast as much as I did. Most players don't even think about eating before noon on the road, but for me, I never missed a chance to have IHOP pancakes or French toast. Part of me wanted to sit down and shoot the breeze with him, maybe understand what made him so dominating. Another part of me wanted to pour the boysenberry syrup over his head in hopes that he wouldn't be able to pitch that night.

When you look at the schedule of pitchers your team will face in the next series, there are a handful that send your heart to your throat. Occasionally this is because the guy absolutely owns you. More often than not, the guy owns just about the entire league.

It matters not if you have become reasonably successful at hitting a baseball. Knowing that you'll soon be confronting one of the best in the business makes you, if only temporarily, worry about choking on your breakfast. Especially if he's almost seven feet tall and has a fastball approaching one hundred miles per hour.

There is a reason these guys are the best. Most likely, they have been around a long time. They have numerous tricks up their sleeves. They know the umpires as well as they know their old high school buddies. They are poised in any situation.

The year-in, year-out success of the best pitchers is all the more remarkable considering the fact that they have been around the block and are much more predictable than their less accomplished counterparts. It's not as if they ever beat you with the element of surprise. They beat you with sheer stability and steadiness.

My minor league teammate Matt Franco once told me: "Why watch SportsCenter? We already know what these guys did last night." He proceeded to rattle off game stats of players from the night before without looking at the TV. Greg Maddux: nine innings, five hits, one run, five strikeouts, no walks. Kevin Brown: eight innings, three hits, shutout. Barry Bonds: two-for-three and a walk, home run, three RBIs. Ho hum. Their performances were like clockwork.

Even though you knew what they were going to do more than you knew what a rookie who just got called up would do, it didn't matter. They still made you walk back to the dugout after a slow groundout to short more often than you could stomach.

Knowing you'll be facing one of these aces, you prepare for the game a little more—spend extra time in the video room, maybe work on your bunting—lest you be embarrassed in front of a lot of people. And when the game begins, you dig a little deeper. Who knows? Doing something magical could immortalize you.

We have a phrase in baseball that we use when we hit a home run off a pitcher: "I put him in the book." When your book is inscribed with the names of the cream of the crop, you now have a bestseller.

It may be hard for fans to imagine that once a player reaches the highest level, there is more hierarchy to traverse. Yet that is the case in the major leagues. You never stop climbing and grasping to reach for the next level, because when you stop, you lose your grip and start going back down. You are either climbing or falling.

Players are constantly trying to gauge where they fit in the giant landscape of baseball. Facing the best is the quickest and easiest way to gain perspective. Of course you want to do well against, say, a team's fifth starter or the new guy who just got promoted from the bullpen. Hits against those pitchers count the same in your career statistics. But those hits don't always firmly place you among the best; those hits don't always let your manager know that you belong in the lineup every day; those hits come with a mental asterisk.

Producing against the best buys you that most precious baseball currency: time. Success against the Randy Johnsons, Greg Madduxes, and Johan Santanas lets your evaluators know that they don't have to take you out of the lineup when a team's ace is on the mound. It lets them know that you can rise to the challenge and that you will not back down, even when your body is all clammy.

Some players believe that the battle between the man with the ball and the man with the bat is so intense that a batter has to be careful about being friends with a pitcher. You don't want to lose an edge when you step into that batter's box or onto the mound.

I guess Randy Johnson was one of those believers. A few years after seeing him in Philadelphia, we were both with the Yankees in spring training. I gave him a Hall and Oates CD to listen to, and he gave it right back. So much for becoming buddies with the Big Unit.

That day in the IHOP, I elected to say nothing. A conversation might have disrupted the karma of the future. Anonymity, I reasoned, has its advantages. Let the guy eat his pancakes. Think about how to neutralize him. Then maybe he won't eat you for breakfast.

When I first came to the big leagues, I learned about the game by listening to my Cubs teammates Shawon Dunston and Mark Grace talk—no, *argue*—about everything. Their backgrounds could not have been more different. Grace was born in Winston-Salem, North Carolina, and had spent his high school and college years in California. Dunston was from the heart of Brooklyn, New York. But they bonded thanks to their shared love of the game, their respect for each other, and their passion for good-natured debate.

Most of these debates started, "If he was black" or "If he was white." Shawon would then say, "Come on, Gracie!" Mark would then say, "Come on, Shay-won!" No one won; no one lost. They just stayed good friends.

One subject brought them to the same side of the table every time. "Barry Bonds is the best player in the game," they agreed. They only argued about by how much.

When Bonds took batting practice, Shawon and Mark would stop what they were doing and watch in wonder as he hit ball after ball over the fence. It was a transformational moment for me to see two such accomplished pros look like little kids watching their baseball hero.

Knowing that these established players recognized that there was a higher power on the field, I was better able to deal with my own insecurity that there were more than a few major leaguers who were simply better than I was. Of course, deep down I had always known that, but I no longer saw it as an impediment to my own success.

Bonds truly was in a league—and mind-set—of his own. He often looked bored as he hit balls four-hundred-plus feet in Scottsdale Stadium in spring training or against the treacherous winds of Candlestick Park during the regular season.

Unlike us regular players, he seemed to have all day to decide whether or not to swing. He was baseball's equivalent of the quarterback who had all the time in the world to throw the ball. Give John Elway or Brett Favre a lot of time, and there was no way you could beat them. Bonds made the ball look like it was moving in slow motion. He had so little movement to his body that he was always waiting for the ball to finish its dance before he would step in and take the lead.

Sometimes a pitcher could change the music's rhythm, but only briefly. In one game my Phillies teammate Bruce Chen kept throwing this loopy slow curveball that Bonds kept missing or watching go for a strike. Bruce walked him on his first at-bat, then struck him out with a steady diet of curves, but between innings I kept thinking, *Bonds is going to figure this out sooner rather than later.* Sure enough, on at-bat number three, all I could do was watch him deposit a pitch into the right field stands. After being fooled twice, the hero made it seem like he'd been planning this revenge as part of his own three-act drama.

While his teammates must have appreciated such feats by Bonds the player, they didn't necessarily appreciate Bonds the man. Once, Bonds infuriated us by stealing second base when the Giants already held a sizable lead, an act that was on the edge of rubbing a blowout in our face. (In his defense, it was early in the game, but since he wasn't winning a lot of popularity contests, it was taken badly.) The next time Bonds came to the plate, our manager, Terry Francona, summoned Ricky Bottalico from the bullpen. Ricky had not even been warming up, so we assumed he was on the mound for one purpose.

Ricky's first pitch ricocheted off Bonds's leg, and the slugger charged the mound. As the two wrestled on the ground, a circle formed around them while hardly a single Giants player moved in to help their superstar teammate. (Then again, we didn't help Ricky much, either; I know I was locked up with Orel Hershiser at the time.) It could have been because they thought it was an easy win for Barry, and it may have looked that way on paper. Nevertheless, various Phillies and Giants bearhugged one another away from the main event and waited for the incendiaries to burn out the oxygen source. Later, there were all kinds of insinuations that no one on his team had *wanted* to help Bonds.

As Bonds confounded the experts by posting better numbers as he got older, there were grumblings that he was getting help of a different sort. During AIDS Awareness Day at Pac Bell Park both the Giants and Phillies met on the field to support this first-of-a-kind event at a baseball game.

Bonds snuck up behind me and gave me a big smack on the backside. Declaring that I needed to get some meat on my bones, he suggested that I should get on his program. I remember thinking it would be tremendous to learn the training secrets of someone of his caliber. I also remember thinking that maybe it wouldn't be so great; there was something fishy about how much better he had become in what were supposed to be his golden years. Watching him on the field, you understood that even his staggering statistics didn't reflect his dominance.

Before a series with the Giants in Philadelphia, our pitching staff determined that their best bet was to pitch him tight. Put the ball on the inside part of the plate. Tie him up.

If pitching tight is your strategy, you hope that the batter will help you out by swinging at balls in the strike zone that are hard to hit or become frustrated and swing at balls that are out of the strike zone. Bonds was too disciplined to do either. He started two of the three games in the series and never swung at a bad pitch. Final tally: two-for-four with six walks.

A seventh walk would have been in order. We held a slim lead in the late innings when Bonds came to the plate to face Amaury Telemaco. With the count 3–1 and Bonds in a groove, ball four was not a bad option. Instead Amaury tried to catch him off guard by throwing a slider. Like a patient sniper, Bonds realized his one chance at his target had finally presented itself. He pulled the trigger and hit a home run to center field.

Because Bonds was already head and shoulders above the rest of us, it's hard to fathom how he got wrapped up in BALCO, the controversial company that had engineered and supplied cutting-edge drugs that had performance-enhancing effects, ultimately finding itself under federal investigation for its work with many high-level athletes. These athletes were then covered in the shadow of steroid allegations. Should it be true, some inner demon apparently drove Bonds to take extraordinary measures to shatter more records and prove he was the greatest. Was it insecurity? Ego? Greed? A need to prove something to his father? We have all been pushed by these emotions one way or another, but steroids is an extreme way to respond.

From a distance it seems so counterintuitive. Imagine if years after painting the *Mona Lisa*, Leonardo da Vinci broke into the Louvre so he could paint it over with a newer, quicker-drying paint. Why bother when you already created the masterpiece of your time?

Bonds finally broke Hank Aaron's all-time home run record under the asterisk-lit dark night in San Francisco. BALCO prevailed as the key story to this historic milestone, tainting any sense of history that could have come with home run number 756. It seems like such a waste. Well before he allegedly began using steroids, Bonds had earned the respect and admiration of fans and the media as a player. Even more important, the star veterans from other organizations had acknowledged that he was hands down the best in the game. Maybe the best ever.

Perhaps it wasn't enough.

There are echoes of the Barry Bonds story in the saga of Alex Rodriguez. A-Rod was, without a doubt, the best I ever played with. There was nothing he couldn't do on a baseball field. It's what happened off the field that, as in the case of Bonds, has jeopardized his standing, his name, and the way history will judge him.

As A-Rod's teammate in Texas for the better part of the 2003 season, I saw firsthand that his work ethic was second to none on the Rangers. At one point in spring training, his neck was bothering him and the team had to practically force him not to practice. When he could practice, he came out early most mornings. On the still dewy field, he'd set the pitching machine to throw wicked curves that 99 percent of the human hurlers in the league couldn't match. He reasoned that if he could handle these offerings, he could certainly handle anything he might face in a game.

Let me put his talent—and his determination—in perspective. We were playing the University of Texas in a spring exhibition game. Players feel like they have nothing to gain and everything to lose when they face a college team, but for college programs, it's a treat. Buck Showalter decided to bat Alex leadoff; he would come to the plate once, go home early, and get some rest.

In the first inning, a crafty Longhorn lefty struck out Alex on a high fastball. As Alex made the walk back to the dugout, he announced,

"There is no way I am going out like that!" He told Buck that he had to get another at-bat. And once the lineup flipped over to the top again, A-Rod was ready.

The Longhorns brought in a hard-throwing right-hander to face Alex. He missed the strike zone on his first three pitches, all of them high, almost at head level.

Alex stepped out of the box and said to the catcher, "Tell him to bring the ball down so I can see how far I can hit it!" From the on-deck circle, I marveled at the bold move. If Alex had said that to a major leaguer, the next pitch would have been in his earhole.

The pitcher did bring the ball down, and Alex hit one of the longest home runs I have ever seen. It went over a giant inflatable Coke bottle well beyond the fence, more than five hundred feet away.

But Alex wasn't done. Before beginning his trot, he turned to the catcher and said, "Welcome to the big leagues." It was a scene right out of the film *The Natural.*

Life off the field has never been natural for A-Rod. He is searching for something. In spring training, my locker was next door to his. Unlike some superstars I've seen, he enjoyed engaging his non-superstar teammates. We talked quite a bit. Among other things, he seemed fascinated by my Ivy League degree, declaring that he would love to graduate from Harvard one day. He talked about this too much for it to have been just a fleeting thought.

At twenty-seven, coming off seasons in which he hit fifty-two and fifty-seven home runs, Alex was already a baseball icon. I could see that he struggled with this. He cared a lot, maybe to a fault, about his image.

Chasing public opinion is a never-ending and dubious task. You can lose your sense of self—something for which Alex has been relentlessly criticized in recent years. As a player, I could relate only on a smaller scale; I certainly wasn't a $252-million man with a bull's-eye on my back.

I sensed Alex was frustrated that he couldn't get people to embrace the image he sought. He wanted to lead his team, and not just because he was better than pretty much every other player. As an armchair psychologist, I concluded that Alex wanted to be universally accepted, ached for what Cal Ripken Jr. had: an aura, a grace, a statesmanship.

The fact that Alex cared enough to try to be this squeaky-clean statesman is commendable for someone who is seen as the superstar of superstars. But his direct attempts often fell flat, leading people to see them as phony or contrived. Once, as the entire team waited for Buck to start a team meeting, Alex jumped out of his chair to challenge the players to answer a situational question that he drew up on the whiteboard. Kevin Mench was asked to provide the right answer. He handled part of the puzzle, prompting Alex to complete the rest himself. On the one hand, Alex was sharing strategy and pushing to be a leader. But on the other hand, from where I was sitting, his seminar didn't resonate with his audience. When you have such great talent and take the time to talk shop and share what could be the secrets to your success, it must be frustrating if you can't bond automatically. When I first came over to Texas, I assumed that Alex would simply be able to walk into a room and command silence; this was not the case. I could appreciate his efforts even if it wasn't a natural fit for him. He certainly commanded silence on the field.

When Alex admitted in 2009 that he had taken performance-enhancing drugs, I was disappointed because I was hopeful for him, but neither was I surprised (although I never saw him juicing or, for that matter, any other Texas teammates since outed). Alex's need for approval and his search for a likable image had likely contributed to the insecurity that led him to the choice to go down the chemical path.

His talent, however, remains unparalleled. Rocket arm, great hands, fast legs, great base stealer, threw with accuracy, hit for average and power. The only weakness I ever saw was on pop-ups drifting into the outfield, nothing an aggressive outfielder couldn't cure.

Alex has a long road ahead of him for the choice he made to enhance his performance. But I think he will do well with the second chance. It may be to a fault but, because he cares about what everyone thinks of him, I believe he will make changing people's minds a high priority. His efforts may end up making the game better, if the fans give him a chance.

Every player who makes it to the major leagues remembers his first game. Your senses amplify everything they take in. Your eyes adjust to the fact that there are actually people sitting in the third deck. Your nose senses foods in the clubhouse that are foreign to a minor leaguer's palate. Your touch feels your name on the back of your jersey, sending a new kind of chill down your spine. Your ears pick up the sound of the ball coming off the bat during batting practice, a sound that can only come when they are using brand-new baseballs as opposed to the rejects from game play.

Once you get that first appearance, you are immortalized. Time now cannot erase your existence. Pop the champagne. You have reached the highest level of your profession.

Not so fast.

What do your teammates think? Keep in mind that there is a difference between staying for a "cup of coffee" and making a name for yourself. Even though you can now say you made it, you must hold on tighter than ever. Until you hang around for a while, you will quickly be forgotten.

The veteran players have seen guys come and go. If you are lucky, you can outlast the average life expectancy of a major leaguer by staying for longer than a few years. Once you do, maybe someone who has been around the block will deem to call you by your first name, instead of "rook."

I remember when Chuck Knoblauch approached me before a spring training game in 1997. He had been a star player for years with the Minnesota Twins. I had been in the majors for little less than a year. He just walked over and said, "Hey, Doug." I looked around to make sure he wasn't talking to someone else. I didn't find

Doug Drabek, so I figured out that he was talking to me. *Chuck Knoblauch knew my name.* Wow.

Hearing that from an opponent is nice, but strangely enough it's often harder to gain such recognition from your teammates. Those in the other dugout have to know you so that they can pitch to you and defend against you. There's no such urgency in your own clubhouse. Sure, the occasional can't-miss superstar rookie who is granted a starting job right out of the gate commands instant attention, but that is the exception, not the rule.

Anonymity is not all that bad. Most players come in on a stealth mission. Stay under the radar, get your work in, hope for a break, and be noticed for what you do on the field.

My break came during a battle for a starting job with the Chicago Cubs in 1997 that started in spring training. Left field began as a revolving door of talent. Among those eventually shown the door were the right-handed power-hitting Ozzie Timmons (traded to Cincinnati the last day of camp), the sweet-swinging left-handed Robin Jennings, and the pure hitting, "roll out of bed and hit" Pedro Valdes. I stuck around, but since I was a pure center fielder, I would be an afterthought as the long-term solution in left.

When I got the chance to play—initially, only against lefties—I held my own. By early May, I was platooning in left with some success. That did not, however, gain me admission to the society of veterans. One game in June, when we faced the White Sox in interleague play, a right-hander was on the mound, so I was on the bench when Sammy Sosa approached me in the dugout, looking for a favor. Sammy and I were cool and he was a fun-loving teammate, but he was also known to haze new players for kicks.

I guess I was next on his hit list. He tapped me on my leg and asked me to get him some water.

I suppose the look on my face gave away my sheer disgust. I may have only been in the bigs for a few months, but fetching a drink was not in my job description. What to do? I put together a makeshift plan to save my dignity. *Oh, I forgot, I need something from inside the*

locker room. I'll get it, and on the way back, I can get Sammy his
water—even though he's sitting five feet from the water cooler and
could easily get it himself.

Apparently, I took too long to execute this plan. Our parched
slugger expressed his unhappiness that I'd left him no time to drink
before he was to go into the field for the next inning. I took a deep
breath and responded, "I am not sure why you couldn't get your
own water. The cooler was right there."

He looked at me as if I had just stolen his pet poodle. Shock, horror, surprise, hurt. He just kept staring at me as I looked out into the
field noting that we still didn't have a right fielder for the upcoming
inning. He emphatically vowed not to bother me for anything after
that and remained true to his word until a rainy day at Wrigley Field
later that season.

During a rain delay in a game against the Phillies, a security
guard approached me as I sat on the bench with my teammates.
"There is someone here to see you," he said.

"Here? Now?" I asked. It was strange to have a visitor in the dugout *during* a game, but there was a "window" during a rain delay.

The guard instructed me to walk toward the locker room. I
took one step, and there was Michael Jordan. Yes, *that* Michael
Jordan.

Three years earlier, during the one season when Jordan played
professional baseball, he played for the Birmingham Barons while I
played for the Orlando Cubs, both in the Double-A Southern League.
As opponents for a solid season of baseball, we came to know each
other. My mother's family hailed from his home state of North Carolina, so we had plenty to talk about on that front. I generally tried not
to bother him, but we would always exchange pleasantries whenever
we crossed paths.

Michael had been in a skybox at Wrigley until the rain delay.
Now with play halted, he'd come down to say hello to me. Remark-
ably, he said he had been following my career since our minor

league experience together. Then he said that I should call him to link up.

When I returned to the dugout, you could hear a pin (or a glass of water) drop. Glanville knows Jordan? How can that be? He just got to the big leagues.

Recognized by the best of the best, I had passed a different kind of big-league test. The response was immediate. A few days later, Sammy approached me in the locker room. This time he didn't ask me to fetch him a cup of water. Instead, he asked if I'd like him to fetch me and bring me to the ballpark in his luxury SUV. I also was invited to hang out with him from time to time. (On one occasion, he took me to see a great salsa performer, Brenda K. Starr, dancing away at the Congress Theater in Chicago.)

Sammy and I had been somewhat close in spring training years prior to our water incident, mostly because we could just have an honest conversation. He talked about his stresses when he first came up with the White Sox without a mastery of English. I had been a little surprised that his proclivity for hazing would trickle down to me, but once players rise to superstar status, even rookies they have known for years can be treated like props.

It certainly didn't hurt my standing that I had friends in high places. After my visit from Jordan, Sammy began to ask me all the time for his fellow superstar's phone number. He wanted to set up a joint interview to send back to his homeland of the Dominican Republic. I never gave it to him.

Maybe if *he'd* brought *me* some water.

Being a Major League Baseball player has its perks, one of which is the wide-open access you can have to celebrities in all industries. In addition to Michael Jordan, I was introduced to other superstars: Mia Hamm, "Stone Cold" Steve Austin, Josh Groban, Jerry Rice, John Cusack, and others. If you added up all the stars I encountered, the sum of their fifteen minutes of fame could fill most of a day.

Thanks to Wade Boggs, I also met a legend by the name of Banks. I'm not referring to Ernie, although our paths did cross in Chicago many times. I'm talking Tyra.

Boggs, the Hall of Fame third baseman, had an amazing career, mostly with the Boston Red Sox. He was a left-handed hitter who used to slap balls off the Green Monster like he was playing tennis with himself. Eventually he found himself approaching his three thousandth hit.

Let me give you an idea of how remarkable that number is. I ended my career with 1,100 hits, and I was an everyday player for most of my nine major league seasons. One year I even had 204 hits in 150 games. Take what I did and multiply it by three. That is a lot of hits.

As only the best dramatists could script it, Boggs stepped up to the plate in 1999 as a member of the Tampa Bay Devil Rays and got his three thousandth hit by homering into the right field stands. He galloped around the bases, and when he reached home plate, he kissed it.

Now, I know the level of nastiness a home plate can attain. It is a smorgasbord of dirt, white chalk, spit, and tobacco—and that's on a good day. So when the columnist Jayson Stark of the *Philadelphia Inquirer* asked my opinion of Boggs's act of passion, I told him, "If they put a picture of Tyra Banks on the plate, I might kiss it." (I should add I was single at the time.)

Somehow that quote made it to the *Los Angeles Times*, and apparently Tyra read it. All I know is that shortly after the season ended, I received a package containing an authentic major league home plate with Tyra's picture airbrushed onto it. An inscription read, YOU DON'T HAVE TO WAIT 'TIL YOU HIT 3,000, YOU CAN KISS HOME PLATE NOW! The plate was accompanied by an invitation to a birthday party for Tyra in New York hosted by *GQ* magazine.

I thought, *Not a bad way to spend an evening during the off-season.*

Still, I didn't believe it. I wouldn't have put it past a teammate to be playing a practical joke on me. But my agent's office was able to confirm that it was not a hoax, and that she had asked her people to find little ole me.

Now I had to figure out what in the world Tyra Banks might want for her birthday. I did a little Internet research and found out that her favorite color was green. I was playing for the Phillies at the time, and we wore green caps for the Saint Patrick's Day game during spring training. One of these caps seemed like the perfect gift.

I rounded up my best friends from college and brought my own mini-entourage to her party. We were escorted to her VIP room, and there she was, greeting us with open arms. I believe one of my friends still hasn't washed the side of his face she kissed. It was a star-studded night. Brian McKnight, Isiah Thomas, you name it. From what I recall, the party also honored her as *GQ*'s first African American cover girl. Great DJ, too.

Meanwhile, I had broken out my "A" game: inside her birthday bag, I made sure to include every possible way a human being could find me if she wanted to. Home phone, cell phone, e-mail, snail mail. I probably would have implanted a GPS chip in my head and given her the tracking device if I had thought of it.

A couple of months later, on a quiet day at Phillies training camp, I was working out with Curt Schilling and decided to take a break and check my e-mail. There was one from an address I didn't recognize. Not until I got to the signature line did it appear that it was, apparently, from Tyra. She expressed gratitude for my taking the time to come to her party and said that she appreciated the gift. It seemed as if I should have been thanking her. Instead, I kept reading the signature line over and over: "tyra banks"—I think it was in all lowercase.

A little skeptically, I wrote back. My first thought was to write "Is this Desi Relaford playing a joke?" but then I wrote her a message thanking her for the invitation and the home plate. Of course, I read what I wrote thirty-six times before I sent it.

To my surprise, she replied. Over time, we e-mailed each other. She turned out to be an insightful and fun e-pal. She even sent me a handwritten thank-you note for the green Phillies cap.

I continue to watch the meteoric rise of her career, and I root for her. She seems to be capturing the hearts of America by her openness and her palpable connection to people—a couple of traits I noticed in the short time I interacted with her. And when I think about some of the more memorable events in my career, I will always think of that home plate with her picture on it and smile.

Still, despite my remark that started all this, whenever I admire the plate, which my wife so graciously has allowed me to display on the basement wall, I will never in a million years kiss the thing. I know too much about where it has been.

Former baseball players are always asked: "Who is the toughest pitcher you have ever faced?" Well, it depends on what *toughest* means. After facing some guys like Kevin Brown, you feel like you may never recover the confidence you just lost. Other guys don't break your confidence, but they do keep getting you out.

Tom Glavine would pat you on the back, then take your wallet. He lulled you into complacency. With his head and his hands, he took the game's obsession with radar guns, speed, and instant gratification and twisted it around you like a pretzel.

You walk into the batter's box feeling good because the odds are in your favor. You may not get a hit, but at least you will not swing and miss or have to make the lonely walk back to the dugout after a strikeout. (Big leaguers do not like striking out.) So you can claim a victory of sorts, even if Glavine just fooled you so badly that you are carrying the splinter of the bat after a weak groundout to short. At least you didn't fan.

That's the pat on the back. Now reach for your wallet and realize that while you may not be losing confidence in your game, you keep looking at that box score and seeing a zero in the hit column. My barely-over-.200 batting average against Glavine tells that story. After he carved us up, I didn't go home with a sense that I may never be able to hit again, but I certainly left the park with a lighter batting average and, most likely, a loss for the team.

Yes, a pitcher achieves greater bragging rights when he can throw his fastball through the side of a barn. The pitch looks good; it sounds good; the radar guns light up; scouts go bananas. The problem is that power is nothing without discipline. I don't care if you throw at a speed of one hundred miles per hour. If you are in the big leagues and you don't locate the pitch, the hitters will light you up like the Christmas tree at Rockefeller Center.

The Tom Glavines, Randy Johnsons, and Greg Madduxes of the world know that pitching doesn't have that much to do with throwing strikes. It is instead the art of throwing to a target. Why throw strikes if the guy with the bat is going to chase a ball six inches off the plate? You want to fool the hitter more than anything else. Throwing strikes may not be a necessity. Of course if a batter is so confused or timid that he can't swing the bat, throw all the strikes you want.

I remember one game when I faced Glavine in Atlanta, and in light of my poor track record against him and my difficulty seeing the ball at Turner Field, I figured I was in for a long, unproductive day. True to form, Glavine kept me off balance with a steady diet of change-ups and late-moving fastballs on the outside part of the plate. But then he decided to throw a pitch inside to keep me honest. Here honesty was the best policy. I hit a home run to left field.

Trotting around the bases in disbelief, I had to steal a look at the Braves' pitching coach, Leo Mazzone, famous for his constant rocking motion, to see if he had rocked himself right off the bench from shock. This was one of those moments when I felt like a true big-league hitter. Make a mistake, even if you're Tom Glavine, and I can really hurt you.

En route to 305 victories over twenty-two seasons, Glavine did not make a lot of mistakes. But those facing him certainly did. He would throw different kinds of change-ups to the point where batters would swing out of boredom. You would rationalize that he has to throw a strike now instead of seeing the ball come out of his hand. Then you'd hit that weak fifteen-hopper to the second baseman.

Despite the fact that you want to take the head off every pitcher you face, you have to be open to learning from your opponent. I watched Glavine carve up the teams I played for as if he was getting ready for a sculpting competition. A handful of guys like Mike Piazza wore him out, but even a superhero has an archnemesis. More often than not, he calmly helped you get yourself out if he didn't decide to do it for you.

In addition to being in a class of his own on the mound, Glavine is a class act. In 1991, during one game between the Phillies and the Braves, the blood was bad and the beanballs were flying. Glavine faced Dale Murphy, his Atlanta teammate from years past. Murphy also is known to be one of the nicest and classiest players to have ever worn a uniform. Now it was Glavine's job to hit Murphy with a pitch to retaliate for what the Phillies had done to his teammates.

Glavine threw four straight change-ups barely breaking seventy miles per hour so that if he did hit Murphy, no damage would be done. He couldn't bring himself to nail his friend. All four pitches missed, and Murphy took his base. Nevertheless, the ump ejected Glavine from the game for throwing at the batter. Glavine just walked off the field, no argument. He had principles that transcended the caveman etiquette baseball can resort to at times.

Glavine also was one of the rare superstars who still took a grassroots, active role in educating younger players about their rights. To avert a players' strike in 2002, I came to the union offices in New York in my capacity as the Phillies' player rep. There was Glavine along with Al Leiter of the Mets, working until the sun came up trying to get a deal done. He was there for the kids coming up and to take care of those who had come before us.

Whether you are the tortoise or the hare, there is more than one way to get the job done. I was fascinated by Glavine's thought process, even if I didn't have an answer for it. He taught my generation that you can succeed with poise, purpose, and patience.

I was recently asked to compile an All-Star team composed of my teammates and opponents. I have played with or against some amazingly talented players, but as I sifted through the rosters of the years I played, I realized that many of the names had been in the Mitchell Report, former senator George Mitchell's independent investigation that named names of alleged users of performance-enhancing drugs and offered recommendations to improve the effectiveness of baseball's drug policy. Although many of these players did some extraordinary things on the field, I found it difficult to classify them as "All Stars." Since I have no idea who was really clean or not, I decided that it would be more fun (and accurate) to list some of the best or most interesting things I have seen during my tenure.

Best Bacon. Coors Field, Denver. Thick, blackened, juicy, and goes great with French toast.

Best Breakfast West of the Mississippi. Café 222, San Diego. This place has its own flavored pancake batter. Try the pumpkin.

Best Breakfast East of the Mississippi. Morning Glory, Philadelphia. Number one French toast in America—after mine.

Best Manicured Grass. Dodger Stadium, Los Angeles. I am not a big golfer, but this is nothing short of a fairway.

Best Hitting Backdrop. Chase Field, Phoenix. Dark green is the color of choice, and it works.

Best Fans for a Visiting Player. St. Louis. The only place where I got compliments for a defensive play I made against their team.

Best Locker Room Chairs. The Ballpark at Arlington, Texas. Black leather recliners with adjustable height and lumbar support.

Best-Dressed Teammate. Bobby Abreu. My Phillies pal loved Tony Montana, and he dressed even better.

Best Class Clown. Yorkis Perez. Another Phillie. He has a future in stand-up; everything was a one-liner, in semi–broken English to boot.

Best Parking Lot. It's a tie. Citizens Bank Park in Philadelphia has double-deck player parking, but I have to give the Ballpark at Arlington some love—two spaces per player. Wow!

Nicest Cars in the Lot. New York Yankees. My Range Rover looked like a Schwinn bicycle next to Ruben Sierra's stark white Hummer with custom everything. Bentleys, Benzes, and anything else that starts with *B* and costs over a hundred grand.

Biggest Video Game Player. Curt Schilling. He has his own company, Green Monster Games, to prove it. At one point we were both playing a game called "EverQuest," and on a day off (and in the days of dial-up) he logged out on the cusp of ten hours of straight play. Sadly, he beat me by only a few hours. Eating at the computer was the key.

Best Practical Joke. In Phillies spring training, the folks in the front office acted as if they were disputing the birth certificate of Venezuelan coach Clemente Alvarez. His current information had him listed as thirty-five years old. The Phillies claimed he was thirty-eight, to which he responded, "I may be thirty-six, but I am not thirty-eight!"

Best Intro to a Game. Pittsburgh Pirates of the late 1990s, using Michael Jackson's "Jam" and a pirate swinging his sword with each beat.

Best Opening Day Ceremony. The Montreal Expos and their imitation of the TV show *Survivor*.

Best Sausage in the Milwaukee Brewers' Sausage Race. Polish, of course.

Best Hot Dogs. Dodger Dogs in Los Angeles. They go down like water.

Best Pregame Music. San Francisco, Hidden Beach Productions. They take great rap songs and convert them into jazz tracks. Smoothest music ever made.

Toughest Fans. San Francisco Bay Area. Pick your poison, Giants or A's. For starters, the Oakland Coliseum had the lowest dugouts in the league; when you stood up, your head was well over the dugout roof, making you an easy target for a fan with long arms. The Rangers ended up in the stands on one occasion. The Giants fans rode you the entire game in the outfield—saying things I prefer not to print here. But maybe you can find them on the *Howard Stern Show*.

Most Ridiculous Mascot. Youppi of the Expos. He was a nice enough guy, but his special move was taking your glove while you were stretching. No, wait a minute, that was his only move.

Most Interesting Fan Contest. Guess Clothing, for a gift certificate in Montreal. People often began to strip down, forcing the camera to reluctantly pan away from them. Of course, we could usually see the ending from the dugout with our own eyes. No one got naked, but plenty of layers of clothing were shifted around.

Best Hotel. The Westin in Hollywood, Florida. Balcony with beach view. Breathtaking.

Best Walk to the Ballpark. Denver to Coors Field. Considering Denver is one of the sunniest cities in the country, it was a nice stroll down an outdoor mall, with pedestrian-friendly car-free zones. Immaculate, too.

Best Pizza. Donatos in Cincinnati. Introduced me to the Square Cut Pizza. Weird cut, great taste. Get the pepperoni.

Coolest Guest I Ever Left Tickets For. John Oates of Hall and Oates. He even changed the bases between innings.

Strangest Items Thrown at J. D. Drew in Philadelphia. Chicken wings.

Longest Walk to Team Bus from Locker Room. Shea Stadium, New York. It was a choice between building a monorail or constructing a new stadium. Hence Citi Field.

Best Clubhouse Assistant on the Road. "Kel" of the Florida Marlins. Moving and shaking at all times, and he made the best smoothies.

Town Where You Lose the Most Money. San Francisco. Cut up those credit cards.

Best Diners. San Francisco. Heaven for a breakfast man like me.

Best Salmon. Seattle. Smoked to perfection.

Coldest Shower. Fenway Park, Boston. Hope it's fixed by now.

Best Headline. "Robbed Ducey" in the *Philadelphia Daily News* after my teammate Rob Ducey got carjacked in a steakhouse parking lot in Philadelphia.

Strangest Attempt to Sell Me Something. A patron at a restaurant in Cincinnati quietly offered his date after Amaury Telemaco and I had shared lunch with him at a Japanese restaurant. Hmmmm.

Longest Home Run. Joe Borchard of the Chicago White Sox off the Phillies' Brett Myers at U.S. Cellular Field. It went over all the seats in right center field. It may have hit the Sears Tower.

Star Who Had the Most Knowledge of Baseball. Marc Anthony, whom I met in Camden, New Jersey, before a show.

Best Tattoo. Phillies catcher Gary Bennett. Simple—a four-leaf clover for his Irish heritage.

Most Shocking Oversight of a Star Player. Running into Ryne Sandberg at NikeTown in Chicago and no one noticing him for an hour.

Best Hotel Lobby. El San Juan Hotel, Puerto Rico. Two clubs, packed house.

Best Nickname for a Player. "Co-Jack" was a great one for the Diamondbacks' Conor Jackson.

Best Nickname for an Umpire. "Low Ball Laz," for Laz Diaz.

Worst Bus Ride to a Stadium. Rear-ending a car in Queens on the way to Shea Stadium.

Most Unexpected Kiss. In Boston a young woman dressed head to toe in Red Sox attire, coming up to me while I was talking to some friends and kissing me on the cheek, telling me, "I am a big fan." I was expecting a passionate Sox fan to stab me before kissing me. I did not press charges.

Smallest Feet on a Teammate for His Size. Mark Parent—six-foot-seven with size nine shoes. With feet that small, he couldn't have been juicing!

9

. . .

THE INTEGRITY OF THE GAME

Organizing a team as a union rep is no joke. You have forty-plus players to represent—all with different opinions, all in different circumstances in their careers. One might be the rising star about to sign that big contract; his concern may revolve around the rules that govern arbitration or free agency. Another could be the young rookie who needs a chance to get started; his issues are more about the minimum salary or the rules by which you can get sent back to the minor leagues. An aging veteran's needs could be entirely different, focused on the pension rights and making sure there isn't a benefit for owners to flood the market with young talent. An oft-injured player may be worried about his rights when he gets released from an organization and how he will be compensated at such a time. As the union rep, you must speak for all of them and help each one to understand that he has the union's ear and the union has his back.

In addition to being the player rep for the Phillies, I served on the Players Association's Executive Subcommittee. This allowed me to work closely with Don Fehr, the union's longtime executive director. During my years as a professional baseball player, major league salaries had risen manyfold, reaching an average of over $2.3 million by the time the collective bargaining agreement was about to expire in 2002. All of this occurred on Don's watch, but his most important impact was in the area of employment rights—particularly his successes with defined-benefit pension plans, which will provide generations of players support after the end of their careers.

Don understood the power of the collective and emphasized to the players the importance of working as one. This approach grew considerably more challenging over time; as more stars came of age in an environment where it was easy to believe they'd be better served as individuals.

When the collective bargaining agreement was nearing its expiration in 2002, things got heated. My Philadelphia teammate Todd Pratt concluded that the superstars' issues were getting all the attention, and he stated publicly that the union did not care about the little guys. After a fiery discussion, I encouraged Todd to talk to Don directly.

After Todd vented at a spring training Players Association meeting with all the top officials from the union in attendance, Don could have listed a thousand items that countered Todd's point— such as how the union fought for *all* players in grievance hearings or how it had defended the rights of players who crossed the picket line as replacements or how the pension Todd will enjoy in his retirement is a benefit for all players, whether they have one day or two decades of major league service—but instead Don simply apologized for not hearing him sooner and looked to make amends.

As the 2002 season moved inexorably toward the deadline at the end of August, the union decided to have a meeting of reps and other players to determine whether to go on strike. It would be the first stoppage since the 1994 strike, which canceled the World Series, so we took this decision very seriously.

From August 30 to September 1, the Phillies happened to be in New York, also the home of the Players Association offices. On our team bus ride there, we had the ultimate conference call. Everyone was invited to get on his cell phone and talk with Don and the other union officials. Despite the chaos of the free-for-all, it was clear that virtually everyone was ready to fight.

Upon our arrival in New York, I went straight to the union offices and stayed there until 5 a.m. We had until late the next morning to reach an understanding with the owners. After hours huddling with Tom Glavine, Al Leiter, other player reps, and the top union leaders, we were ready. I went back to the hotel to get some rest, and when I woke up I learned that we had come to an agreement. Later, I found out that the Boston Red Sox' refusal to get on their team bus had put the exclamation point on the players' resolve. A deal had been struck fifteen minutes after that defiant act.

This was a moment that framed the power of the collective. Players united and worked hard to find common ground in a way that preserved history—a history that began with players who never enjoyed the benefits that our generation of players has enjoyed. In this fight I had a taste of what it means to fight for rights and to keep moving forward while building on the efforts of those who came before us. It was the present preserving the past for the future.

If there's one issue that has caused fans and pundits alike to scratch their heads and wonder if the Major League Baseball Players Association really cares about the future of the game, it's steroids. "How can the players be so shortsighted?" goes the conventional wisdom. "Don't they realize that if they resist efforts to police and punish, they risk killing the golden goose?" The union's efforts to protect the names of those who failed a drug test administered to all major league players in 2003 is cited as proof positive of the players' shortsightedness, if not blindness.

I can understand why there are so many calls for the names—and then the heads—of the 104 players on the so-called list. It seems that publishing this list once and for all would make us all feel better. We could put this chapter behind us, convince ourselves that everyone not on the list is as clean as a whistle, and rest assured the game would never return to such disgrace.

But it would be a Pyrrhic victory, at best.

The 2003 drug test was a "survey" test. It was devised to establish the extent of the drug culture in baseball. Instead of just running with innuendo, rumor, and guesswork sparked by certain off-the-cuff remarks by former players like José Canseco and Ken Caminiti, the Players Association decided that it needed to actually find out for sure.

So this test was put in place to get a true number. It also allowed players a safe place to be truthful (or sloppy). And it can be assumed that the assurance that the results wouldn't leave the premises persuaded some players not to try to mask their samples to hide a potential positive result. Here was a chance to be forthright and give baseball officials a true sense of the extent of a problem that needed to be addressed. Ironically, the players who may have found ways to beat the test seem to be better off today. Those players are quietly in the "clean" column, and those who were either lazy enough or open enough to provide a real sample, which helped move this testing policy forward, are about to get a Scarlet Letter.

The tests were contingent on some semblance of confidentiality. I can't imagine that any player in the game, clean or not, would have ever agreed to a collectively bargained drug policy if he had been told beforehand that the results would end up in the public domain. Neverthess, years later, we are seeing a chronic leaking of confidential and anonymous information, with select players on the list being "outed." Kind of shady and illegal, at that.

If this is for such a good cause, why the negative approach? Why pick and choose who gets sent to the stockade? How about leaking the names of the one thousand players who didn't test positive? That would be a nice change of pace, but whoever is leaking this information isn't playing nice at all.

I have no love for the drug culture in baseball—it was pervasive and, by raising the performance level in the league, probably helped to shorten my career—but systems have to be put in place to curb what will be an ongoing problem. No list of 104 names posted online will change that.

Still, people are outraged and I understand. Something dear has been lost. The culture of a game that had the rare ability to bridge generations of fans and players has been broken. Before the steroid era, a home run was a home run, and we could look at and admire and compare the achievements of Mantle, Aaron, Ruth, Schmidt, and Mays and feel like we were speaking the same language. The steroid era wipes that out: the magic created on the field starts to seem artificial, patronizing us, appeasing us, making us doubt whether we are truly seeing what we are seeing.

But we need to pay close attention to our outrage, because the precedent set by breaking the confidentiality of collectively bargained tests is a bigger problem. It creates the impression that agreements between employers and employees can be thrown out at any time, just because someone felt they had the right to know. In such a world, what would prevent your employer from taking a drug test result of yours and slapping it up on the Internet tomorrow?

Granted, somewhere in the morass is a federal investigation, which often changes the rules of these things. But as the government investigated the players wrapped up in the BALCO affair, all players ended up cast in its shadow. This led to the samples obtained in the 2003 survey test not being destroyed as planned, since the union was concerned about destroying what could have been evidence in an ongoing investigation. The union was just following the law. (And if the test was anonymous, you might ask, why is there some key out there to match up the names with the numbers? I've learned that the answer is because there had to be some way to trace back in the event someone lost a sample, or it got tainted, or there could have been a false positive, giving the players a right to retest.)

I don't know who or which organization is leaking these names. But I find this act more outrageous than that of the players who tested positive. At least these players helped the game take a step toward putting a better policy in place. It may not have been out of nobility, but at least it was effective. I do find it curious that whenever a player is arrogant and bold enough to declare his "cleanliness," he quickly gets nailed by his 2003 positive test. To me, it appears more like a targeted impeachment process. I am not crying for those players' choices, but what is happening to them is telling.

Certainly, I can understand the frustration of the investigators. When all is said and done, these players are simply "users," low men on the totem pole of a drug scheme. Players lying at hearings and in the media are creating a distraction and getting in the way of the investigators' ability to do their job. They are also inhibiting their need to focus on the more significant pieces of this puzzle, like the suppliers and the source of these drugs.

I think it would be a travesty to release the list of 104 names. The promise of confidentiality was in place to allow players to be more willing to provide a true test. We can't go back and change the rules after the fact and then claim that we are noble and honorable. I want drugs out of the game, too, but we should seek a more effective, sustainable way to go about it that doesn't trade long-term gains for short-term gratification, privacy for a mugshot-riddled Web site, confidentiality for an imagined right to know, or anonymity for the rebirth of witch trials. That 104 baseball players are hiding something does hurt our game; but throwing a collectively bargained agreement out the window disturbs a precedent that has served as the backbone of labor management relations in our country.

I have been asked on many occasions whether I think players known to have taken performance-enhancing drugs before or after the 2003 survey test should be eligible for the Hall of Fame. My answer? Sure, they can be eligible, but I would not vote for them if I had a vote. If they are statistically worthy of getting into the Hall, odds are they probably enjoyed a lot of the benefits of performing so well: winning teams, winning contracts, entries in the record books. They did well, so they can skip the Hall.

I know that I played clean, but I also know that with a career batting average of .277 and fifty-nine career home runs, I'm never going to be enshrined in Cooperstown for my numbers, but I often wonder whether a player who gets into the Hall should be automatically considered successful. And whether one who doesn't should be seen as unsuccessful.

In 2009, two players were voted in, Rickey Henderson and Jim Rice. I had the pleasure of playing against Rickey. He drove teams crazy by stealing bases and scoring runs. He wrought havoc on defenses that could never relax for a second when he was on base. In effect, he ran teams out of house and home.

Also known for his quirkiness, Rickey often talked about himself in the third person. But take my word for it, playing against him made you feel like there were three of him on the bases anyway. His induction was a no-brainer: all-time leader in stolen bases, walks, leadoff home runs, and runs scored.

Jim Rice was a hitting machine, driving in runs like he was some sort of taxi service. Playing left field, in front of the Green Monster at Fenway Park, he was also a master of deception. When a ball was hit over his head, he would stand and watch without enthusiasm, and the batter would assume that the ball was going to end up somewhere on Lansdowne Street. Think again. Rice was just setting him up so he could throw him out at second base, after the latter had lost a crucial step admiring his shot. You could make a great video of all the shocked faces of base runners who were cut down at second because they fell for this trick.

When a career is over, we reflect. I reviewed mine as if I had a fifteen-year video reel in my head. I'd think about what I could have done better or how I could have handled a situation differently. Maybe I should have bunted more. Maybe I shouldn't have charged that pitcher in Double-A. But all in all, I feel good about my career.

I know it could have been better, but I also know it could have been worse.

Still, somewhere in that internal dialogue you ask yourself, *Was I a success?* I suppose it is safe to say that if you are inducted into the Hall of Fame, you probably would answer *yes*. But I tend to believe that personal success is much more elusive than that.

Yet even personal success in the game is hard to define without input from the masses. Baseball has a love affair with numbers; it's how players are measured and, often, how we measure ourselves. Statistics are flipped around, analyzed to the nth degree, placed in boxes of homemade recipes. *What did I hit on Astroturf? How many stolen bases did I have in day games? What did I hit against lefties from east of the Mississippi?* Before long, it's easy to find an angle that makes you the either the greatest player on the planet or the worst in history. I finished my career with a 293-game errorless streak on defense. I also hit .210 that last season. Still, can I get a vote for the Hall?

But there are a few universally accepted measuring sticks that no one can escape. A World Series ring is one of them. Players come to spring training year in and year out obsessing about a championship season. If you hang up the spikes without a ring on your finger, you can't help wondering, *Did I fall short?* Even if you are about to enter the Hall of Fame.

The more years I played, the more essential that ring came to seem. In my first year of free agency, in the winter of 2002–03, I preferred a place where I would have the opportunity to play the most. So I headed to Texas. After I got that out of my system, two seasons later, I went to where I thought I had the best chance to win: the New York Yankees. I wanted to end my career emphatically. Finish it off as a winner and enjoy the ticker-tape parade into retirement. That was the plan, until the Yankees' plan didn't include my services.

Maybe I would have approached free agency differently if I'd had more playoff success earlier, before I'd earned the right to test the market. When all is said and done, I made it to the playoffs only once. There were a few second-place finishes, and a winter league championship in Puerto Rico, but in the major leagues, I nearly always spent the off-season watching the playoffs on television.

I may not be on the committee that votes players into the Hall of Fame, but I can think of a lot of players who will never be inducted into the Hall, and who never were part of a world championship team, but who nevertheless make you rethink what it means to be successful.

I saw the Cardinals' Mark DeRosa at an Athletes Against Drugs function, where he was speaking about leadership. He mentioned that if he had ever won a World Series when he played for the Cubs, he would first have celebrated with his teammates and family—and then he would have looked to hug Ron Santo.

Santo is a Chicago Cub legend—an All-Star third baseman during the 1960s and early 1970s—who has become a rallying cry against the subjectivity of the Hall of Fame voting system. He has, so far, narrowly failed to be voted in, yet he is recognized for his statistically amazing career, including being a nine-time All-Star selection with five Gold Glove awards and more than three hundred career home runs. If there is any criticism, it's that he never made the playoffs. Not necessarily his fault.

Santo may not (yet) be in the Hall, but listen to DeRosa and you'll hear a current player wax poetically about how Santo—retired now more than three decades—exemplifies success and passion. Santo lost both his lower legs to diabetes, yet as an announcer for the Cubs he makes all the road trips and, when the team is at home, hikes to the top of Wrigley Field to get in the booth. The city of Chicago loves him. And it is safe to assume he went about the game in the same fashion that he goes about his business today. As my dad used to say, "How you do one thing is how you do everything."

So what is success? Maybe it's Rico Brogna playing every day, generously and with a smile on his face, despite having a debilitating disease called ankylosing spondylitis. Maybe it's Terry Shumpert crediting his faith for his commitment to put his family first—to the point where even when he had a half day off in Triple-A, he would be sure to stop home in Kansas City. Or maybe it's Tuffy Rhodes, from the rough side of Cincinnati, who didn't find what he was looking for here in the States and went to Japan—where he tied the single-season home run record and became fluent in Japanese.

Maybe you played drug-free and left it to nature despite what some players were choosing to do. Or you could be like my minor league teammate Scott Weiss, a Stanford grad who walked away from the game because a promise of advancement wasn't kept. Or it could be someone like Amaury Telemaco, who grew up in the Dominican Republic without running water but with a need to help take care of his siblings; he made it to the top as a pitcher and was one of the most honorable people I met in the game.

I will venture to say that gaining awards and accomplishments doesn't always mean you will sleep well at night. The players with the most internal peace are those who know who they are and, as a result, have found personal success more accessible than the players who chase the illusions of the quantifiable.

A few years ago, it was a given that Roger Clemens, one of the greatest players of all time, would be voted into the Hall of Fame during his first year of eligibility. Now his ascendance has stalled. If Major League Baseball had a starter kit for players, it would no doubt contain a fortune cookie. Crack it open, and you would find a little slip of paper with the message "You have to believe in yourself or no one else will." In general, good advice. But follow it too closely, and you may end up believing in yourself so thoroughly that you trust no one else. This is usually where your problems begin.

Exhibit A in this discussion is Clemens. The Rocket Man's stubborn belief in himself seemed to grow as he fought to clear his name from accusations of steroid use made public in the Mitchell Report. Maybe, by insisting on his innocence, he thought he was pushing against a downhill-rolling snowball to get it back to the top of the hill; instead, he may have unleashed the worst avalanche of his life.

As the evidence against him mounted, he escalated his defiance, ultimately landing in front of Congress and federal prosecutors. In testimony riddled with inconsistencies, information was exposed that connected his wife to human growth hormone use. The evidence eventually devolved into a he said, she said debate over assertions of his past personal trainer Brain McNamee and reading between the lines of the fine print in Andy Pettitte's affidavits—neither of which shed Clemens in the light of playing cleanly.

Most baseball players develop a special kind of shell that forms around them as their careers unfold. It probably isn't that different from an eggshell. It is fragile, but no one is really allowed inside until the player is ready to share his secrets, or until something terrible happens, causing the protective layer to crack. Inside this shell, a player justifies his need to be secluded. He perceives that the court of public opinion will either build him up or tear him down, and that either way, when his time comes, no one will remember him. So he uses this barrier to protect himself from the fickle judgments of the peanut gallery and to make it through his world.

It is a fairly typical and primitive form of defense. It is too complicated for a player to comb through the press and millions of fans, each of whom has an opinion of him. It is even more complicated to share with family and friends or nonbaseball colleagues the idea that his life can't be perfect—even with the fame and the seven-figure (or eight-figure) salaries. So he turns inward.

That is where things get a little weird. Ego kicks in, and inevitably you end up listening only to your own voice or the voices of the ordained elite, those you've given the key to get inside. It becomes an alternate reality where even though you think you are saying things that make sense to the outside world, most of your true thoughts and ideas just bounce off the inside coating and end up right back where they started.

To those outside Clemens's protective shell, he seems to be fighting ghosts. We must understand that he stopped listening to the outside world a long time ago, partly because ignoring those voices was integral to his survival. So if he seems out of touch, it's probably because he *is* out of touch. This process of defending his reputation cast shadows on his wife and others close to him, pretty significant collateral damage, especially considering that, in the end, his legacy is still hanging in the balance. All under the auspices of a principle of honor that I am sure he firmly believes in because throughout his career, like most players, he has been reinforcing it in his own head out of self-preservation.

Clemens fought a great fight on the baseball field, racking up unheard-of accomplishments that statistically place him among the best pitchers of all time. Yet his methods of obtaining that success are in question. Like all who have achieved greatness, he has found that the top of the mountain is a lonely place—because you're not only standing alone but also listening only to your own voice.

When I first came to the Phillies in 1998, I ran around saying yes to every request. Pretty soon, I felt like a rag doll from agreeing to do every appearance, every interview, and that was the year my eggshell grew the most. I learned that as a player there are a lot of demands on your space, and when the situation becomes overwhelming, the easiest way to deal with it is to tuck your head safely inside the shell.

In this environment, it is easy to overcompensate. Clemens may end up destroying everything dear to him by maintaining his bull-in-the-china-shop approach—even destroying those who have been with him since day one. What makes it even more difficult is that he is sparring in an arena where he has no experience. This is not Fenway Park; this is Congress and the Department of Justice, and they don't miss hanging curveballs. To bust out of the shell without acclimating yourself to this new world is nothing short of a kamikaze mission, no matter if your story checks out.

Most likely, he will reach the point of no return, where he will shun even those who would come to his rescue. He will end up hard-boiled, congealing everything inside including his most trusted inner circle.

When the show stops for a baseball player, it is hard for him to accept that there is no longer a microphone amplifying everything he says. Suddenly, no one is listening, so he speaks louder. It becomes critical to have people around him he can trust. They will be the ones to let him know when he is off-track. If at that point he still ignores them, he shouldn't be surprised to end up as the scrambled egg special of the week. Pass the salt.

Sammy Sosa, like Roger Clemens, has also been tainted by the steroid scandal. Now his entry into the Hall of Fame, once deemed automatic, is also in question. As soon as he declared that he would "calmly wait" for his call for his induction to the Hall, I knew he was in trouble.

During the 1994 players strike, Larry Himes, the general manager of the Chicago Cubs, called a meeting in the outfield of Tinker Field in Orlando, Florida. Since the big-league team was not playing, the Cubs had sent all their top staff to the Double-A team, which was carrying many of the up-and-coming stars in the system. The Orlando Cubs had a few first-round picks (Derek Wallace, Brooks Kieschnick, and me), and the home office wanted to teach us how to be big leaguers during this precarious time in the game.

As part of his motivational speech to my teammates, Himes raved about the aura in a major league locker room. He spoke of its "swagger," reminding us that it is the only place you want to be. And we listened.

Himes was also known as the man behind the trade to acquire Sammy Sosa from the White Sox, for whom he'd also served as general manager (and had also acquired Sosa from the Texas Rangers). Bringing Sammy to Wrigley had earned him kudos as a dealmaker. But when he brought up Sosa in the meeting, he lost me and, I am sure, a few of my teammates.

"Have you ever seen Sosa with his shirt off?" Himes asked us. "Don't you want a Sammy Sosa body?"

That season, 1994, was the first year I heard questions about players who may have been using steroids. Even though I was still in the minors, I heard the rumors about who might have been doing what. I also formed some conclusions based on observations. I had no hard evidence, just a sixth sense that came with being a professional.

When a player competes every day, he knows exactly how far he can hit a ball, how fast he can throw a pitch. And he knows his opponents almost as well as himself. Based on how the ball came off the bat from hitters, I could tell how far it would go with a high degree of accuracy, since my job as an outfielder required me to be at the right place at the right time.

So when a guy you played against for game after game all of a sudden consistently hits the ball substantially farther, and all that changed was his age going from thirty-three to thirty-four, questions do come to mind.

I played against Jason Giambi in the Southern League in 1994. Our scouting report was that he was a good hitter but had trouble turning on the ball, so we played him to the opposite field. He was a doubles machine. Gap to gap, line drives into the alleys, warning track power.

A few years later, when I saw the numbers he was putting up in the big leagues, I thought, *Hmmm, something is not adding up.* But I wasn't a physician; I was a ballplayer who did not and could not be expected to fully understand the capacity of the human body.

I had heard about players hiring super strength coaches, then stating the all-too-common line: "I am in the best shape of my life." Maybe Giambi just got stronger through a regimen of training. Or maybe that hitting coach he hired told him something that clicked. *He's a fun guy, we have the same agent, so I will give him the benefit of the doubt,* I told myself.

Funny, I worked hard, too, and as a first-round draft pick, I had some skills. Since I was always a slim guy with good hands, I assumed that I just had a certain kind of frame and that I was as strong as I could be. That was fine since I was getting smarter, improving mechanically, increasing my endurance, getting more flexible. In the equation for power, it is all about strength, speed, and flexibility. I had improved in all those areas.

By the time McGwire and Sosa went on their home run record assault in 1998, I was too busy worrying about my own game to think about what others were doing to their bodies. I had to survive every day, and that took self-centered focus. Like everyone else, those of us who were clean were fans during that amazing summer. We loved watching McGwire take batting practice, and for a few moments, we were unquestioning twelve-year-olds who wanted to believe in magic.

As I looked around the locker room, I also came to the conclusion that I really didn't know who was clean. My skepticism about certain newly minted behemoths never went beyond a few words or a wink to my Phillies teammate Kevin Jordan. In our little circle of two, we spoke openly and emphatically against the juice culture, accepting all the while that it was difficult to fully assess who was clean, but we also tired of the whisperings that the culture of the game was an excuse to artificially enhance. That seemed like a cop-out to us. At least take responsibility for your choice and the consequences that come down even if your kidneys fail at age forty. KJ was not big on shifting responsibility. Don't blame everyone or everything else, he said; too many players faced the same kinds of adversity (sick family members, declining security, aging, injury) and made the choice to be clean. But we were talking to ourselves or to a brick wall, mostly.

There was only minimal "Does he use or doesn't he?" conversation in the clubhouse or dugout. It was a dirty little secret.

Baseball's unwritten code translates to unspoken words. Players are reluctant to share with anyone the type of orange juice a teammate likes, let alone rally other teammates around the idea that someone is cheating. The game, with its in-house policing mechanism, discourages even the purest purist from crossing the brotherhood— teammate and opponent alike.

José Canseco's revelations about certain players are the most public example. It matters not that he has turned out to be credible in many instances. No doubt there are some players who would love to catch him in a dark alley, maybe even guys who were clean. It's not that different from a loose-lipped player triggering an in-house feud by talking about someone's philandering on the road. People do dirt, but we don't talk about it outside the circle. It isn't our business to judge, be the jury, or offer a public opinion.

When I signed as a free agent with the Texas Rangers in 2003, I received a call from the manager, Buck Showalter, welcoming me to the team. Then he wanted my advice about some players the team was thinking of adding to its roster. He told me that the Rangers currently had a player for whom they needed a strong backup, because they were unsure about his bat (a typical assessment for most up-and-coming players who weren't "appointed" to the job). Having spent seven seasons in the National League, I had no idea who this player was, but I listened to what Buck had to say.

We proceeded to go over some possibilities as insurance for this player. Buck mentioned several names I knew from the National League. I made some recommendations, and that was the end of the conversation.

At camp in Arizona, the player in question looked spectacular. Balls jumped off his bat. He hit a couple onto the roof of the workout facility. Wow. *Looks like my backup suggestion wouldn't have played much anyway*, I thought. This guy could really hit. Based on my conversation with Buck over the winter, this display caught me off guard, but then again, we hadn't played a single game.

During one batting practice session, I was standing within earshot of another teammate, Kevin Mench. Kevin was never shy with the commentary, fun trash-talk and all. In assessing this player's showcase, he chimed in, yelling, "Holy Andro!"

Was he joking? I did not know Mench well at the time, but I have come to learn that he is definitely part clown, part football fan. But at that moment, I wondered whether this player we were watching at the plate was somehow different from the player of years past, who had inspired Buck's doubts. I had no previous reference point to judge him and no evidence. As far as I know, his name has never come up as a user in the years since. Yet the sad state of affairs of the steroid era has created doubt everywhere, even in that sixth sense we all have. Fairly or not, suspicions arise and questions linger when you hear a teammate make what may be a joke, and when you see statistics improve dramatically. Now no one is beyond suspicion, and we don't know what we are seeing or what to believe, even when it is pure. That is truly unfortunate.

When Barry Bonds went on his assault of the home run record books, there was still some of that blinding awe that comes from watching a player be so much better than everyone else. You get caught up in the moment—as in that scene from the movie *Good Will Hunting* when the lifelong mathematician is blown away by the skills of Matt Damon's character. You forget about the baggage that comes with this "once in a generation" performer; you just needed confirmation that someone like him exists. It minimizes you in a way that almost gives you relief. Sort of like when you sit at the ocean and realize how small you really are; part of you feels less responsible for the world. Then you say, to yourself, *Whew, now I can just play my game, I can't ever be that good.* (Unless, of course, I buy a "new" me at the drugstore.)

But something else crossed my mind as I watched Bonds. His age. I knew what it was like to get out of bed day in and day out as a base stealer. By the time I was thirty, my body was changing. I needed to stretch more, and I had days when my legs were just tight. And Bonds was six years older than I was.

No one all of a sudden just gets exponentially better at a time in your career when you are hurting all over and supposed to be slowing down, unless of course you find a way not to hurt, and not to age. And last time I checked, no one has yet found the fountain of youth. Yes, Barry Bonds was probably the game's most all-around talented player for years, but even he got older. My eyes don't believe his stats for 2001: seventy-three home runs (more home runs than singles) and a .515 on-base percentage. Sabremetrically shocking, but fun to read.

Although the best test of a player's legitimacy may well be that sixth sense all players have, it still is not evidence in a court of law or even that of public opinion. I was suspicious of a lot of guys, many of whom have ended up in the Mitchell Report or have been called out one way or another, and I am suspicious of some whose names have not been revealed. But to destroy someone's reputation on suspicion is irresponsible and bad family etiquette.

I've heard some pundits say that even the "clean" players have some responsibility for the steroid era because they kept their mouths shut. This accusation stands only if you assume that a clean player knew who else was clean and then, in the next step, could actually build a movement of clean players to take action against their teammates (leaving aside the ever-shifting list of what substances were banned in the first place). That's difficult on several levels. First, several guys who proclaimed their cleanliness have turned out to be dirty. And for every legitimately clean player who was outraged, there were five who wouldn't dare break the code. In fact they might have even left you out to dry once you "sold out" your teammates.

Remember, players are brothers. You no doubt have a relative whose decisions you don't approve of, but you never forget that you are both in the same family. A verdict against this relative on the basis of your evidence will change the family forever—and change is scary. It's especially scary in a den of insecure egos, even when it's for the good of the game of baseball. So do you turn in a fellow player with only circumstantial evidence?

The twelve-year-old fan inside me still feels pain for the state of the game. I don't even know where my favorite players fit in the landscape of today's players. It was fun to see Mike Schmidt hit his home runs and to look at his accomplishments relative to players of earlier eras. It seemed pure, but maybe that is the conclusion of a wishful twelve-year-old. Truth is, it's very likely that the players of yesterday would have made the same kinds of choices as those in my era, and Schmidt and the great pitcher Bob Gibson have said that they might very well have done so. I am sure there were times in the game's past when the owners might have issued an ultimatum: Take steroids or else find work at the local factory. What choice did players have in the 1930s?

So let's look at the kinds of clean players on a roster.

Faith-Based Clean Players. These players choose not to take any illicit substances out of principle. Thus they express their opinions about drugs through quiet conversation and faith-based caucuses.

I Use Other Drugs (But Not Steroids). Although these players may have been on amphetamines or other drugs of choice, they consider steroids too risky or believe that steroids are on the other side of their personal line in the sand. They feel some guilt from hypocrisy and fear the microscope will end up on them. In some cases, they are even more dogmatic about the fact that the line should have been drawn where they drew it.

I Will Never Break the Code. Players of this type see everyone as part of a brotherhood and cannot compromise the integrity of the fraternal order for fear of anarchy and isolation. So they say nothing and are critical of those who may speak out against their brothers.

I Will Let Everything Fester and Be Bitter. These players just mumble to themselves in frustration, often getting extra bitter when they lose their job to someone who may be using steroids or when their team offers them a minor league contract yet rewards juicers. Case in point: in 2003, I spent two months on the disabled list with a hamstring injury, but I came back and contributed to a playoff team. Yet when I went looking for a new contract after the season, few teams were interested. I signed on as a part-time player with the Phillies in 2004, and at the end of spring training in 2005, the Yankees offered me a ticket home. In contrast, Fernando Viña, who we later learned (thanks to the Mitchell Report) was linked to performance-enhancing drugs, had been limited to only sixty-one games in 2003 due to the same injury, but signed as a free agent with the Detroit Tigers for a reported six million dollars over two years. Same kind of hamstring injury, similar career numbers, two very different contract offers. After hearing about Viña being in the report, I had a direct comparison to my career to consider. It just made me wonder, *Does the league in some way prefer users over nonusers?* The system rewards performance, and the users generally performed better than the nonusers. Not to mention that the users could be perceived as being more committed to earning that paycheck. But the big assumption is that the system knew beforehand who was clean and who was not—a leap that puts a sizable hole in the conspiracy theory, which is why this category of clean players tends to rant without clear direction (although we now have the benefit of looking at free agency after the Mitchell Report was published).

I Don't Know Whom I Can Trust. Although these players are strongly opposed to the steroid culture, they have no idea how to build a movement or a case, so they stay quiet out of paranoia.

Let Manny Be Manny. These players just worry about themselves. People do what they do; they are grown men who have to take responsibility for their own actions; I know who I am or what I have done.

Crazy Man in the Room. This rare fellow causes havoc in union meetings or in closed circles, but since everyone dismisses him as crazy, no one really pays attention and therefore he is a lone wolf.

Show Me the Science. These players are not convinced that there is clear proof about the effects of steroids and what is legal or not legal.

During my career, I fell into many of these categories at one time or another, but as I got older, I found myself to be festering with annoyance or trying to capture consensus through one-on-one conversations like the faith-based clean players.

I made the choice to play clean because this was something that was important to me. But who could have imagined the drug issue would get so complicated?

The players who use steroids and other performance-enhancing drugs made a different choice, and whether they are caught or not caught, there is always a price—despite the money, championships, and fame that may have come. Many of them deal with a nagging inadequacy. They believe that to cope with challenges of their profession and to hold on to what they love to do, they need something from a bottle. They may or may not realize that every time they pop that pill, they lose an opportunity—one that could have bestowed the gift of self-awareness. With that gift comes empowerment and peace, for you know what you are truly capable of when facing challenges with raw, honest vulnerability.

In fairness to them, they are just mimicking what our culture teaches us. We cannot age; we cannot lose a step; we cannot fail; we cannot show our frailties; we must be the best at all costs. So we find quick fixes to avoid the human condition, failing to realize or ignoring the fact that the most divine inspiration comes from showing what we can do in the face of our greatest challenges with the tools and gifts we already have within us—whether it involves hitting a Randy Johnson slider when your father is gravely ill three thousand miles away or trying to turn around a public school that the community has given up on.

I would not for anything in the world trade places with my juiced brethren because I know that they will wake up one morning and wonder if it was worth it. Was it worth the self-doubt, the destroyed marriage, the record you broke that puts you alone on that mountain, the anticlimactic destruction of the legacy of the game, the disappointment of your fans when they find out about your steroid use?

I hope the game can reset itself and find a new life, but in the end I firmly say, "No, Mr. Himes, I do not want a Sammy Sosa body, but I pray for the game's soul."

10

. . .

TOWARD THE LAST GAME

We've all been in situations where we are just "playing out the string." You're working for a boss you know is about to get fired. You're nearing the end of a month of dance lessons and realize you still have two left feet. Or maybe you handed in your senior thesis and you're wondering why you need to go to class the rest of the semester.

So how productive are you really going to be until the inevitable happens?

Unfortunately, like it or not, there are a lot of teams in Major League Baseball that are not going to make the playoffs. And most of those teams know it by the middle of August, when there are still six weeks left in the season.

Mathematically, they are not out of it. We could crunch the numbers and find a scenario that allows for a team that is twenty games out of first place to win its division. But we know that ain't gonna happen. Same thing goes for a lot of other teams with dismal records.

So if you're on a team with no hope of seeing the playoffs, what do you do? I have been there. I remember one summer when my Phillies teammate Scott Rolen pulled me aside and ran the numbers. We were once again staring at the backs of the Atlanta Braves as they cruised to another division title, but Scott was the first on our club to quantify the futility of chasing them.

At the time he broke this all down, about a month after the All-Star break, his math told us that we needed to win about 70 percent of our remaining games and the Braves had to lose just over half their games for us to tie them at the end of the season.

Given that we hadn't played even close to .700 baseball to date, and the Braves, with their pitching rotation of Cy Young winners, were not about to play below .500 ball, the challenge was daunting. But never say never—unless, of course, you are the Phillies trying to catch the Braves during their run of fourteen consecutive division titles. The evidence was overwhelming, and frustrating.

So was Scott giving up? Was his realism a knock on his ability to be considered a "winning" player? He certainly performed well all the time I played with him, even when the math didn't look promising. He dove for balls; he ran like a freight train; he played hurt throughout those years. On top of that, he now has a world championship under his belt.

Denial is an important part of baseball. If you take it one day at a time, you may actually avoid what seems inevitable. Someone on the first-place team could get injured; you could find your swing in the second half; your clueless manager might get fired; you could nail that cha-cha step that blew out your ACL from last year. Stranger things have happened.

We can't forget that teams like the Colorado Rockies in 2007 rattled off fourteen wins out of fifteen games at the end of the season, ultimately propelling themselves to the World Series after they had been left to rot on the side of the road in mid-August. Making something possible in the face of the impossible is what keeps this game interesting. But still, aren't some teams just done?

I was on a few teams that had a huge uphill climb, and I found there were still many reasons to be productive.

For starters, baseball is both self-centered and team-centered. On one side of the coin, it is hitter versus pitcher. No one else, on either team, can do anything about it: mano a mano, me against you. That is the self-centered side. But flip that coin over, and you find a shared cause, a dependence, a need to work together to succeed. Defense does not work alone; base running needs coaches; bullpens need to be managed.

Baseball is rare in that you can focus hard on being selfish and still be helpful to the team. If I keep hitting, it is bound to help the team one way or another. Sure, I could do things just to pad my statistics, like steal bases when we are losing by ten runs, or not reach for a ball so that I don't risk making an error, but that will get policed in a New York minute. No teammates would let that go on for long.

Besides, you could get traded to a contender and find new hope; or by playing well you might end up a sought-after free agent in the off-season; or maybe it's only year one of your manager's three-year deal, and you want to stay in his good graces. In short, giving up and rolling over is not an option, not if you want to be around for the glory of next season—when your last-place team might become a high-flying first-place team. Besides, the competitor in us wants to keep battling and enjoying the game we still love. That doesn't happen when you play halfheartedly.

I remember my teammate Brian Hunter from the Arizona Fall League. He put up some amazing numbers in Triple-A (.372 batting average, 49 stolen bases, 113 runs scored) before our fall season. In Arizona he wasn't playing quite as well, but we made the playoffs, and he announced, "Now, everyone will see the real Brian Hunter!" After this declaration, his next eight at-bats yielded mostly strikeouts—he basically got his head handed to him. I have been there, and I know that you can't turn it on and off. Better to stay on until the end because when it is off, the roaches get in position and take your job.

So if you have a favorite team that you feel in your heart is completely out of it, hang in there. They may well be done, but you still may see some magic out there. It could be the rising prospect who will help them next year. It could be the rebirth of a veteran player who has found his swing and wants to be sure he has a job for another season. It could be a team that is young and learning to play the game together for years to come—and still smiling ear to ear. Numbers may not lie, but they don't tell the whole truth, either.

The vast majority of players at the major league level were legends somewhere before they hit the big time. Many also may have had a whole lot of championships to go with their personal successes. I brought home my fair share of trophies, but the big ones escaped me more often than not. Especially once I put on the professional uniform.

In college, I rode in from high school to a team that had won the year before, and I, in turn, helped keep a mini-dynasty going by earning two league championship rings of my own my freshman and sophomore years. These resulted in an equal number of NCAA tournament bids. Going into the 1991 amateur draft, I was now a "winner"—a two-time college champion to go with whatever the scouts measured on the stopwatch.

Professional baseball was not so rewarding in the trophy sense. There is so much talk about being a champion, winning, doing whatever it takes, sacrificing, leaving it all on the field, giving 110 percent, that you come to understand that your career can be considered insignificant if you can't find a way to help a team win it all.

The minor leagues left me empty-handed when the last out of each season was recorded. My teammates and I were sent packing instead of into a locker room with champagne pouring over us. In fact, most of my teams didn't even come close to winning. We were well out of the race with a lot of games to go. *Was it me?* I sometimes asked myself. I'd always been a "winning" player. What happened?

I did, however, find success in the off-season. In 1994, during my time in the Arizona Fall League, my team made it to the finals only to lose to the Peoria Javelinas and their star player, Jason Giambi.

But at least we won our division. I was encouraged. The next winter, the Cubs sent me to Puerto Rico for the winter season. There I put it all together by playing my best baseball and also finding a way to be a key cog on a team that was knocking off top-notch opponents with regularity.

Most players head to winter ball to work on their craft in some way. A player may try to learn a new position. A pitcher may try to add a slider to his repertoire. A free-swinging hitter may try to develop more discipline at the plate. I was there to work on getting on base more, but I also had another goal. As my Mayaguez Indios manager, Tom Gamboa, clearly stated, "We are here to win."

After so many middle-of-the-pack finishes in the minors and the accompanying self-doubt, I had to reboot. Thinking back to the glory we had achieved at Penn helped renew my confidence and reminded me of the tangible and intangible things that are necessary to win. For starters, I had to remember the burden wasn't just on me; it took collective responsibility with selflessness and execution mixed in. It took big play making, timely hitting, solid defense in a critical inning. Talent was important, but it certainly wasn't everything.

My first winter in Puerto Rico gave me reason to be optimistic. When I returned, however, the Cubs general manager, Ed Lynch, was skeptical. Although he was happy that I came back with an MVP trophy, his unequivocal message was: *Do it again during a professional championship season.*

What I had gained from my experience in Puerto Rico meant the world to me, but it apparently only meant what the brass would allow it to mean stateside. Fair enough; I'd have to show that I could do it in a Cubs uniform. As my Indios had lost in the finals that year, I did have some unfinished business.

My second year on the island would finish the job. I had an entirely different approach after deciding that I had to go down there and get better, not just produce and earn trophies. The albatross I carried with me was about getting on base and, in particular, walking more.

I had been aggressive my entire life—understandable, as I was hitting in the middle of most lineups right until I signed a pro contract. But in the minors I was groomed to be a leadoff hitter. Moving to the top of the lineup required an entirely new mind-set: set the table, work the count, get on base, and let the big boys knock you in.

In Puerto Rico, I worked as many counts as I could, trying to force a walk or at least cause the pitcher to throw a lot of pitches. The greater the variety of pitches you and your teammates see early in the game, the better you'll all be prepared to deal with whatever comes your way. You'll see the movement on the ball, gauge the speed, and get a sense of what the guy throws depending on the count. Of course, the more pitches the man on the mound throws, the sooner he'll reach his pitch count and be pulled from the game. I had a chance to see top-of-the-order hitters like Rickey Henderson and Craig Biggio drive teams crazy by fouling off great pitches time and time again. Then, when they got on base, they would wreak havoc on defenses. I aspired to do what they did. And by the time the season ended, we were atop our division and I had tied for the league lead in hits after having led the league the year before. No MVP trophy, but we were in a great position to win a championship.

This time, we would not falter, knocking off the Caguas Criollos in the semifinals and then triumphing in the finals over a star-studded San Juan Senadores lineup that featured Juan Gonzalez, Roberto Alomar, Candy Maldonado, Carlos Delgado, Hector Villanueva, Rey Sanchez, and others. Our team was more grinders than heroes: Luis DeLeon, Charlie Montoya, Alex Diaz, Edwards Guzman, a young Bengie Molina, Pedro Munoz, Wil Cordero, José Hernandez, and a five-star closer in Roberto Hernandez.

We poured the champagne quickly and furiously in the locker room and danced the night away at the center of town when we got back to Mayaguez. I was a champion again. It felt good; it felt right.

I would have another opportunity to taste the postseason in 2003 when the Cubs brought me back to Chicago in that midseason trade with the Rangers. The pennant race went down to the wire, with the Cubs battling the Houston Astros and St. Louis Cardinals for the National League Central Division title. We won the division on the next-to-last day of the season, clinching with a doubleheader sweep of the Pittsburgh Pirates at Wrigley Field.

One nice thing about nearing the end of the regular season is that teams can carry up to forty players on their rosters for the month of September. In a playoff push this is a considerable asset; you have someone for every situation times two. Need a pinch runner who is a great base stealer? Got that. Need a left-handed pitcher who keeps the ball elevated in the zone? Got that. Need a defensive shortstop who switch-hits? Got that. A manager can get spoiled and the players can get stressed when the roster has to be pared down to twenty-five again at playoff time.

I didn't think that the Cubs would go to the trouble of trading for me, watch me contribute to the division title, and then declare me inactive for the big dance. But that is what happens to a lot of players. Do the math.

Was I on the bubble? When Dusty Baker called me into his office in late September, I surmised that I was. "Can you play infield?" Dusty asked me.

At first I thought this was a trick question. Then I put it together. Our middle infielder Tony Womack had slid into home, tearing a ligament in his elbow. With Womack out, we only had three middle infielders: second baseman Mark Grudzielanek, shortstop Alex Gonzalez, and backup Ramon Martinez. As we were keeping an extra pitcher on the roster, we needed another position player who could be the emergency second baseman or shortstop.

Facing the reality that I either answer Dusty's question in the affirmative or be the twenty-sixth man watching October games in Wrigley wearing a parka in the dugout, I hesitantly said I could indeed play infield—although I sensed from Dusty that an acceptable answer was that I *would* play infield. I would have failed miserably at the poker table since I am sure my jaw hit the ground with tremendous force right after he asked.

I borrowed an infielder's glove from Martinez and started taking ground balls before each game. Oh yes, I also began praying that it would never come to this in a real game. A championship game at that.

I tried to separate ego from objectivity, but it was a tough task. I had been one of the hottest hitters in the American League when the Cubs traded for me, so I thought I could contribute to the team's success in some way. But I also knew that Tony Womack with one arm might be a better second baseman than I was with a fully functioning arsenal of limbs—even if he had to kick the ball to the first baseman. At the same time, I really didn't think about how my teammates would react. We all were playing out of position in some way. Platooning, pinch running, starters pitching in relief. Why not me?

Only when I heard about Womack's elbow situation did it fully register that I almost didn't suit up for the playoffs. So many players who had made this trip to the playoffs possible didn't make the final twenty-five. Shawn Estes had a few key starts; Augie Ojeda played great defense; Josh Paul kept everyone loose. They all had a role, and all still were respected. Champagne would be poured on their heads, too, should we win, but there's no denying that come playoff time the difference between being number twenty-five and number twenty-six was significant.

After I made the cut as an emergency infielder, I quickly had to learn all kinds of infield etiquette. Back in my minor league days, Jimmy Piersall had instructed me that when an inning ended and a fellow outfielder was left stranded on the bases, I was to bring him his glove so that he didn't have to make the trip back to the dugout. Now I had to revise a rule that was burned into my consciousness. I was now the ultimate utility player, and if pressed, I would (I shudder at the thought) have to carry an infielder his glove.

Alex Gonzalez got irritated with me when I took ground balls while wearing spikes. I was already a wreck trying just to field the ball; now he wanted me to use turf shoes with no traction because my spikes were messing up the infield. I'd played a thousand major league games in the outfield and was clueless on that score. I had done the equivalent of putting my grass cuttings on his lawn, and now I had to call a landscaper.

I don't remember taking any extra time to master bunt defenses or cutoffs and relays. I got a crash course, but in the end, if I was ever on the field as an infielder, my plan was to call timeout and ask someone what to do.

I figured that I would not have to worry about this situation. This was just a drill, a test of the emergency broadcast system.

In the National League Division Series against Atlanta, Dusty pumped us up by explaining the mind games he was playing in the paper. He employed the "shy" guy routine as if he was trying to lure an attractive woman across the room. He talked to the press about how the Braves had a huge edge. They had home field advantage, and they had won twelve division titles in a row. But once the press was gone, he told us not to pay attention to anything he said in the paper; he wanted us to put a foot in these guys.

As I held my outfield glove close to me in Game One, things got hairy. In a rare (and early) move, Baker pinch hit for shortstop Alex Gonzalez in the sixth inning. Ramon Martinez replaced him. It suddenly registered that I was a double switch or a sprained ankle away from making my infield debut in the middle of the playoffs. I almost passed out. I already hated hitting at Turner Field, so now I was going to add insult to insult by potentially making the most errors in one inning—in baseball history.

I don't even remember the rest of the game. I was in an altered state thinking about how I could put Martinez and Grudzielanek in protective armor until the final out. Fortunately they survived double switches and bad hops all night long.

As it turned out, through the five playoff games against Atlanta and the seven versus Florida that followed, I never had the opportunity to help (or hurt) the team in the infield. I did, however, have such a chance at the plate in the eleventh inning of Game Three against the Marlins.

After barely making the playoff roster and then with only one at-bat in the division series we had won three games to two over the Braves, it was a long shot that I would even get a plate appearance in the National League Championship Series. The odds were even longer that Dusty would send in a righty like me to bat against a right-handed pitcher in extra innings. But the game was tight, and we were running out of hitters.

When Dusty (through bench coach Dick Pole) told me to get ready, I was at least in a familiar place. Having spent five years with Philadelphia in the same division as the Marlins, I knew how their home field played in day games, night games, rain, and more rain. I could even tell you a lot about the batter's box—which had these big white markings and signaled me to position myself in a more closed stance to see the pitcher better. And since the Marlins' roster hadn't changed much since I'd last faced them, I knew the team well, including the man on the mound, Braden Looper.

My numbers against Looper weren't spectacular, but I generally had good at-bats against him—especially if he threw me something other than his featured pitch, the sinker. As I have said before, only two things happened when I hit a sinker (neither of them good). Either I hit a ten-hopper to the third baseman or shortstop, or I fouled the ball off my left ankle. To this day, I still have a weird sensation in my left leg from a foul ball I hit off Derek Lowe years ago.

The score was 4–4 with one out and the speedy Kenny Lofton on first base when the "secret weapon," Doug Glanville, came to the plate. With the count 2–1, Kenny took off to steal second. I got the sinker that I dreaded, but somehow I managed to get nothing but barrel on it. Surprise number 1—a line drive instead of a grounder.

Surprise number 2 was even better. The liner traveled right through the spot the shortstop had vacated to cover second for a play on Lofton. I had the best view in the house to know that there was a great chance that ball was going to go all the way to the wall. It did. Lofton scored easily, and I cruised into third. I had knocked in what became the winning run when the Marlins failed to score in the bottom of the eleventh. We were now up two games to one.

There were more than sixty-five thousand people in the stands, many of them Cubs fans, and millions watching at home. After the game I got the royal treatment with numerous interviews, including one before I could even leave the field. Lost in the shuffle was my teammate Randall Simon, who had hit a big home run to get us into that extra inning.

To this day, I can't say for sure whether Kenny was running on his own or if the hit-and-run sign was on. I did see him take off, and I was already geared to take a more contact-oriented swing, partly because I was sure Looper would try and sink one on me at some point. But having that kind of foresight usually didn't help me. I just didn't have a sinker-ball swing.

Immediately after the game, there were questions about whether it was a hit-and-run. Dusty squashed any effort to address this; he didn't want to give away our strategy in postgame interviews. He told me not to let anyone know.

The truth was that I didn't know myself. I certainly knew the signs, but when I got in that batter's box, I was locked in. I'd had only one at-bat since the season had ended over two weeks earlier. I needed to focus every ounce of concentration on the pitcher.

I'm sure I looked at our third base coach, Wendell Kim, but I don't remember actually seeing him. Have you ever driven down the highway and realized you were on autopilot for a few miles? All sense of time and distance absent? That was me in that at-bat. I probably read correctly whatever signs he gave and just stepped in and reacted to the situation. Once Lofton was running, all I had to do was get the bat on the ball, and hope it had eyes to find the hole.

So, as I am often asked, was it the biggest hit of my career? I suppose being a step away from the World Series and getting a hit that propels your team even closer has to rank right up there. But I also remember the home run I hit off Mike Wilkins in Little League when he was twelve and I was nine. I floated around the bases, and I still haven't lost that feeling. That was pretty big. So was the homer I hit off Mike when he was a high school senior and I was a sophomore. "I still can't get you out," he told me.

The one thousandth hit of my career certainly was big, not because it was a nice round number, but because it happened the same day my father passed away. This was the last game of the season, and I knew it was unlikely that he would be with us come April the following season.

Timing is everything. So, too, is context. When I slid into third base after hitting that triple in the NLCS, I was floating just like I was when I hit that very first Little League home run. I didn't know that it would seal the victory for my team, but I knew it represented overcoming a lot personally: midseason surgery, being buried on the Phillies bench the year before, coping with the death of my father (although he was still inspiring me from beyond). Conquering the challenges I had in my life was the true victory; the fact that it happened in front of the entire world and helped the Cubs just made it sweeter.

Had the Cubs gone on to win the NLCS or even won the World Series for the first time in ninety-five years, I could probably get free drinks for the rest of my life in almost any bar in the Chicago. As we all know, that didn't happen. A lot of people blame a young man named Steve Bartman for the Cubs' stunning defeat in the series against the Marlins. Not me.

When I was with the Cubs the first time around in 1996 and 1997, our hitting coach, Tony Muser, and outfielder Luis Gonzalez had a playful relationship. Underneath Muser's gravelly exterior, he understood people very well. But it was Gonzalez who put a smile on his face and seemed to remind him why he was doing his job year in and year out. Luis worked tirelessly, kept the Cubs locker room loose, and was always clowning with Muser.

One day Muser took it upon himself to be a TV segment producer. With the help of our video guy, Fast Eddie, he made the "excuse" video. It was a montage of Gonzalez's errors and blunders underscored by that merry-go-round whining circus music. When the music was nearing its end, Muser scrolled every excuse under the sun as to why things didn't go right. *I didn't feel well. The sun was in my eyes. It's too cold. It's too hot.*

As a young Cub, I learned a few key lessons from Tony Muser. He was a veteran presence with years of knowledge and high expectations for his students. Under Tony, I began to understand there wasn't an excuse—ever. Sure, there may be reasons things happen. But in the end, the things you can't control, you can't control. Conversely, when you mess up the things you can control, that is on you.

Fast-forward to the 2003 playoffs. With such a commanding three-games-to-one advantage over the Marlins in the best-of-seven series, we certainly had reason to be optimistic. When a player wants to get tickets for playoff games for his friends and family, he has to order them ahead of time. I wasn't so bold as to think we had the pennant wrapped up, but in my head I was counting how many tickets I would need when we faced the New York Yankees for all the marbles.

In Game Five, Josh Beckett shut us down in Florida in a way where all you can do is tip your cap. Now it was three games to two, but we were still in the driver's seat. Heading back to Wrigley Field, we only needed to win one of two games at home, and our ace starters Mark Prior and Kerry Wood were poised to take the mound.

In Game Six, we led 3–0 going into the eighth inning. Prior had been outstanding, allowing just three hits. With one out and Juan Pierre on second base, the Marlins' Luis Castillo came to the plate. On a 3–2 count, he hit a foul ball down the left field line, where the stands edge right up to the chalk line. As the ball curved toward the field of play, our left fielder, Moises Alou, jumped near the wall in foul territory to attempt the catch. At the same time, a fan wearing a Cubs cap and headphones reached for the ball. Alou closed in, reaching his glove into the stands, seemingly ready to make the grab. Instead, the fan—Steve Bartman—deflected the ball. Alou came up empty-handed—and furious. He threw down his glove and spit out a few choice epithets.

After the ensuing argument and lost case for fan interference, Dusty Baker and Alou returned to their respective perches. On the scoreboard nothing had changed. But on the field everything was different. The momentum had shifted from Prior's cruise control performance to the cigar-smoking manager, Jack McKeon, and his youthful Marlins.

Florida proceeded to rattle off eight runs before I could come back from the water cooler, and we lost 8–3. The turnaround reminded me of the fog rolling in at Candlestick Park—except this time, the temperature didn't drop thirty degrees, only our hearts did.

There is nothing like going from complete control of a situation to being flat on your back counting stars and sheep. I went home to my apartment in disbelief, not even thinking about fan interference, but wondering how Robin Hood had just picked our pockets.

Still, I woke up confident. In Game Seven, Wood would have a definite edge over the Marlins starter, Mark Redman. We were home; we were destined; we would get back up from that rabbit punch and return the favor. Nothing to worry about; it was our time.

But it was the Marlins' time, too. They found a way to pull it out, rallying from a 5–3 deficit to win, 9–6.

An oceanful of Fish swam onto our field to celebrate. Where was the justice? The Marlins had only come into the league in 1993. They had already won a World Series in 1997. We hadn't won a World Series since 1908. Wanting to erase the disaster from my mind, I left the dugout as soon as possible.

So, did Bartman cost the Cubs the World Series?

Tony Muser would have looked at the foul ball Castillo hit, and said, "It was just a foul ball." And it was. The count remained the same. We had the same opportunity *after* Bartman reached out that we had before. Indeed, if we had held the three-run lead and gone on to win the game and the pennant, no one would ever have known the poor guy's name.

Unfortunately for Steve Bartman, human beings—particularly athletes and their fans—are driven to look back in time and find a reason why something happened. The football pass dropped in the end zone. The technical foul in the first quarter of the basketball game. Bartman. It is easy, if painful, to pinpoint the moment when the game went from getting ready to pop champagne to wondering if you were drinking the bubbly during the game.

I don't blame Steve Bartman for my game-winning eleventh-inning triple in Game Three going to waste. I don't consider him the reason why my wedding band is the only ring on my fingers. He did what any fan would do with a ball that started well into the stands and began to hook toward the field: try and catch a lifetime souvenir during the time when the ultimate curse on your favorite team will be reversed. Just like everyone else near him attempted to do, too. (A sadly forgotten fact, especially since some of those same fans booed him out of the ballpark.)

So was it Bartman? Or was it the error that our shortstop, Alex Gonzalez, made later that inning on a potential inning-ending double-play grounder? Or maybe it was that Alou and Baker argued too long, or that Dusty should have taken Prior out earlier. Maybe our catcher should have called for a curveball instead of the fastball that Derrek Lee ripped into left field. Maybe it was bad luck to have champagne on ice prematurely. Maybe Glanville should have started at shortstop.

We just don't know. It could have been all of the above and none of the above at the same time—just as it is in every game. In the end, there really is no excuse for things that happen beyond our control. All we can do is adjust after they happen. We lost. The Marlins played well and won a world championship. It is okay to not have a reason.

Sure, I would have loved to have won a World Series, but I don't blame Steve Bartman for why I didn't.

The planets may not have been properly aligned during our run for the championship, but the stars were out in full force the entire time.

There exists a constant gravitational pull that can draw people in entertainment together. Actors, supermodels, X-Games champions, NFL quarterbacks, musicians, movie producers—all find ways to the light. No one is shocked that Brad Pitt decided to be with Angelina Jolie as opposed to an unknown woman that he met at Starbucks. There is a perception that people in the spotlight understand other people in the spotlight and therefore should stick together.

Although baseball is a major player in the entertainment world, only the game's elite get the type of exposure that ensures the opportunity to mix with Hollywood starlets or make cameo appearances in a sitcom. No offense to most of the other tens of players named Rodriguez in professional baseball, but it's only A-Rod who's partying with the likes of Kate Hudson and Madonna on a regular basis. Most players are still fairly anonymous in those celebrity circles unless they fight their way in.

And how do you do that? By having your agent put you in touch with the right contacts or dating someone in the sought-after echelon. Nothing gets you in the circle like finding a truly significant other. Before C. C. Sabathia was married, rumors surfaced linking him to Serena Williams. As a result, C.C. became an A-lister. His street cred went through the roof.

As I found out in 2003, there is one exception that levels the playing field for everyone from the All-Star right fielder to the twenty-fifth guy on the roster. Make the playoffs, and you get a hall pass into the coveted circle, even if for just a minute.

Economists should use the postseason as a case study for the law of supply and demand. Celebrity demand for behind-the-scenes access is at a peak. Stars clamor for the chance to be in the mix and, they hope, in the clubhouse. The national anthem is sung by recording artists like Beyoncé, not the local talent that is typical of a regular season game. The number of suppliers who can meet that demand—players and certain team functionaries—is small. As a result, they can work an insider deal to their liking, so they swap status and spaces—at least for October.

Players' celebrity status begins to escalate during the push to the playoffs. While battling for the division title in 2003, the Cubs got police escorts. I started getting recognized throughout Chicago, whereas weeks before it would happen only when I gave my name for a reservation. Almost overnight we became rock stars.

Our locker room was filling up as never before. Instead of dodging empty chairs in the close quarters of our sanctuary in Wrigley Field, I was dodging reporters from every media outlet in the country. Where did everyone come from?

For most of my career, it took almost three weeks to refill a bat order. But in the 2003 playoffs, I ordered some bats (as the twenty-fifth player on the roster), and they literally came the next day (personalized, at that). I imagined UPS and FedEx engaged in a duel to determine which company would have the privilege of assigning an employee to sleep outside Louisville Slugger's headquarters until someone on the inside finished carving my order. For all I knew, maybe Louisville Slugger had opened a new factory in Chicago, just for the playoffs.

My voice mail was overtaxed, and my e-mail was overloaded with messages from everyone under the sun. Most of the words were incoherent from screaming cousins or "blast from the past" acquaintances whom I hadn't heard from in a long while. But of course, the first message was "your voice mail is full." Everyone was watching. Kind of cool. Kind of eerie, too.

As a role player, my game contribution mostly involved eating sunflower seeds on the bench. Still, I suspect someone who paid close enough attention could recite that I preferred the jalapeño-flavored seeds over the BBQ ones. More TV cameras meant more face time for every player.

Those tuned in would also have noticed that celebrities from TV and movies, the media, corporate America, and politics were filling up every empty space available at the stadium. If you are claustrophobic, this was not a good time to be there. It was cool that many of these people were actors whose work I knew or liked. During one game my brother sat near Marg Helgenberger from the hit television series *CSI*. He conducted his own thorough investigation and still hasn't stopped talking about her blue eyes.

When we played in Los Angeles late in the season, the insane became mundane. Usually there is a rule that outsiders can't be in the clubhouse until a certain amount of time has elapsed after the game, but in L.A., when we came in after a win, our locker room was full. I must admit I was a little uncomfortable when I was trying to come out of the shower and change into my street clothes while trying to work my way around a few actresses whose names escaped me. Actually, I never knew who they were, but it was interesting that they were gaining street cred from us, not the other way around. They probably knew my name. Then again, I would rather they didn't, since I eventually gave up and dressed in front of them.

Even my former minor league buddy Michael Jordan joined us from time to time. When we won the division series against the Braves, he tried to avoid the spotlight and let us savor the moment. He also tried to avoid getting doused with champagne, but we found him and drowned him in bubbly. The greatest basketball player of my era, and quite possibly, ever, was cheering my team on. Wow.

It was nice to see how these top stars were everyday fans of the game. There was very little bravado. They were often dressed in fan paraphernalia while wishing us the best. (Certainly if someone asks me to play an extra on *CSI*, I would do it!) The game can reduce any of us into little kids.

Bright lights attract brighter lights as stars from far and wide, baseball fans or not, come to see what is going on. For a short period of time, while my teammates and I were doing what we had always done, we, too, were stars at the pinnacle of our profession. Success attracts the successful.

Our new support group understood the significance of winning it all. A world championship would be our Oscar. Unfortunately, we ended up with Oscar the Grouch inside his garbage can, but as people say: it's an honor to be nominated.

I did take the field for one World Series game.

For Game Five of the 2008 World Series between the Philadelphia Phillies and Tampa Bay Rays, I had the honor of bringing out the ball for the first pitch, to be thrown by the former Phillies great and current U.S. senator Jim Bunning. The world did not know what I knew at that moment: the Phillies were ordained to win this game, no matter how many days it took. Why? Because that moment was the convergence of all the magic of my youth.

When I came out on the field, I hit the trifecta of my childhood dream. I was at a World Series; the Phillies were primed to win; and my favorite singer and good friend John Oates was singing the national anthem.

I knew no one could lose with all that power.

It was also fitting that I was in Philadelphia for the moment. I had played five of my best seasons with the Phillies, but then I fought and scrapped my way out of town as a free agent. I was like a defiant teenager who had the world figured out at eighteen and, much to the dismay of my "parents," escaped to sign with the Texas Rangers to be their starting center fielder. Then I got hurt, got traded to the Chicago Cubs, and returned to the Phillies a year later as a bench player. I tried one more time to make it to the game's biggest stage by catching on with the Yankees in 2005, only to be cut at the end of spring training.

After that experience, I decided to come back home. I signed a one-day "exploding contract" just so I could retire as a Philadelphia

Phillie. My World Series appearance three years later was the giant cherry on top.

The Phillies are a family, and it doesn't matter if you are a popcorn vendor, a fixture like Vince, who handled dugout security, or an MVP like Jimmy Rollins—you might as well be wearing the uniform.

I suppose this was something that I was drawn to as a young fan of those Phillies teams in the 1970s and '80s. Year after year I saw the same players wearing the uniform. Maddox, Schmidt, and others played for the team until their bodies gave out, and I could count on cheering for my favorites year after year.

When I joined the Phillies family, I found out that this was also true for everyone from parking lot attendants to announcers. When you are in, you are in. You are a Phillie for life whether you like it or not, and that family loyalty originates with the group of families that owns the organization.

The owner I came to know the best is David Montgomery, the team's president and CEO. (In addition to our Phillies bond, we are both Penn alumni.) He is responsible for the organization's philosophy: to stand behind the players "through thick and thin, in sickness and in health." In the glory years of the 1970s and '80s, this mantra was hailed as genius, though when times were tough (many of those years when I was there), the organization drew criticism because it "stuck with people too long."

When my father passed away, ten Phillies representatives attended his service. David Montgomery led the way. When I got married three years later, once again David and his wife made the trip to Asheville, North Carolina, along with the team's community relations director, Gene Dias, and a slew of former teammates. They have been consistently supportive and dependable through every phase of my life and the lives of many others who have worn the red and white.

When the Phillies won the National League pennant in 2008, I received a text message from my old pal Mike Lieberthal: "Are you going to the World Series? I am going to all the home games!" I wrote back saying that I hadn't planned on it, but if the team had a ticket for me, I would see if I could get out there last-minute.

Within hours, I received a long e-mail from the Phillies' former PR director, Larry Shenk. He invited me and my family to town and said that the Phillies wanted to give me the honor of bringing out the ball for the first pitch for Game Five. It turned out that Senator Bunning's toss to home was the beginning of the game that would bring the first World Series title to Philadelphia since 1980.

Once I arrived at the stadium, the red carpet never stopped rolling out. I met with former teammates, chatted with U.S. senators, reunited with my favorite security guards, kicked back with Mom, and spent time with John Oates. And that was all before I got on the field.

Just before the 8:25 p.m. scheduled first pitch, it was time. Time to walk out that first ball in front of the frenzied, towel-waving Philadelphia fans. Everything came together: a passion, a pastime, a love, the music, my family, my friends, and my life's commitment— all on one canvas. A true homecoming of the greatest kind from a tough city that still has big love in its heart.

It took the Phillies two days to complete the rain-interrupted game, but when closer Brad Lidge knelt in celebration after tossing that final strike to clinch the Series, the Phillies family knelt with him. A prayer of thanks, a prayer for the city.

11
· · ·

REFLECTIONS ON THE GAME

I have frequently thought about making a T-shirt that reads, 10 THINGS YOU FIGURE OUT IN THE OFF-SEASON. Players become experts in everything under the sun when they suddenly have an abundance of time on their hands.

I suppose that's part of the deal. During the season, you barely have time for everyday life; then, in a flash, you have too much time, you start to overthink everything. And your epiphanies are absolute: you don't just find an answer to a problem; you find *the* answer.

That is probably why you break up with your girlfriend, or get back together with that ex-girlfriend, or discover, while engrossed in a late-night game of Texas Hold 'Em, the precise problem with your swing. You figure everything out in the blink of an eye. And that is not a good thing. Boredom is your enemy, and it's often fertile ground for the ridiculous.

Because you can't go into total stasis, I did what I could to keep the off-season fresh. During the first few months you have to at least lightly stay in shape before ramping up to a full regimen. But some players trained from the moment the season ended. Royce Clayton, who married an Olympic sprinter from England, jumped right into the fire, and I found out firsthand that working out with them was serious business. Up to that point, I'd never fully appreciated how much form mattered.

Gregg Jefferies was famous for swinging a bat underwater to create resistance. I guess it made sense. At the worst, he could find a gig at SeaWorld if the off-season became permanently "off."

Somewhere in the middle of my career I started hearing the phrase "There is no off-season anymore." As if 162 games, winter ball, and a six-week spring training don't earn you some downtime to kick back.

Early on, I often moved out to Arizona or some other warm-weather place during the winter, just to get a head start. I would do the standard training routine at the team complex—running sprints, lifting weights, eating healthfully—but soon realized that I had another ten hours of the day to burn. Usually a recipe for disaster.

As time went on, I got more creative with that extra time. Even before *Dancing with the Stars* was a hit TV show, I had my own adventures in cha-cha. I took a class with a dance company for an entire off-season—almost five months. I learned fox-trot, salsa, swing, rumba, you name it. I figured it was a fun and unique way to stay in shape instead of the same old sprints and push-ups. But I was before my time and, unfortunately, before reality TV. Otherwise I'm sure I could have at least gotten voted off some show because of my horrible waltz.

Anything and everything goes in the off-season, especially when you get spoiled having the resources to burn and the time to burn them. In the off-season of 2003, my college mentor, Vukan R. Vuchic, offered me a chance to teach a seminar on urban transportation with him—in South Africa. I had a few days to decide, after having just lost Game Seven of the National League Championship Series. But I agreed to go and was in Cape Town less than three weeks later. Why not?

There is an easy way to tell who has way too much time on his hands: he buys something that may work for him, but that is absurd to many others—a time-share in a war zone, or an alpaca farm—but instead of conceding the point that, say, alpacas don't fare well where you live (like Philadelphia), he tries to sell you on the idea, too. Sorry, Billy Wagner, I can't do alpacas in Chicago either.

The off-season would not be complete without creating the ultimate drill to fix your broken swing. Hit with one eye. Hit blindfolded. Hit with your back to the pitcher. Or maybe kneel on one hand while biting a piece of tree bark, and then swing. The best part about these homemade drills is the special bats or strange machines players invent so the drills can be executed correctly. Landfills near major league cities are full of ballplayers' discarded off-season mock-science contraptions.

I remember the "strobe" drill. That was a good one in Cubs spring training. You had this disco light going off as you hit with these funky glasses with slots. The theory was: if you can hit in these conditions, you can hit in any condition. I wish I could give you an example of a specific device that made it through the Patent Office, but more than likely someone got hurt from it, and I don't want to be subpoenaed.

When I was in the minor leagues, I had the brilliant idea to work for some extra spending money over the holidays. So I took a job at a Barnes & Noble in North Jersey. I had my Penn engineering degree, so in many respects I was considered overqualified for my job as a cashier. Still, I figured I was a ballplayer who was keeping busy and making some Christmas money—that is, until a guy walked into the store wearing a Penn Engineering cap.

He was young, maybe a sophomore, and when I told him that I had graduated from the engineering school, his face fell. Then I pieced it together: I had shaken his hope for getting a job commensurate with his Ivy League degree.

But I was only doing what ballplayers do in the off-season: something that makes no sense whatsoever.

I have heard of teammates falling out of tree blinds (Carlton Loewer), getting lost on mountains (Turk Wendell), flying fighter jets (Turk again), dating supermodels (pick anyone), gaining a hundred pounds of muscle (see Mitchell Report), going back to some motherland (I guess that would be me), or working out with Arnold Schwarzenegger's personal trainer (Mark Smith). After a while, no tales I might hear that first day of spring training could surprise me. There's nobody better than a ballplayer to put the "off" in off-season.

Durante el invierno, jugué dos temporadas en Puerto Rico, donde mejoré en muchos aspectos de béisbol. Entonces . . .

I remember my father telling me the story of when he first landed in New York, having emigrated from the island of Trinidad, in the West Indies. He was proud of his spanking-new suitcase until he reached customs and couldn't find the key to the lock, and the customs agents had to break it open to search his belongings. My father's heart sank. After all, he saw the opportunity in this new world and wanted to make a good impression with the best he had to offer.

New Jersey–born, I couldn't grasp the emotions of going to a new land full of hope and fear at the same time. That was until I was invited to play in Mayaguez, Puerto Rico, for my first stint in winter ball. Think of it as baseball's equivalent of continuing education.

It was 1995. I had most recently played in Des Moines, Iowa, at the highest level in the Chicago Cubs' minor league system. It had been a rough year, between having to adjust to a new level of professional baseball after a labor strike and play for a manager who didn't exactly care for me. Even so, I was only one step away from the big time. And from what I was being told, a lot was riding on the success of my tenure as a member of the Mayaguez Indios.

Before the trip to Puerto Rico, the Indios' new manager, Tom Gamboa, warned me that "things there are not like they are in the States." I'd been to Trinidad many times, and I had seen some challenging conditions, so my mind raced with images of sleeping on a bed of roaches with no roof. Nevertheless, I kept saying to myself, *How bad could it be? Puerto Rico is still part of the United States.*

I arrived at the Mayaguez airport with a suitcase, a big baseball bag containing the tools of my trade, and the hope of furthering my baseball education enough to make it to the major leagues. But even as I walked through that airport, I couldn't help thinking about my father and his sunken heart.

Armed with relatively strong book knowledge of Spanish and foot speed that would eventually earn me the nickname *la gacela* (the gazelle), I made my way to the small town of Cabo Rojo at the southwest tip of the island, and to my new home: Tony's Restaurant, which doubled as a motel. The front part of the property had a fantastic eatery. Its walls were covered with photos of Puerto Rican legends, from salsa singers to the brightest and best baseball players in its history—Vic Power and Juan Gonzalez, among others. Deeper within the property were small rooms with window air-conditioning units that seemed to blow mosquitoes into your bed as much as cool you off. Within a week or so, I moved next door to Don Carlos Cabañas, which became my apartment for the winter.

I was thrown for a loop immediately: my new digs didn't include consistent hot water, air-conditioning, a phone, or a TV. When people wanted to reach me, the calls had to be routed through my landlord's line to a pay phone on the street. I slept on a mattress covered in plastic, and I would wake up in a cold sweat to the sound of an obnoxious rooster next door. But in some ways, I was happy that I didn't have any reason to stay home. I'd saunter around town and visit the mall, practicing my Spanish every chance I got. And most important, I was focused.

Over time, Puerto Rico became home in the truest sense. The people embraced me like family, and I played the best baseball of my professional career to that point, leading the league in many categories—all while finding the most wonderful personal peace I had ever experienced.

To top it off, I had gained a true mentor in Gamboa, who was fond of saying, "We didn't lose; we just ran out of innings." His optimism spread through the team and gave some rising stars like Mark Loretta, Bengie Molina, José Hernandez, Enrique Calero, and me a newfound determination to reach our potential. I responded by racking up an All-Star appearance, a fastest-man award, and an MVP trophy in Puerto Rico. I could taste a promotion to the big leagues.

In baseball, as in any other profession, it often helps to spend time perfecting your craft by playing while others are sleeping. My Puerto Rican sojourn lasted two off-seasons, and in that period I was a part of close to five hundred games combined between there and the United States, with only a week's break between seasons. I never grew as much as I did in that time period, as a person and as a player.

To this day, I have so much love for the people of Puerto Rico and the gift of my experience there. They gave me so much, and I have never forgotten.

Nor have they. Years later, when I went back for vacation, I made a stop at my old stomping grounds in Mayaguez. Other than having a new dance team to entertain fans at the ballpark, everything was the same. The same fans were supporting the team, and they even sat in the same seats. As I caught up with some old friends, the announcer stopped the game to recognize my contribution to the team's championship season in 1996. It was a moving moment.

Give me a plastic-covered mattress in a room and a rooster over a season ticket riding the pine any day of the week. No one likes sitting on the bench. Sunflower seeds start to burn the inside of your mouth after a while. You realize how exhausted you are at around 8:45 p.m. every night game. And there is nothing worse than going into the game in the third inning because some player ten years younger than you tweaked his hamstring.

Turning an everyday player into a sub is like trying to domesticate a wild animal. Maybe you can get him to wear a leash or sleep in a cage, but every time you close your eyes, you really aren't sure what will happen to you if he ever gets loose.

The first time the cage doors closed on me was in 2002. I had played baseball since I was seven, so I had a twenty-five-year run as an everyday starting player (except for the time I spent platooning as a rookie with the Cubs). But I had started the 2002 season as cold as April in Philly, in part because of the stress of watching my father's health deteriorate. By June, I had lost my job to a platoon of Ricky Ledee, Bobby Abreu, and a sprinkling of Jason Michaels. I wasn't happy.

When you lose your job, you can't help but look around. Certainly I wasn't the only one struggling. Most of our team started off horribly that year. Scott Rolen, Mike Lieberthal, Travis Lee, even Abreu were all struggling. Lee and I were benched, while the rest were given the time to play through their slumps. Here was that clear moment when the game shows it can be as arbitrary and even political as anything else.

It made me think back to a gathering from the year before. On this occasion, our manager, Larry Bowa, called a meeting with Rolen, Abreu, and me to ask us why we didn't come out early to take extra batting practice before the game. We had just returned from Los Angeles, where our bats had been lethargic and our batting averages had fallen even lower.

Rolen had a routine where he hit off the tee, Abreu studied video, I hit soft toss. We all explained to Bowa that we were doing our part to rebound from this slow start. After more circular dialogue, Rolen eventually asked Bowa if he was questioning his professionalism. Bowa emphatically denied his point.

The meeting went nowhere after that because each one of us had been around the block and had a customized program to work through bad times. Bowa shuffled the papers on his desk, clearly not happy how the meeting had turned back on him, but it was a heads-up that people were watching and we needed to produce.

In this particular season, I wasn't so sure I had the cover that Rolen may have had. My numbers had declined the last two years, and when the manager is looking for answers, someone will have to be part of the "change" to shake things up in the lineup. Given the fact that I was on a one-year deal and was the least likely of the threesome to be considered a franchise player, I suspected that I would be that someone. Nevertheless, the most important part after working "smart" through a slump is for the manager to give you time to see your work come to fruition.

Still, I hoped my defensive play would be that extra something to give me the time I needed, but it wasn't to be. I was out.

Benching me didn't help. As a team, we didn't get any better. We just had too many problems other than my poor on-base percentage as the leadoff hitter. Our starting rotation was struggling, we weren't getting timely hitting, and we had a cloud of mistrust floating around. Everyone was on pins and needles. Is Rolen getting traded? Is Bowa going to explode? Fairly typical of the challenges facing a team that is trying to find itself.

Shortly after losing my starting job, I had a revelation. I had been very focused for the first six years of my major league career. I rarely went out; I got my rest; I ate breakfast every day. Even including my escapades in Montreal, there had been only one team-witnessed departure from sobriety.

A couple of seasons earlier, on a team flight from Atlanta to Miami, I had not noticed that I had gradually downed a full bottle of chardonnay while yapping away with Rolen and Kevin Sefcik. Part of why I had lost track of my drink count was the soothing effect it had on my anger (toward myself, no less) at going oh-for-five and, worse, allowing the bigoted reliever John Rocker to strike me out. In my altered state I apparently decided to cap off my self-flagellation with a toast. Even more interesting was that all this was done in sunglasses after midnight.

"How could I strike out against a man who offended everyone on Earth, especially on a pitch that bounced halfway to home?" I asked. "Was I trying to imitate my father in his cricket career in Trinidad?" Robert Person and Sefcik laughed so hard at my barrage of self-criticism that they had to be picked up from the floor. To top it off, our manager, Terry Francona, let me know that I was asking these questions at nearly the top of my lungs. (Actually, I was "slelling"— half slurring, half yelling.) Thank goodness I was in the self-contained airplane cabin and not on the streets of Montreal.

Riding the pine in 2002, I realized that I hadn't smelled the roses very often during my career. Like many players, I was so focused and concerned about producing every single day that I forgot I was doing what I had loved to do since I could hold a bat.

So I changed. I started going out a little instead of staying in my hotel room after games. I even did a little sightseeing from time to time, something that you miss out on while visiting the greatest cities in the United States and Canada. I said to myself, *Maybe the glass is half full.*

No more stress of having to get two hits a day, no more moving barely interested corner outfielders to a better defensive position, no more blame, no more scrutiny of my on-base percentage. I had proved for several seasons that I could start at the highest level and, better yet, be a dominant force in my glory year of 1999. I couldn't control that my days as a starter were numbered in Philadelphia because I certainly couldn't do much from the bench other than be well prepared.

Since I was also grappling with my father's illness, I had plenty of stress to dissipate anyway. The decline of my numbers over the previous couple of years could not be explained by any physical decline; instead of being one step ahead of the pitcher, I was now one step behind. Our hitting coach, Hal McRae, said to me, "Well, it is a credit to your talent that you are still hitting close to .270 when your heart and mind are clearly with your father."

As I started ramping up my nightspot appearances, I surprised a few people. At one point when we had an end-of-the-year party at a popular nightspot the players frequented, the regulars were shocked to see me. One woman said to me, "I never have seen you out in Philadelphia."

This is not to say my work ethic disappeared when I was benched.

I put in a couple of months of work to try to earn my spot back. I ran with the pitchers, I hit extra, I was superprepared, I became a pinch-hitting guru with multiple hits in a row at one point. As a result, I was told that I would "play a little more" the second half of the season. It was a strange statement, but at least Bowa was communicating something to me. Eventually, I did get a chance to play every day again, going on a near-.400 tear to close out the last six weeks of the season.

Sure, a player wants to play every day, to be in the lineup no matter what, but if that should not happen after years of being the go-to guy, it's okay to exhale and absorb the amazing journey of a life in baseball. You get to see the game from another perspective. It's a great way to learn how to become a manager or a coach one day because you have to constantly be in tune with what the manager is thinking and doing. When you may have to go into the game at the drop of a hat, it helps to understand the tactical side of the game to help you anticipate those moments. After a while, I knew when Bowa was going to double-switch me into the game well before he made the move.

My advice to those who find themselves in this position? Even though deep down you know you should still be starting, should you find yourself on the bench, start smelling those roses. Get an autograph from the player you always admired, talk to the ball boy for an hour before the game, answer all that fan mail that is piling up in your locker, and find out when your favorite spot closes. And should you go out to the Fluid Lounge in Toronto, order something other than chardonnay.

Whether you are a regular or a role player, there is always a moment in baseball that makes you question whether you have lost the love for the game. It could happen when, after riding the bench for months, you finally find yourself starting—against last year's Cy Young winner. It could happen when you take that first step toward fielding a ground ball and something twinges. It could even happen on a 3 a.m. bus ride from Seattle-Tacoma International Airport to your hotel at the beginning of a two-week road trip when neither family nor friends will be coming to visit you.

My love affair with the game survived that disappointing 2002 season in Philly. It remained true throughout the 2003 season with the Rangers and then the Cubs. But then along came 2004.

Following the Cubs' playoff loss to the Marlins, I re-signed with the Phillies with high hopes of continuing my hitting revival that had begun in Texas. But here I was again rotting on the pine in the City of Brotherly Love, and no matter what I did on the field, I wore the stamp of DEFENSIVE REPLACEMENT on my uniform. Since it wasn't my first rodeo, I knew that few veterans can escape the virtually inevitable move from starter to backup. Still, playing once every two weeks was for the birds.

One evening, from my all-too-familiar seat in the dugout in Citizens Bank Park, I watched as our ace Eric Milton pitched a gem against my former team, the Chicago Cubs. His high-riding fastball was supernasty, and he reached the ninth inning with a no-hitter intact. He had already thrown one earlier in his career. We're talking history here.

Following the timeworn etiquette of putting his best defense on the field to preserve a 2–0 lead, Larry Bowa sent me out to center field to replace Ricky Ledee in the ninth. I'd grown accustomed to dusting off the cobwebs and entering games in the late innings, but going in for defensive purposes during a no-hitter was new to me, and, I confess, scary. It seemed inevitable that the ball was going to find me.

Sure enough, the Cubs' catcher Michael Barrett hit a high fly ball my way. Unable to pick up the trajectory of the ball, I froze for a millisecond, then leaned back toward the outfield wall to protect against the hit sailing over my head. This instinctive reaction might have in some ways pleased my outfield coach; you never want to get beat deep in the late innings with a slim lead. But this was a no-hitter.

After that back-leaning freeze step (which looked even worse on instant replay), I realized that the ball was going to drop in front of me unless I did something about it—now. I broke in at full tilt while watching our second baseman Chase Utley flail away in a futile attempt to make an over-the-shoulder, diving circus catch. I was still the closest to the ball and knew it was on me, but my diving attempt was doomed from the start. The very first move I made had closed the window of opportunity to catch that ball. I never even got a glove on it. Base hit.

The fans booed me relentlessly.

I wish I could say that was the end of it. Unfortunately, after striking out the next two batters, Milton gave up a single to Mark Grudzielanek, and then Corey Patterson hit a game-tying double over my head and off the center field wall. Bowa pulled Milton. No no-hitter. No win for Eric.

We escaped without giving up the lead run. After Jim Thome led off the bottom of the ninth for us with a walk, my job was to bunt him into scoring position. Cubs reliever LaTroy Hawkins threw the first pitch at my head, sending me onto my back to get out of the way. This yielded a big cheer from our home fans. Ouch. I eventually got down a good bunt, and Pat Burrell ended the misery by singling home the game-winning run, which had moved over to second base on my sacrifice.

I had a good relationship with the press, but I knew the reporters gathered at my locker were not interested in asking me about my bunt. As much as I would have liked to avoid them, I knew I'd have to explain what had happened on Barrett's fly ball. Players dream about breaking up no-hitters, but not ones being thrown by their teammates. All I could say was that I needed a great jump to get to the ball and that the split-second freeze had changed the play, but even then, I didn't want to totally concede the point out of frustration.

There is nothing as demoralizing as getting booed by your home fans. I had heard catcalls before on a play or two, particularly in my first year in Philadelphia, when I was replacing Lenny Dykstra, but this was by far the most enduring and emphatic expression of disapproval in my career.

I questioned it all at that point. Maybe I would have felt differently if I had been a few years younger or if I were a starter and could get back in the lineup the next day to make amends, but that wasn't the case.

The space I was in reminded me of the "Why am I doing this?" look on Brian McRae's face in 1997 when he was traded less than five months into his three-year deal with the Cubs. He had already bought a house in Chicago. He had reserved a skybox for the season. He had customized his license plate to read CUBBIE. He had his jersey hanging in the nearby legendary restaurant, Murphy's. But now he was off to New York, traded to the Mets. Blindsided.

After the near-no-hitter fiasco, we had a trip to Miami for a series against the Marlins. There I talked to my mom on the balcony of the hotel, rambling about the exhaustion of being center stage all the time and the expectations of the masses. Normally, I would have moved the conversation to another topic, but this night was different; something had changed for me.

I had been in love with baseball ever since I could remember. There had been times when I'd questioned my relationship with the game, but at the end of the day, I had always remained true. Now, however, it was hard to imagine us growing old together. Or more accurately, I was growing too old for the game. In one moment I had caused Milton's paradise to be lost—and mine, too.

My last day in uniform came the following spring when the Yankees cut me. After fourteen professional seasons, I didn't want to exit the stage wearing the pinstripes of a team for which I'd never played a single regular season game.

Because I'd grown up an avid Phillies fan, it had been a dream to play for that franchise. So after I decided to walk away from the game, I contacted the club and asked if there was any way for me to retire a Phillie, even though I spent the last spring training game of my career as their opponent, in the Yankee dugout.

The first hit of my career was a base hit to left against the Phillies. The last hit of my career that final spring training was a base hit to left against the Phillies. The Phillies were everywhere in my baseball life.

It turned out to be a little more complicated than I had anticipated. Legal wrangling was required to address liability, severance issues, and roster spot regulations, even if you wanted to draw up a contract that for all intents and purposes was designed to explode after one day. After a few months of figuring out a sound legal structure and resolving scheduling conflicts, the Phillies finally gave me a couple of dates to consider for a formal retirement ceremony at Citizens Bank Park. When I saw that one choice included a showdown against the Boston Red Sox in June, I jumped on it.

It was an easy decision. Boston's manager, Terry "Tito" Francona, ranks at the top of my list of the game's good guys. I base this not on the baseball history he has set, but on my personal history with him.

Tito was the Phillies' manager when I first was traded to the team in the winter of 1997. I proceeded to play for him for the next three seasons—from 1998 through 2000—as the team's starting center fielder. Under his tutelage I played the best baseball of my career, and I owe a lot to the environment he created in the locker room.

There is much debate about the value of a manager to a major league roster of professionals. Many managers lose points when they work for an organization with bottomless resources for obtaining talent. Joe Torre, for instance, always seemed to get an undeserved asterisk next to his record whenever someone evaluated the Yankees' reign over baseball for so many years in the late 1990s and early 2000s. But make no mistake about it: when you have so much talent on a team, it can just as easily turn into an imploding festival of egomania. You have to know what you're doing. And in this respect, Tito was a master.

It is all about understanding people—their roles, personalities, and skill sets—and doing what you can to put everyone in the best position to be successful. A bit oversimplified, but that is the gist of it.

Francona understood this as well as anyone I ever played for. From the day I met him in 1998 to his last day in Philadelphia in 2000, all he did was get better and better at managing people, while putting in his time to master the game's strategy.

Francona was a positive and even-keeled person throughout the roller-coaster ride that is the typical baseball season. He only chastised us when he saw us going through the motions or not hustling instead of giving our best. He didn't obsess about the bottom line; he didn't live and die by scores and statistics. His top concern was how we went about our business to achieve this bottom line. If we did it honorably, he had nothing but words of encouragement for us.

When I was traded to Philadelphia, I was coming off a nice season in Chicago, but the jury was still out as to whether I could be an everyday contributor to a major league team. After I edged out Lenny Dykstra for the starting center field job, Francona proceeded to run me out there every single day. His confidence in me was unwavering. Toward the end of the season he finally confirmed what I already knew: "It looks like the bat is swinging you instead of the other way around. I'm going to give you a day off." (I still led the National League in at-bats.)

I took an interest in trying to help Tito be successful, too, something I never attempted with any other manager in the major leagues. He was often criticized for being "too nice" and for not being able to make the tough decisions regarding personnel. So after my first season with him, I bought him a copy of the movie *U-571*, in which Matthew McConaughey portrayed a gung-ho, up-and-coming submarine commander who couldn't make the decisions that were best for the mission if they came at the expense of his crew. Today, after Francona has led the Boston Red Sox to two World Series championships, his "too friendly" critics are nowhere to be found.

Only once did I ever have any tension with him. After my father had suffered his major stroke that fateful day in the 2000 spring training season, I was distracted to the point that in one game I forgot how many outs there were in the inning and let the winning run score. Francona defended me to the press, telling the reporters to "give the kid a break; his father had a major stroke a couple days ago." I was upset, because I didn't want the press to know the details of my personal life. When I asked Tito about why he spilled the beans, he explained, "I was just trying to protect you." Which he sincerely was trying to do. So, after sitting with him for a while and getting that casual don't-worry-about-it-because-I-will-take-the-heat smile, I just had to smile with him.

He also kept the locker room as loose as possible. He joked with the players and joined in on practical jokes. His one-liners should be in the Hall of Fame one day—he could disarm anyone. I laughed when I read his quote regarding Kevin Youkilis after Kevin was named the "Greek God of Walks" in Michael Lewis's book *Moneyball*. The reference was to Youk's extraordinary ability to see the difference between a ball and a strike. Francona's reaction: "I've seen him in the shower, he isn't the Greek God of anything."

His humility and modesty were inspiring. One off-season, I called him after hearing he'd had a near-death experience during a "routine" procedure on his constantly swelling knees. He just shrugged it off, saying, "Things happen, I'm fine." And when news of his firing from the Phillies at the end of the 2000 season unfortunately leaked out a few days early and ended up on a press release in our lockers, he managed right to the end—even when one of our coaches was so offended by the leak that he refused to work the last few games.

So I made the right choice to retire with Francona on the field. That day he graciously invited me into the Red Sox locker room, and I actually spent more time there than in the locker room of the organization I was retiring from. I talked to some of my old opponents— John Olerud, David Ortiz, Manny Ramirez, Matt Clement—and my former teammate Curt Schilling, among others. For a second, I almost thought I was in the lineup, but that is how Tito did it, warm and inviting, all of the time. Even before I officially retired, he had an opportunity to play in the minors waiting for me if I ever wanted to get back in the saddle.

The day I retired was special. I walked out on the field in front of a sold-out crowd at Citizens Bank Park and received a wonderful ovation. Tito took the time to talk to my wife-to-be and my mother, greeting them behind home plate. As I threw out the first pitch, I was equally moved to see all of the Red Sox stop what they were doing to come out and give me a standing ovation. Something like that tells you a lot about their manager.

On paper, I was ready for my ride into the sunset. I had a nice Ivy League engineering degree, a wonderfully supportive family, some coins in my pocket. My transition to the other side was supposed to be smooth sailing to blissful relaxation. But I didn't really know much about this world I was entering. I had a Ph.D. in baseball, but in every other realm that involved making a living, I was stuck at my college graduation ceremony, thirteen years before.

And I was one of the more prepared players.

There are no institutional services within Major League Baseball to help baseball players move on to that next life. You get the pat on the back, the thanks for the memories, and the "you are going to be fine because you have money" platitudes while the door closes behind you. I don't expect tears of sympathy—there are many causes more worthy of attention than the plight of millionaire athletes. Then again, it's worth noting that the majority of professional baseball players never leave the minor league ranks and never make even close to six figures a year.

I spoke recently to my former teammates about life after the game and its challenges. Every one of them had struggled in one way or another. No matter how your career ends, once it does, it feels like the rocket you rode to the top has been abruptly stopped by an errant asteroid. There's nothing to fill that void of competing every single day at the highest level.

The former professional football player Eddie George noted to CNN.com, "What people fail to realize is that when you make a transition away from the game—emotionally, physically, mentally, spiritually—you go through something. You change, and you're constantly searching for something." Who will understand that a transitioning athlete needs help? There are few soft landings when you've been flying high.

Failed marriages are a huge part of the sports culture. I have heard some astonishing statistics. In 2007, an organization called the Professional Sports Wives Association reported that "a staggering 80 percent of pro athletes are divorced and are a quarter of a million dollars in debt after they retire." I certainly know many teammates, coaches, and opponents who have gotten divorced at some point. And divorce frequently occurs right after a player retires.

You return home, and there isn't a ticker-tape parade for the homecoming king. In some ways you're a stranger to your own family; you need to learn how to be consistently present. And how do you accomplish that while dealing with the trauma of missing the only way you've ever made a living, or the depression of feeling forgotten?

Shortly before I left the game, I invested in a real estate development company. Ask any ballplayer in transition; odds are they have at least "dabbled in real estate." It is the fashionable investment of choice. It is also tangible and real, as you're able to slap your name on a development sign and have the world know you've accomplished something. My methodical nature told me I should get an M.B.A. and then work for a builder, learning the business and working my way up the ladder, while plotting my own projects on the side. (I was interested in the development side of building baseball stadiums.) Instead, I jumped in feet first, providing both my capital and my time to someone who was almost a total stranger.

Now, I had been pitched before by a million other people, from video gaming companies to health clubs to nonprofits. But this person caught me at a time when I needed something. My father had passed away, my career was declining, and I realized that I had to find a way to redirect my competitive energy.

The venture collapsed amid inept systems and the more general collapse of the markets. My options were limited. To preserve my investment (and those of others), I became a one-man bailout package: I formed my own company along with a childhood friend and took over the projects without having any idea how to run that kind of business. In some ways, my release from the Yankees in spring training propelled me further into my blind home-building foray; it would have been hard for me to stomach ending my career with a rejection and then having a business implode six months later. So, newly married, I had to make this work somehow, even though the red flags were everywhere.

I ended up learning more about corporate law than I ever wanted to know, while navigating a complete morass of misinformation and broken business plans. Not very easy when your name is a familiar one and it isn't difficult to imagine the headline of your own financial demise. I misinterpreted the emotions that arose from responding to constant crisis as the thrill of competition. My new company had to complete a fleet of single-family homes while learning the building codes, finding subcontractors, calming investors, and dealing with the burden of escalating carrying costs—all on the fly. Worse yet, we were picking up the pieces of someone else's inability to deliver.

If you were fortunate enough to have had a nice run in the big leagues, you probably made a lot of money and often heard that you were "set for life." And if you took the time to learn the nuances of the stock market, surrounded yourself with a trusted team of investment brokers, accountants, and financial planners, and avoided taking ridiculous risks with your money, you probably would be in great shape for decades to come. But who teaches classes on these topics that I can trust? And which players are actually willing and listening participants? I had a father who challenged me, well before I was in junior high school, to write the price of Oppenheimer shares daily in a notebook, so by the time I was drafted, I knew about mutual funds, bonds, even options. It was a good base, but I would say that this experience is rare—and it didn't protect me from my own real estate investment nightmare.

Managing finances is just part of the problem. An even bigger issue is what to do with your time. The pleasure of a hammock at age thirty-five only lasts so long for someone who likes to be engaged. Like most players, I had been on the go for decades. I only had one gear, and when I retired I discovered that it had nothing to do with the beach and a glass of iced tea.

On top of that, most players are not set up for "real life" at all. Having been nearly invisible for a decade between March and October, you have no idea how to be an ever-present father or a spouse, no idea how to create a résumé or handle a job interview, no idea what is required to run a business or even what to do in the summer—a season with, suddenly, an inordinate amount of time. Plus, because you can no longer perform athletically, you're probably fighting a strange emptiness that you can't talk to just anyone about; with a million dollars at your disposal, your complaints don't resonate.

Because you probably played for several teams, there's no single organization around that knows you that well. Your agent says hello once in a while, maybe. The union is busy dealing with current issues, and the institutions for retired players are more focused on promotions or destitute players—great causes, but they wholly miss the sweet spot of the typical baseball player after his career is over. Meanwhile, the game goes on, with younger, more marketable faces filling your slot. The mix-and-stir friends have disappeared, and no one can tell you what to do to help you get back into society. It's a story that touches anyone leaving a career before they choose to do so.

As I've spoken with former teammates and opponents, many have described themselves as feeling disowned and ignored, scrambling to find some direction and support. Their disillusionment is powerful enough to make it hard to get off that couch and take on the new day. *Where did all my friends go?* It would be nice to see the organizations that surround a player during his career—the league, the union, the alumni association—do more to help athletes transition into a new life.

I was able to get back on my feet through trial and error and with the support of my family. My degree also gave me some options that most players do not have. And after years of navigating the real estate market, there was now light at the end of the tunnel for my homebuilding business. My partner and I survived and built a few solid homes (Craftsman style is my favorite) after taking our lumps, which is a source of pride for me.

But the more typical story is one of ongoing distress, and that seems so unnecessary given the resources a player can amass during a successful career.

Even after their careers end, these players still have a place in the memories of a generation of fans and can be powerful mentoring influences. In many ways, they are an untapped resource, one that could be wonderful for a community. But first each player needs to find a new home within himself, and that will take a little help.

Every holiday season, after getting our fill of eggnog, my family and I enjoy a tradition of watching one of our favorite movies: *A Few Good Men*, starring Jack Nicholson, Kevin Bacon, Tom Cruise, and Demi Moore. Its most famous line is Nicholson's: "You can't handle the truth!" But the one that always sticks with me is spoken by Cruise's character, Lieutenant Kaffee, his parting words to one of the defendants: "You don't need a patch on your arm to have honor."

In the world of baseball, a player's uniform carries with it a history and a commitment. Putting it on calls up the honor of baseball's past, as if within its fabric is the spirit of everyone who has contributed to the team's cause. The longer you wear it, the harder it is to stop wearing it. It is as if it seeps into your soul.

My old friend, teammate, and mentor Shawon Dunston played at the major league level for eighteen years. And he often repeated to me this one indispensable piece of advice: "Never give the uniform back. Let them rip it off your body." Once you give it back, he insisted, it will never be the same, and neither will you.

All of us, no matter what dream we pursue, hope for a storybook walk into the sunset, where we end our journey on our own terms. Imagine, for instance, what that might mean for a ballplayer: the magic of winning a World Series in your final season and heading home to a ticker-tape parade.

But for most players, that is not the ending at all. Either you have to turn in the sacred uniform after floundering at some point—as I found out firsthand from Joe Torre and Brian Cashman after getting my Yankee spring training pink slip—or the door seems to slam in your face arbitrarily, PAST DUE is stamped on your career, and you reluctantly walk away. Either way, it rarely feels like it's happening on your own terms.

Even the gift of longevity in professional sports brings a burden. Each year that you survive and earn the right to wear the uniform, you find it harder to define yourself without it. It begins to feel that you are wearing the uniform twenty-four hours a day.

Our uniform is our patch on the arm, a badge that becomes our ticket to social acceptance, fame, financial security (maybe), and admission to an elite club of "success." But it's also a ticket into the theater of self-doubt. A doubt that turns most players into awkward Clark Kents without their Superman costumes. Because with that uniform comes the responsibility of representing cities, towns, family names, team legacies, and even your own childhood hopes. And all that can confuse your sense of where the uniform ends and your real self begins.

I remember walking into the locker room at my first major league spring training and seeing my jersey hanging next to that of the future Hall of Famer Ryne Sandberg. I knew something had changed. It was no longer about promoting high school or college pride; I was about to wear baseball history on my sleeve, and that was not for the faint of heart. The moment I put on that uniform, I was Doug Glanville the Ballplayer. That became the quickest and most direct way to describe who I was and who everyone would want to be if they were in my shoes.

For the most part, players embrace being the Ballplayer. This label allows you to be what you always dreamed of being. The wait is over—you get VIP treatment. You can even stop working on the side of you that isn't a ballplayer, just as long as you are wearing that uniform. You might resist becoming wholly defined as a ballplayer by laying claim to more than that (father, artist, neighbor), but such attempts are often hollow. After a while, it is just easier to accept it. After all, we are living the wonderful dream of many people, including ourselves.

I began playing baseball from the moment I could hold a ball. And when I finally took off the uniform, I had played fifteen seasons in the pros. I was thirty-four years old and had essentially played baseball my entire life. I was fortunate to be able to study engineering and do other things along the way, but I wore the uniform the whole time. I'm surprised I didn't find pinstripes on my body when I jumped in the shower after I retired.

In the end, I had to find honor outside the game—or, more specifically, outside the uniform—and I had to find it in areas where I'd had little exposure. I had to learn how to get access to opportunities without the sex appeal of being a "current player," without great tickets to offer, without hot information about the workings of the locker room, without the ability to invite someone into the inner circle of the famous. I could no longer just flash my "badge" and watch the rest unfold automatically.

It takes a lot of introspection to avoid this Superman effect, of feeling heroic and powerful in uniform and ungainly and lost outside of it. Often it is more comfortable to just keep finding ways to wear the uniform, by playing for as long as your body, mind, and soul will allow, or by remaining close to the game (and in uniform) as a coach or manager. Players all share a love for the game, so why not stay on for as long as possible?

Eventually, many players find honor outside the uniform—even as their game-winning hits and diving catches fade to memories. But it takes a lot of work. I had to fight for it and to trust that it would happen. It also takes time to truly comprehend that while there is a history and a legacy behind every baseball uniform, each player who wears it adds something to that history—something that was inside him long before he joined the team. And that this same "something" can be found again when the uniform is put away.

When I was feeling invisible without my uniform, I thought about an actress friend of mine. Not long after she came to Hollywood, she won a large role in a blockbuster movie alongside *A Few Good Men*'s Kevin Bacon. Then she hit a wall. After ten years of running from audition to audition, she finally decided to take off her track shoes and leave Tinseltown. Crossing over to the other side is really difficult, she told me, but once you get through the barbed wire, you can't help but exhale now that the burden has been removed from your shoulders.

So I carried on, as many do, without the pinstripes or the Major League Baseball logo on my cap. I reflected and saw a career that I was proud of, a life that I was proud of, still surrounded by the people who supported me all along. I followed my heart and found peace, and I prepared to make it through the barbed wire to get to the other side.

It was time to head home.

EPILOGUE

. . .

An alarm clock did not ring, nor did an alert beep from my cell phone text messaging system. Nevertheless, I knew it was time.

After my first child was born in 2008, my freshly acquired nesting instinct told me that I finally had to address the basement closet full of dust-collecting memorabilia.

Previous attempts had failed, as thoughts of team yearbooks falling on my head discouraged all sense of motivation. But this new phase of my life pushed me over the top; necessity finally met readiness.

At least I knew what was in there. Old newspaper clippings, game balls from Little League, every uniform I had ever worn. But the real treasure was boxes of unopened fan mail from when I couldn't muster the energy to read every letter. Here lay the result of that exhaustion (with a twinge of laziness), in paper form.

If I were to put a number on it, I'd say that I probably replied to 90 percent of my fan mail over the course of my career, and the remaining 10 percent I had saved at the end of each season. Even though I knew there would be moments like this, when the 10 percent would be laughing in my face.

Still, most important right now was the sudden need for space to accommodate stroller accessories, ExerSaucers, and other baby plastics. And all that stood in my way were boxes of fan mail from as far back as 1994.

Now that I think about it, 10 percent may have been a low estimate.

So I went on the attack. I began opening mail at a frenetic pace. I had planned to open all the letters and then decide in each case what to do next. Answering them all was a possibility, but I reserved the right to toss some in the trash, realizing that a number of these letters were nearly fifteen years old. Also, I was on the clock: bulk packages from Babies R Us were about to demand the extra closet space.

But I softened my stance when I thought about the eight-year-old fan happily receiving a letter from a player he once took the time to write to and request an autograph. Such requests often involved baseball cards tucked inside self-addressed, stamped envelopes.

Then it sank in. That eight-year-old kid may already have graduated from college and in any case has probably moved five times since he wrote me. Besides, updating the postage from 1994 would force me to take out a second mortgage.

But I decided to continue, so that everyone who had taken the time to write would know, at least in spirit, that I read every single letter that was sent to me. Maybe the morning I mailed the mountain of replies, a smile would cross the collective face of my pen pals.

The fun part was being able to paint a picture of my entire career through the eyes of others. People remembered the most subtle moments.

There was the story of a man who was wearing a halo following an automobile accident. I threw a ball to him before a game in an effort to lift his spirits, and after overshooting him I went back and threw him another, this one landing softly in his hands. His wife took the time to write me a thank-you letter.

There was the nine-year-old who told me to make sure I signed his baseball card by hand, demanding, "Write it yourself—don't stamp it."

There was my self-appointed "Jewish mother," who was upset

that the Phillies weren't selling jerseys with my name on the back. Not only did she write me, but she photocopied her letter and sent it to the Phillies front office. My jerseys eventually did end up in the team stores, despite the fact that the photocopy of her letter intended for the front office also ended up in my basement mail closet. (Shhh . . . don't tell her.)

For the most part, the mail was a wonderful collection of positive energy. Kids were inspired; teachers requested signed cards to reward students (sorry so late!); fans sent thank-you notes for when I took just a split second to shake a hand or smile back. It was a joy to know how much doing what I loved to do really mattered to people, and to see it in written form.

After reading these letters, I shocked a few people by picking up the phone and calling them. One was a college teammate who wrote me during the Chicago Cubs playoffs in 2003. His wife answered, and she seemed to know right away that I was calling because of his letter. Her husband, Tod Sweeney, had always said in college that he would become a doctor and move back to Colorado, which he called his only true home. The business card enclosed in the envelope confirmed that he had done both.

Not all of the mail could be classified as "fan mail" per se. I served on the Executive Subcommittee of the Players Association, which was not a fan favorite in the near-strike year of 2002. One fan wrote a "plea" to save the baseball players with a mock fund-raising campaign to help supplement our "exorbitant" salaries by donation. The letter was actually very creative and well researched.

There was also a missed opportunity: a grassroots organizer at my alma mater, the University of Pennsylvania, wanted my approval to start the Doug Glanville Fan Club. Since I was ten years late in getting back to him, I told him he could start a Facebook page fan club if he wanted.

One of my favorites was from a guy from Ohio who was on disability and in jeopardy of defaulting on his mortgage. So he took the time to mail me his payoff letter with an address where I could donate money to his fund-raising drive. I didn't send him money, but I wished him well.

It was a joy to walk down memory lane arm-in-arm with the stories inside my fan mail. I had managed to save mail representing all fifty states, Guam, France, Japan, Canada, Bulgaria, and Puerto Rico. As I cleared everything out, I saved a few of the letters so that, one day, my children could enjoy the stories and the gracious efforts of people who used to watch their dad play ball.

In some ways, this closed a big chapter in my life. After all, there will be no more fan mail, at least not because of a new moment we shared on the baseball field that moved someone to write me. All my uniforms are now neatly hanging in the closet (or in the nursery), never to be used again.

This was my small attempt to finish what I had started and give a little bit back, postcareer. I hope the three weeks I spent getting Sharpie marks and paper cuts on my hands and cleaning the post office out of three- to five-cent stamps was worth it to the few who received back their self-addressed, stamped envelopes—from the collector in Brookings, South Dakota, to the woman in Tokyo who loved pink envelopes. Even if it was fifteen years later.

And if they stumble across this book, I want to let them know that, despite the delay, I have always been thinking about them with gratitude. A small thanks for fifteen years of letters inspired by playing this fan-friendly game while crisscrossing the United States, Canada, and Puerto Rico. It was a quite a run, and a heckuva paper trail.

APPENDIX: IN THE BOOK

. . .

Doug Glanville
Chicago Cubs / Philadelphia Phillies / Texas Rangers
Last series—5 for 12, 1 HR, 2 SB

At the plate
Glanville hit the ball well this past series. Pitchers got hurt with mistakes up in the zone. Must throw breakers off the plate, low and away, and then bust him in for chase. Stay away from patterns, he picks up on them quickly, variety with off-speed pitches leaves him vulnerable. Dead fastball hitter, so if you must throw it, move the fastball around but throw trash first to set it up.

—Sample scouting report by Hank King,
advance scout, Philadelphia Phillies

When you hit a home run off a pitcher, you put him "in the book." More than likely, those pitchers in my book didn't heed the scouting report above; their strengths matched up with my strengths so they just stayed with what they knew, or they were actually human and made a mistake and I was able to capitalize.

I was a high-ball hitter, plain and simple. Pitches that were at the letters of my jersey and up: I could hit those. But a pitcher who kept the ball down in the zone, like Brandon Webb or Derek Lowe, drove me crazy—especially if he had a sinker.

As I have mentioned, a coach in the minor leagues was upset at me for chasing the high pitch and told me, "You may be able to get on top of the high pitch down here, but when you face Roger Clemens, you'll have no chance at hitting that." Thank goodness I didn't listen, because I survived on that high pitch (aka "French Toast," a term cooked up by Hal McRae) for fifteen seasons.

In this, my first book wearing the hat of a writer, I want to officially list the pitchers who made it "in my book" when I wore a baseball cap. Initially, I was worried that they would take it the wrong way, but baseball players, of all people, know about traditions, and they understand that if you have the good fortune to have someone publish your book, it is very fitting to include this section. (Although I have never really heard about a book for pitchers, I assume that whenever they strike you out, it is sort of like being put in their "book." Since I struck out 502 times in my career, you could fill a library with those books!)

Although I did not do the research, it is likely that the vast majority of those pitchers listed below struck me out, too. So we're even. You'll notice that I only hit more than one home run off a handful of pitchers. I spread it around. I also spread it around geographically. I always wanted to hit one home run in every stadium, and for a guy with only fifty-nine career home runs, I was an equal opportunity slugger. I hit one at Jacobs Field, the new and old homes of the Milwaukee Brewers, Enron Field (now Minute Maid Park), Three Rivers Stadium, Riverfront Stadium, the Vet, Citizens Bank Park, Bank One Ballpark (now Chase Field), the Astrodome, even that aggravating Turner Field, among others. In the first couple of years of interleague play, I quietly had the most hits of any player against the American League for a stretch, including my home run at beautiful Camden Yards.

You will notice that if you have the name Bobby Jones, I would have hit a home run off you. The two pitchers by that name couldn't have been more opposite. There was Bobby J. Jones: right-hander from Fresno, California, a mainstay of the New York Mets rotation, a first-rounder out of college whose motion was one of the more fluid in the game. He had great control and hit his spots for years. And there was Bobby M. Jones: from the opposite coast (Orange, New Jersey), drafted out of high school, pitched for the Rockies for most of his brief major league career; he was left-handed, African American, and "herky-jerky" in his motion. In only a few at-bats against him, I hit for the cycle.

So here are the pitchers in my book, in no particular order. (A number in parentheses means I hit more than one off this pitcher.) I think there are a few future Hall of Famers in there, too!

Al Leiter (3). He woke a sleeping giant by saying to me, "You used to be a tough out."

Steve Trachsel. He used to drive me to Wrigley as my teammate in Chicago.

Rick Reed. I hit it right after two Mets fans yelled at me in the on-deck circle. Take that!

Bobby J. Jones. Off a curveball no less. Never to repeat this feat.

Bobby M. Jones. Dead center field at Coors Field. Clearly the altitude helped me.

Oswaldo Mairena. Off the bench and close to a thousand hits, this was career hit number 998.

Ryan Dempster. Home run on Opening Day; I was among the league leaders for a day.

Hideki Irabu. Only home run where I hit the foul pole. Also revenge for hitting me in the back at Yankee Stadium with the first pitch of the game.

Rocky Biddle. First walk-off home run ever at Citizens Bank Park.

Kevin Brown. I could never explain why I hit against him so well because he was the nastiest pitcher I have ever seen.

Vladimir Nunez. Tried to get cute with a sidearm delivery.

Mark Petkovsek (2). A rare sinker baller that I could hit.

Mike Timlin. I liked high fastballs, and he threw one at old Busch Stadium.

Juan Acevedo. Another high fastball at Busch.

Kevin Tapani. Sweet revenge against my Cubbies on a slider, no less, at Wrigley.

Jeff Fassero. First home run ever. Onto Waveland Avenue. Woohoo!

Terry Mulholland. Got my first hit off him and then bombed him at the Vet.

Micah Bowie. My two hundredth hit of the season and against my old team, the Cubs. Trade revenge!

Scott Elarton. I lied. He hung a curveball at the Astrodome.

Dwight Gooden. Most memorable home run. I watched him while growing up in Jersey.

Octavio Dotel. Into the cheap left field seats in Houston.

Javier Martinez. A young opponent from Puerto Rico. We met in winter ball.

Randy Johnson. Finally got the Big Unit. Say no more.

Curt Schilling (2). Two in one game. He killed my computer game character, so I got him.

Tom Glavine. A rare hit off Tom. Shocked myself.

John Burkett. He left a cutter up in the zone, I was on a home run roll at the time.

Russ Springer. First-pitch fastball, up in the zone; it just worked out.

Woody Williams. He loved high fastballs, and I loved hitting them. Good match.

Oliver Perez. I can now say I hit one of those palm trees at Jack Murphy Stadium.

Kevin Jarvis. He had a no-hitter going, and I broke it up in the rain.

Denny Neagle. He tried that quick-pitch move, and it didn't work.

Darryl Kile. May he rest in peace. Fantastic pitcher. Best curve I saw in the big leagues.

Kirk Rueter. Generally, he owned me, but not on this day.

Andy Benes. Had my best batting average against any pitcher against him.

Brian Rose. First at-bat of the second half of the season at Fenway.

Juan Guzman. First Canadian home run. SkyDome.

Bill Risley. Second Canadian home run. Same game.

Pat Rapp. Finally figured him out in beautiful Camden Yards.

John Smiley. Interleague home run at Jacobs Field.

Victor Santos. Off my old teammate in Texas in Miller Park.

Pete Schourek. Home run at Riverfront Stadium in 1997.

Brett Tomko. High fastballs always make me look like I have some pop.

Tim Wakefield. Finally got that knuckleball up in the jet stream.

Gil Meche. Early homer in Seattle during my inaugural American League season.

Ramon Ortiz. Tomahawked a fastball onto the rocks in Anaheim.

Jason Grimsley. Hit one for my then-girlfriend in Texas.

Rocky Coppinger. County Stadium in Milwaukee on a pitch over my head.

Rick Helling. Inside-the-park home run called by the wonderful Harry Kalas.

Archie Corbin. During a day game not on TV. Maybe it didn't happen.

Vic Darensbourg. My only pinch-hit home run.

Antonio Osuna. Fastball inside that I caught flush. Waveland Avenue.

Glendon Rusch. Hit him well in the minors, carried over into the basket in Wrigley.

Gabe White. Took a good swing, and the ball went out. Nothing exciting here.

Armando Almanza. Didn't even remember this one, but it was at the Vet.

Masato Yoshii. Had to look this one up, had no recollection, but it was a leadoff homer.

Honorable mention:

Bobby J. Jones. Surprise! Another Bobby Jones sighting. This was the should-have-been home run that the official scorer ruled a double and a two-base error by Dante Bichette. Oh, well, stuck at fifty-nine.

Defense was more my strength. Here's the rest of that sample scouting report:

> *In the field*
>
> Glanville is known for his good instincts in the outfield complemented with his speed and quickness. He has a strong arm partly because he charges the ball well and is accurate with his throws. He takes good lateral routes and is not afraid of the walls. His quick release and his discipline in hitting the cut-off man suggest that you should not take the extra base unless you are sure.

ACKNOWLEDGMENTS

• • •

Little did I know that when the Mitchell Report was released in December 2007, I would get a golden opportunity. My college friend Alan Schwarz, who is now a reporter with the *New York Times*, encouraged me to talk with the opinion team at his newspaper, and soon I was writing an online column for the *Times* called "Heading Home." After deputy editorial page editor David Shipley demonstrated the faith to give me a column, editors Tobin Harshaw, Peter Catapano, and George Kalogerakis taught me lessons in big-league writing. Toby red-penciled my first entry so heavily that it looked like I'd lost a bad fight, Peter kept the balance, while George read my mind to make my words make sense.

The column created another opportunity: this book.

As a rookie in the world of publishing, I was helped by numerous men and women whom I am proud to call my mentors and teammates. Paul Golob, the editorial director of Times Books, saw the possibility of an original book springing from my perspective on baseball and life. Tim Hoy, the in-house counsel of my old baseball agents, Arn Tellem and Joel Wolfe, threw out the first pitch by helping me learn my new industry through an introduction to Helen Eisenbach, who is well versed in the publishing arena. Shortly after Paul contacted me, I had interviewed a few literary agents and was fortunate to team up with Dave Larabell of the David Black Agency. With his invaluable help (and that of David Black, which continues to this day), I crafted a proposal that resonated with Paul.

Eventually, we would get the book in motion. I was racing another clock, the birth of my daughter in August, so, to Paul's surprise, I told him I would finish early. I met my goal but, like a crafty left-hander, Paul had thrown the change-up, giving me a date on the early side just in case I thought to stroll into the deadline party fashionably late. It turned out—as Paul knew—that we would need the extra time to take care of the edits and revisions.

I also had a Mariano Rivera–like closer because of Paul's foresight to pair me with writer/editor Steve Fiffer, who helped guide the project and touch up my words. We were on the same page from day one and the friendship we developed is a delightful by-product of our collaboration. (Thanks, too, to Steve's wife, mystery novelist Sharon Fiffer, for providing tea and sympathy while we worked at their kitchen table.)

My new double-play combination became Larabell to Fiffer to Golob to go with a deep bench of Alex Ward, Dan Farley, Nicole Dewey, and Maggie Richards at Times Books. Inspiration came from my late father, Dr. Cecil E. Glanville, an accomplished poet, who taught me the importance of writing long before a career in baseball seemed a possibility. Whatever talent I initially displayed was refined by my powerful tenth-grade English teacher, Jean Sumner, at Teaneck High School.

Once we had a real first draft together, I became paranoid as a fact-checker. In a way, it was one of the best parts of writing this book. I called on teammates and friends I hadn't spoken to in years. Shawon Dunston (the wise man), Ozzie Timmons, Kevin Orie, Ron Gant (who referred to my language skills as being "cinco-lingual"), Brian McRae, Kevin Mench, Michael Carter, Royce Clayton, Carl Everett (aka "Playa"), Mike Lieberthal (aka "Thal"), Alex Rodriguez (thanks for the note), Curt Schilling, Desi Relaford, Wayne Gomes, Kevin Roberson. I let them know that as players we are just conduits to the human story, and to be effective advocates for empathy and understanding, we need emotional honesty—and they gave it.

To my media friends: Jayson Stark, who has everything ever known about baseball at his disposal, thank you for keeping the game fun and funny. Paul Hagen and all my beat-writer friends in Philadelphia and Chicago have given me nothing but love and, little did they know, inspiration to do what I am now doing. Dave Kaplan, thank you for sharing the story of your life at McDonald's during the Cubs' horrible start in 1997. Thanks to Jimmy Greenfield at ChicagoNow.com for digging up what happened when Lance Johnson took my number. Dennis Deitch, thanks for giving me an honest assessment of the reporter's side of the coin and breaking it down, even though when you first came on the scene we were calling for your head. Thanks also to John Perrotto in Pittsburgh for helping me figure out that Derek Bell's pants apparently approached size 46 when the league stepped in, and to editorial page editor Harold Jackson of the *Philadelphia Inquirer* and Phillies intern Craig Hughner for helping me track down the article "The Skinny on Glanville." And, to George Castle, thanks for your relentless intensity and your advice on how to be a writer. Finally, a note of gratitude to XM Radio and the Power Alley team of Seth Everett, Jim Duquette, and Billy Ripken for letting me ramble on the air at will.

The Major League Baseball Players Association gave me a lot of support and made sure I had my information together. Allyne Price e-mailed me time and time again to give me history lessons, and Melissa Persaud's efforts helped me track down some old friends. Speaking of history lessons, my thanks to umpire Mike DiMuro for deciphering the rule book and its evolution for me.

My hometown people in Teaneck were solid as I took a walk down memory lane; thanks to former mayor Jackie Kates and family friend Carolyn Witherspoon. I also thank my friends from Teaneck, including Assad Koshul, my business partner, who allowed me to focus on my writing as he held down the fort with my business team of Nick Sabanovic and the masters of all things Web Irfan Akram and Aamir Noman of Mechtechnologies. Then there is my longtime off-season workout partner, Seth Bendian, who listened to my theories—some of which made the book, some of which ended up in the toilet.

My Puerto Rico connection Steve Melendez tracked down numerous blasts from the past. I found Sandy Alomar Sr. to be full of his usual wisdom, and thanks to James Ramos and Fred Mohedano for helping me with my Spanish for this book. Thanks as well to Nahir Lugo, who helped me remember some baseball moments in Puerto Rico that had escaped me.

Margaret Sandberg allowed me to refer to her as the "Queen Bee." Thank you, your grace is well appreciated. Lisa Harrison Rogers let me use her name even though I never bothered combing my hair when we hung out in my Texas years. And I thank the quasi-anonymous tag team of "the Lady in Blue" and "Ms. San Diego" for allowing me to share their stories.

I want to express my deepest gratitude to all my friends in the Phillies and the Cubs organizations who helped me dig up little tidbits. Leigh Tobin, Dan Stephenson (aka "Video Dan"), Hank King, and Frank Coppenbarger unearthed some good ones, as did Mary Dosek with the Cubs. They must have thought I was a little over the top when I called to make sure that Mark Parent had used Velcro to keep his pants down. I think that in the end I got the facts right but, if I missed, I apologize. Rest assured, I certainly drove everyone crazy trying.

I look forward to working with my new Chicago mentors who have helped me flesh out where to go from here. Thanks to Stedman Graham, for his leadership and tips on how to build a market; his right-hand woman, Lisa Ridolfi, who is constantly hustling in Chicagoland to give my name some weight; and Lee Hillman and Tolbert Chisum for making the introductions. Then there is Shannon Jones, who listened to my ideas while I was in his barber's chair, letting me know that it can all get done, just keep the faith. I thank Burton Rocks, Jackie Harris, and Jeff Wernick, my new bicoastal hustlers in New York and Los Angeles, for all the calls on my behalf to find a broadcast home for me, and I thank Charlie Schumacher and Lissa Christman of Comcast SportsNet for giving me some time as an analyst.

I also want to recognize the Baseball Factory for becoming my partner in sharing all the lessons the game has to offer with young student-athletes. Fielding the youngsters' questions and those of their parents has been such a joy. It has been an inspirational way to give back to this game. Thank you Steve Sclafani, Rob Naddelman, and Jason Budden.

To John Oates, the unsung half of the greatest music duo in history, thank you for your efforts, for your music, and for sending my articles out to all your friends.

For all of the wonderful fans of the game, I want to recognize you for all the years of support and undying commitment to this great game. It is truly a game that transcends; we all just have to do our part to keep it that way. I hope we can all find patience in our heart to see the humanity in a life in baseball, once we peel back the layers and emphasize the common space we share.

Finally, the key cog in the lineup was my loving family. I have been so fortunate to have such a wonderful support system. My mom, who, at seventy-three years old, still needs a personal assistant to balance her active schedule. Thank you for your amazing spirit, strength, and positive energy. I am nowhere without you showing me that anything is possible.

To big bro, Ken, my big-league brother, it has been a long way since the days of Intellivision. I love you; you are the passion point of our family and have always been in my corner, no matter what. Keep playing. Keep that innocence; there is enough skepticism to go around. To Gabe and Lydia, aka "Glydia," thanks for helping find all those baby items on eBay, so we could stop pulling our hair out. It has been a pleasure to have another brother with such kindness who likes video games and iPhones as much as I do. To my good friend and cousin, Yvette Thompson, thank you for your words of patience and support.

To my in-laws. Ma Lynn, I thank you for being the calm force of nature, warm and real and loving your grandkids with all your soul. Pops, when I lost my father, I lost a soul mate and the greatest man I knew, but to have you as my new father is the equivalent of lightning striking twice. Thank you both for your daughter, Tiffany, my wife, my heart.

To my wife, thank you for giving me balance, purpose, love, and direction, and our wonderful children, Vaughn and Nadine. Thank you for Vaughn, who is so full of life and enthusiasm and has such a kind soul and, like you, has a bottomless heart for love (and thanks for jumping at the chance to give him his middle name, Robinson, in honor of Jackie). Thank you for Nadine, who could lay still in my lap as I typed over her head into the wee hours, and who is so young but strong. I need you to help "Lady" celebrate every day that her middle name honors her wonderful grandfather. Thank you for sharing your attorney's eyes and making sure I was consistent with my assertions and that what I wrote resonated with nonbaseball fans. You helped refine the ending and made sure I kept the stories fair. Your input was priceless and so is my life with you. It has been a game from where I stand and I will always choose to stand with you.

INDEX

• • •

ABOUT THE AUTHOR

Doug Glanville played outfield for the Philadelphia Phillies, Chicago Cubs, and Texas Rangers from 1996 through 2004. From 2008 to 2010, he wrote the online column "Heading Home" for *The New York Times* and provided baseball analysis for XM Radio's MLB Home Plate's *Power Alley*. In the spring of 2010 he joined ESPN as a baseball analyst, contributing to *Baseball Tonight,* ESPN.com, and *ESPN The Magazine.* He serves on the executive board of Athletes Against Drugs, the fundraising committee for Boundless Readers, and advises high school student athletes as a special consultant to the Baseball Factory. Glanville grew up in Teaneck, New Jersey, and is a graduate of the University of Pennsylvania. He lives with his family in Chicago.

For more information about Doug Glanville, you may visit his Web site at www.dougglanville.com.